Cyber Crisis Response

Cyber Crisis Response

Leveraging The SONAR Method™ to Accelerate Response and Recovery

Andrew Gorecki and Christopher Scott

CISO DRG Publishing
P.O. Box 928115
San Diego, CA 92192-8115
<www.CISODRG.com>
info@cisodrg.com
ISBN 978-1-955976-20-6

To contact the authors, write the publisher at the address provided above, "Attention: Author Services."

Editor Bill Bonney
Technical Editor Matt Stamper
Copy Editor Nadine Bonney
Production by Last Mile Publishing

Acknowledgements

Andrew Gorecki

Writing a book is like embarking on a long journey. It requires tremendous effort, personal sacrifices, and unwavering determination to get to the finish line. Going through the process is challenging, if not impossible, without a supportive environment and sacrifices made by your loved ones. For this reason, I am grateful to everyone who directly and indirectly helped to make this book a reality.

First and foremost, I'm grateful to my colleagues and mentors who helped me embark on my professional journey and shaped who I am professionally. I want to thank Himanshu Wickramasinghe, who introduced me to cybersecurity, mentored me in my early years, and guided me on the consulting path.

I am also grateful to Wendi Whitmore and Ahmed Saleh, who took a chance on me in 2017 and brought me to the U.S. to join IBM X-Force. I am also grateful to Kurt Rohrbacher and many of my former X-Force colleagues, who were a source of inspiration and motivation that allowed me to grow as a professional. Finally, I want to thank Charles Henderson and Chris McCurdy, who believed in me. I could always count on them for support.

A special thanks to Chris Scott, who introduced me to cyber crisis management, acted as a mentor over the years, and has been a role model of an exceptional professional and human being.

I am particularly grateful to Bill Bonney, whose valuable feedback and guidance were instrumental in getting this project over the finish line. I also want to thank Matt Stamper for reviewing the material, providing valuable comments, and contributing content.

Finally, this book would not have been possible without the support of my wife Marie and my daughter Alicia. I want to thank them for the support, encouragement, and sacrifices that allowed me to make this book a reality!

Christopher Scott

This book is a testament to the journey I've undertaken in the realm of cybersecurity, a journey made possible by the faith, guidance, and support of remarkable individuals and teams who believed in the vision of creating a safer digital world.

My professional journey took a significant turn in 2012 thanks to Wendi Whitmore, who took a chance on me by bringing me into the fold at CrowdStrike. This opportunity marked the beginning of an impactful contribution to the world of cybersecurity, setting the stage for the work that would define my career.

I am deeply grateful to George Kurtz, Shawn Henry, and the rest of the leadership at CrowdStrike. Their trust in me to tackle significant challenges and explore new frontiers has been instrumental in my growth and the advancements we've achieved together in the field.

At IBM, Koos Lodewijkx stood as a beacon of what it means to be not just an exceptional professional but a great human being and friend. His example has been a constant source of inspiration and guidance.

Special thanks are due to Andrew Gorecki, whose unwavering professionalism and drive were pivotal in turning the concept of this book into reality. His dedication and commitment to excellence have been key factors in the successful completion of this project.

The team at CISO DRG Publishing, especially the amazing support from Bill Bonney, has provided incredible backing throughout this endeavor. Their insights, encouragement, and assistance have been invaluable in bringing this book to fruition.

Last but certainly not least, my heartfelt gratitude goes to my family—Sarah, Elizabeth, and Edric. Their love, understanding, and sacrifice, allowing me to travel the world to combat cyber threats and assist organizations in strengthening their security postures, have been the cornerstone of my resolve. Your support has been my strength, and I love and appreciate you all more than words can express.

This book reflects not just my journey and insights but the collective spirit and dedication of everyone mentioned and even those unnamed. Together, we contribute to making the digital realm a safer place for all. Thank you.

Table of Contents

Foreword

Since I co-founded CrowdStrike in 2011, I have witnessed first-hand the devastating consequences that a breach can inflict on victim organizations. In recent years, high-profile breaches have sent shockwaves across every industry and serve as a wake-up call for many leaders.

As the threat landscape has become more complex and sophisticated, cyberattacks have increased with dramatic velocity. Data theft and ransomware have become commonplace, while nation-states increasingly conduct cyberespionage and misinformation campaigns to undermine democratic processes in the Western world.

At the same time, cloud-conscious adversaries increasingly target and exploit cloud environments, while the explosion of generative AI makes it easier for low-skilled adversaries to move faster and launch more 'state-of-the-art' attacks. Adversaries leverage stolen identity credentials and use interactive tactics with hands-on keyboard operators to evade legacy defenses. No organization is fully immune to cyberattacks. The battle is no longer about stopping malware - it's about stopping the breach.

That's why, since co-founding CrowdStrike, my mission has been to stop breaches and improve security outcomes for our customers. While CrowdStrike secures tens of thousands of organizations, from small businesses to large Fortune 50 clients, many organizations still rely on legacy, out-of-date solutions that are ineffective in stopping sophisticated adversaries. Unfortunately, those organizations are hit the hardest when they experience a breach. This is why I believe that being prepared for a potential crisis is so essential.

This book distills years of experience from the trenches of cyber crisis response into a framework that organizations can use to plan for a cyber crisis proactively. Andrew and Chris have taken their decades of combined experience in breach response, remediation, and executive crisis advisory and engineered a framework to help security, technology, and business leaders better prepare to handle breaches and their aftermath.

This book also provides a unique and multidimensional perspective on responding to large-scale events. It covers topics ranging from stopping the bleeding, starting the response process on the right foot, handling investigations and recovery, managing brand reputation, and working with regulators.

I have personally worked with both authors over my career. Andrew and Chris have done a fantastic job of distilling their years of experience into a crisp guide that can be used by security technologists as well as senior executives.

If you are looking for a comprehensive crisis response guide rooted in a practical understanding of the domain and written by authors with plenty of battle scars, this book is for you. My hope is that you read this book to preemptively prepare yourself and your organization before a crisis ever materializes. However, if you find yourself knee-deep in the middle of a full-blown incident, this book will be your definitive guide to weathering the storm and recovering.

Stay secure,

George Kurtz,
Co-Founder and CEO of CrowdStrike

Preface

In our shared experience, we have observed that many organizations struggle with crisis response, particularly when facing a significant cyberattack for the first time. This struggle often encompasses a disconnect between technical and business-level responses, poor coordination and communication, an insufficient understanding of competing priorities, and inadequate containment before business recovery.

Moreover, building crisis response capabilities based solely on industry standards and high-level guidelines is challenging. These are often penned by scholars and academics who lack practical understanding of responding to a cyber crisis, and more than theory is needed. In crisis response, experience and "battle scars" are more valuable than degrees, certifications, and other formal qualifications that only prove knowledge of concepts and theory.

Over the years, our numerous conversations and client meetings have highlighted concerns about insufficient preparedness for potential crises and a lack of practical resources. Despite catastrophic cyberattacks becoming almost daily events, the cyber crisis domain remains a relatively uncharted territory among business and technology leaders. This realization led us to write a book together, a decision we both enthusiastically embraced.

We have spent years in the trenches of crisis response, serving in technical, management, leadership, and advisory capacities. We aim to convey our practical understanding and experience of this subject in simple language, avoiding technical and esoteric jargon, and provide the industry with useful guidelines to help enterprises build cyber crisis response capabilities.

Over the years, Chris developed and refined The SONAR Method™, a framework that includes five phases in responding to a crisis:

Stabilize, Organize, Negotiate, Articulate, then Remediate/Recover. Having worked together helping companies respond to crises, we knew we could use it as the basis for organizing this book and explaining cyber response concepts to our audience. The SONAR Method framework (SONAR) provides a fundamental structure and guiding principles for building cyber crisis response capabilities while allowing you to construct your program according to your organization's size and the intricacies of your regulatory requirements, available resources, and culture.

Our book introduces a framework for managing incidents ranging from singular events to complex cyber breaches and crises. Crisis response requires coordinating multiple, often conflicting activities. Therefore, the framework introduces concepts such as stabilizing an environment during a cyber-attack, organizing teams and resources, negotiating with stakeholders, and communicating effectively across various parties, including regulators and third-party entities. It emphasizes the importance of engaging with these external groups for compliance and collaborative efforts, alongside detailing actions for remediation and recovery. As experts who have lived in the trenches of crisis response, this book describes many of the common pitfalls we have seen and potential solutions. Of course, there is no better way to learn than to do it yourself, but understanding the paths others have walked can help you better prepare for the journey.

Writing this book has been a journey. We hope you will enjoy reading this book as much as we enjoyed writing it and find it a valuable source of information regardless of your role and experience with this domain.

We wish you all the best and success in your cyber crisis response journey!

Andrew Gorecki and Chris Scott

Introduction

We live in a hyper-connected world with no geographical boundaries restricting information flow. The same technology that allows us to exchange information, facilitate e-commerce transactions, and collaborate globally also enables malicious actors to conduct their operations and cause harm to organizations and individuals. Cyberattacks are no longer a hypothetical threat but something that can happen to any organization regardless of size, industry sector, or geographic location.

Cyberattacks, with ransomware leading the charge, have taken the media by storm in recent years. Organizations across all industries, including Norsk Hydro, AXA, Nissan, and Epiq, suffered significant losses due to cyberattacks. Moreover, cyberattacks also pose a serious risk to critical infrastructure and essential services. For example, the Colonial Pipeline ransomware attack in May 2021 severely impacted fuel delivery on the United States East Coast. Following the attack, Colonial Pipeline turned off the spigot out of concern that malware could impact operational technology systems supporting fuel distribution.[1] Another example includes a ransomware attack on the four Scripps Health Hospitals in California that led to almost $113 million in losses for the institution.[2]

Cyberattacks can severely impact business operations and have data privacy, legal, and brand reputation implications for the victim organizations. For example, double extortion is a common strategy

1 New York Times, "Pipeline Attack Yields Urgent Lessons About U.S. Cybersecurity," published May 14, 2021, available at https://www.nytimes.com/2021/05/14/us/politics/pipeline-hack.html.

2 HIPAA Journal, "Scripps Health Ransomware Attack Cost Increases to Almost $113 Million," published August 11, 2021, available at https://www.hipaajournal.com/scripps-health-ransomware-attack-cost-113-million/.

that cyber criminals employ, combining data theft with ransomware deployment to increase their chances of getting paid. Even if the victim organization recovers business operations, releasing confidential information can damage brand reputation, lead to class action lawsuits, and have profound data privacy implications.

As experts who have lived in the trenches of response, we have witnessed firsthand catastrophic cyber events and how a lack of adequate preparation led to chaos, delays in response, and impeded recovery efforts. Incident and crisis response plans focusing on checklists to satisfy compliance requirements are no longer enough. Instead, you need to take a more pragmatic approach to crisis response and build capabilities to accelerate response instead of impeding it.

A cyber crisis is no longer a hypothetical event that can only happen due to bad luck. We live in a digital age where cybercrime is a lucrative business, and a successful cyberattack is as inevitable as death and taxes.

We have worked with clients who told their senior leadership, "We looked at different threats and determined it is highly unlikely anyone would like to attack us." At the other end of the spectrum, we also encountered clients with a false sense of security, believing that deploying a silver bullet solution promised by a security vendor would solve their security headaches. This thinking is naive and out of touch with reality.

Sadly, cyberattacks hit organizations that think they are immune the hardest. When a cybercriminal deploys ransomware to your environment, it can impact business operations for weeks and cause massive financial losses and regulatory headaches. Cybercrime is a lucrative business, and you can no longer assume your organization is exempt from being the target of a cyberattack.

How your organization manages a cyber crisis can define brand reputation for many years to come and, in extreme cases, can spell the difference between the life and death of the enterprise. However, it is not all doom and gloom. A well-thought-out crisis response strategy and preparation can help you endure a storm and an emotional roller coaster when your organization becomes the victim of a ferocious cyberattack.

How this Book Is Organized

Andrew and Chris worked together at a leading cybersecurity company. They successfully employed the concepts described in The SONAR Method framework to assist major clients in responding to and recovering from a cyber crisis. We organized the book into six sections, including a section to define a crisis and then the five phases according to The SONAR Method. This book reflects our experience using this method. The six sections are as follows:

Defining a Cyber Crisis – defines fundamental concepts underpinning crisis response, including a cyber crisis definition and defining crisis parameters. This section also provides an overview of the threat landscape and some essential guidance for organizations that want to build crisis response capabilities.

Stabilize – how to stop the bleeding so you can properly activate the Crisis Response Team. This phase focuses on the initial decisions during a cyber crisis to contain an event and prevent its exacerbation in your IT environment. We discuss how to stabilize the initial chaos when a crisis event occurs and get the situation under control. However, stopping the bleeding is just the first step in the response process.

Organize – how to organize a crisis response, including setting up technical and business teams, the role of executive management in the response process, crisis management and coordination, and response planning and execution. We conclude this phase with an overview of breach response investigations and remediation and recovery considerations.

Negotiate – how to negotiate with key stakeholders, especially with conflicting priorities and activities. This section also touches on negotiation with a threat actor and aligning responses to business priorities to ensure everyone works in concert towards the same goals. In the Negotiate phase, you sit down with other leaders behind closed doors and agree on concrete actions to control the crisis.

Articulate – As part of the Articulate phase, you must communicate decisions and actions to internal stakeholders, provide clear direction, articulate roles and responsibilities, and ensure everyone is marching in the same direction. Furthermore, you must also communicate with external stakeholders where appropriate. Otherwise, a negative perception could amplify the crisis and cause your organization a Public Relations nightmare.

Remediate – The last phase in The SONAR Method framework is to remediate the compromised network and recover your systems to an operational and secure state. This part will guide you through considerations and approaches to eradicating the threat actor from the compromised network and securely recovering systems so the actor cannot easily return to continue their operations.

Note that the Remediate part of the SONAR framework is an overarching term encompassing the remediation of security weaknesses that led to a crisis, system restoration, and recovering the impacted environments to an operational state.

The framework may appear linear at first. However, you should use it iteratively and incrementally when responding to a crisis. Figure 1 highlights this process.

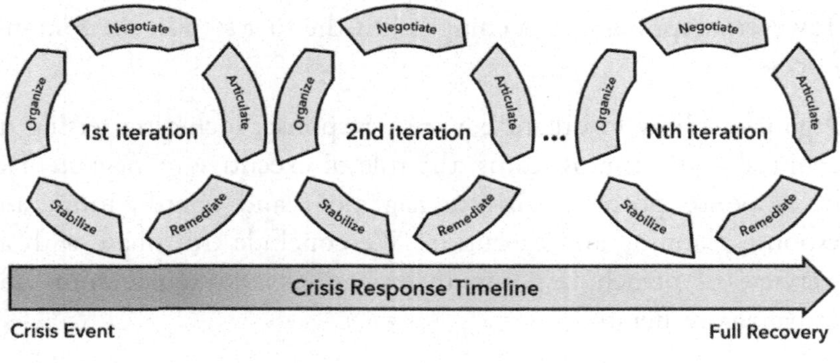

Figure 1 – Crisis Response Timeline

Crisis response is often a messy and convoluted process. The purpose of this framework is to provide you with a structure and guidelines to handle a cyber crisis event. However, feel free to tailor the framework to your response needs. Apply your judgment and critical thinking and leverage the framework based on your unique context.

Section 1

Defining a Cyber Crisis

"If I had only one hour to solve a problem, I would spend up to two-thirds of that hour attempting to define what the problem is."

~ Mathematician and theorist, Albert Einstein

Chapter 1

What Is a Cyber Crisis?

Crisis response deals with the reality of a rapidly unfolding cyber event that can impact business operations, severely damage your brand and reputation, lead to financial losses, and cause regulatory headaches stemming from data breaches.

In our experience, the term *cyber crisis* is often misunderstood in the cybersecurity industry and among business leaders. Moreover, we frequently encounter even seasoned professionals using *crisis response* and *crisis communications* interchangeably. While the former deals with the reality of a significant cyber event, the latter is a subset of crisis response focused on managing the **perception** of that reality by shaping internal and external opinions about the unfolding event.

There is no universal definition of *crisis* or one-size-fits-all criteria for declaring it. We strongly advise you to work with your business leaders to define the parameters of a crisis for your organization based on your business context and potential loss scenarios. However, for this book, we define a cyber crisis as follows:

A significant cyber event or a series of compounding events that negatively impact business operations, threaten the health and safety of employees and customers, lead to material financial losses and brand reputation damage or breach of regulatory requirements, or cause other material impacts.

Remember, how you define the term crisis is specific to your organization. However, the critical aspect of this definition is identifying what a material impact means for your business. A material impact is what often distinguishes a crisis from an incident. It refers to a significant or high-magnitude loss, whether caused by a single event or the compounding of multiple events. Later in this chapter, we explain how to define crisis parameters for your organization.

Differentiating Between Crises and Incidents

While this book primarily focuses on addressing crisis events, it is important to understand the difference between an *incident* and a *crisis* because an *incident* you do not address adequately can cause a *crisis* to unfold before your eyes.

An *incident* is a small-scale event that does not severely impact an organization and is addressable at the tactical level as part of day-to-day operations. For example, suppose a malicious threat actor compromises a user workstation. Your security team contains the intrusion before the threat actor establishes a foothold and moves laterally to other systems or gains access to confidential data. In such a case, the event does not have a material impact on your organization, and there is no need for a strategic-level response.

A particular type of incident is a *major incident.* A *major incident* often leads to a substantial, temporary impact and requires an "all-hands-on-deck" response. However, you can contain it relatively quickly without causing high-magnitude losses and prolonged business impact. For example, suppose a threat actor launches a distributed denial-of-service (DDoS) attack against a web application that handles large volumes of business transactions, causing financial losses and negative publicity. In such a case, the response will require an "all-hands-on-deck" approach from your technical functions to contain the incident and recover the impacted application. The senior leadership will be informed about the response but may not actively drive it from a strategic perspective.

Incident response mainly revolves around technical response and can be contained relatively quickly, followed by timely recovery and a short-lived impact. A cyber crisis, on the other hand, leads to a prolonged impact on operations, with recovery times often exceeding pre-established Recovery Time Objectives (RTO) and Recovery Point Objectives (RPO).

In other words, while incident response mainly focuses on technical activities, crisis response considers a more strategic and holistic approach to managing the state of affairs. This book is all about managing crisis response.

Chapter 2

Defining Crisis Parameters

The parameters for declaring a crisis are organization-specific and dependent on factors such as scope, revenue at stake, industry norms, applicable regulations, risk appetite, and human life and safety.

Impact criteria that we often leverage in our consulting engagements include:

- **Operational** – an event that negatively affects the operations or availability of critical systems, applications, data, or even an entire business process, causing a severe impact on business operations.
- **Legal and Data Privacy** – an event that leads to the unauthorized access to or disclosure of a substantial amount of confidential information, causing a materiality impact and the requirement to disclose the event to regulators and the affected parties. The impacted data may include client data, Personally Identifiable Information (PII), confidential business information, intellectual property, and other data subject to local laws and regulations.
- **Reputational** – an event that can lead to severe and long-term brand reputation damage, often with significant national media coverage and widespread social media exposure.
- **Financial** – an event that leads to significant direct or indirect monetary losses. Those losses can include lost revenue, response costs, litigation costs, damage compensations to victims, and regulatory fines.

In reality, a cyber crisis often leads to one or more of these impacts. For example, an extensive ransomware attack combining double extortion tactics can lead to operational, data privacy, reputational, and financial impacts. Double extortion refers to a tactic where a malicious actor exfiltrates confidential data from the compromised environment before deploying ransomware to increase the chances of payment.

We have observed that some clients attempt to quantify certain impact types, such as the amount of data leaked or financial losses. We strongly advocate risk and impact quantification as part of preparedness, and frameworks such as Factor Analysis of Information Risk (FAIR) are available to assist you.[3] However, potential losses and impacts cannot always be quantified at the onset of a crisis event. For this reason, we recommend establishing crisis parameters based on qualitative measures for the impact criteria outlined earlier in this section.

As part of crisis preparedness, we recommend collaborating with business stakeholders, Risk Management, Legal and Data Privacy, Business Continuity (BC), and other necessary functions to establish crisis parameters for your organization. For example, we frequently engage Risk Management as one of the first steps in defining crisis parameters for our clients. We observed that Risk Management departments in larger organizations often have a risk matrix established with thresholds for event severity, including crisis criteria. This approach has the following benefits:

- Saves time on knowledge discovery and development effort
- Aligns crisis parameters to the organization's risk appetite
- Establishes consistency and a common language among stakeholders

[3] The FAIR Institute is a research-driven not-for-profit organization dedicated to advancing the discipline of cyber and operational risk management through education, standards, and collaboration. Available here: https://www.fairinstitute.org.

A word of caution. Although we encourage you to leverage a sound process and methodology to determine various impact levels, your cyber crisis definition must be succinct, clear, and straightforward. Avoid analysis paralysis! Instead, keep it simple and create a definition that any employee can understand and use to recognize crisis precursors and symptoms and notify the right stakeholders to activate a crisis response.

The next chapter explains what factors often lead to and contribute to a cyber crisis.

Chapter 3

Activating Crisis Response

Depending on the scope and nature of a crisis event, you can partially or fully activate the Crisis Response Team. We explore this topic more in the Organize Phase. However, in this section, we want to emphasize that the activation criteria should serve as guidelines.

Every situation is different, and even the most detailed playbook cannot cater to all scenarios or replace critical thinking. Consequently, the person responsible for activating the Crisis Response Team must rapidly assess the situation and use the criteria combined with their best judgment when making decisions regarding the team activation. Sometimes, it is better to ask for forgiveness than permission.

Also, note that a responsibility assignment may differ for partial and complete activation. For instance, a Chief Finance Officer (CFO) may be informed about the event during a business-impacting DDoS attack. However, during a data breach event, the CFO will likely be consulted and responsible for approving expenditures on resources and external vendors to assist with the investigation and containment. We explore this topic in-depth in the Organize section of this book.

Based on our experience, organizations fully activate the Crisis Response Team under the following conditions:

- A cyberattack severely impacts multiple core applications and business services globally or in a specific region, causing a significant operational impact.

- Disaster recovery and business resumption are the top priorities, and time is critical.
- An "all-hands-on-deck" response is required that takes priority over day-to-day job duties.
- Each hour of downtime leads to significant financial losses, and time is critical.

In contrast, you may partially activate the Crisis Response Team when a cyberattack causes data privacy or reputational impact. However, an "all-hands-on-deck" response may not be required, and your company can still conduct business operations while responding to the crisis. For example, when a threat actor gains access to confidential customer data, leading to data privacy and potential legal implications, the organization can still serve its customers and process transactions while investigating the event, managing public relations, and working with regulators.

It is essential to establish who determines whether partial or complete activation of the Crisis Response Team is required. Furthermore, as part of planning, determine who decides what roles you should activate as part of the process.

Of course, the guidance above is based on large-scale events where we assisted the impacted organizations with the response. However, we encourage you to establish criteria specific to your organization based on your unique business context.

Chapter 4

Understanding the Threat Landscape

The term threat landscape refers to an ecosystem encompassing the cyber threats that can negatively impact your organization and lead to material losses if not managed adequately. The ecosystem includes threat actors, also called threat groups or adversaries, vulnerabilities, malware, and the tools, tactics and procedures that enable a threat actor to execute a successful attack.

We no longer deal with individuals and small groups hacking for notoriety or fun. On the contrary, in the age where information is often considered a natural resource and information technology underpins many business processes, we face threat groups reassembling modern businesses with highly organized and structured operations. The following paragraphs briefly describe common threat actor types and their motivations.

Advanced Persistent Threats

Advanced Persistent Threat (APT) refers to sophisticated threat actors often associated with nation-states and foreign intelligence agencies engaging in cyber espionage to advance the domestic agendas of their countries, including political, economic, and military gains. Sophistication, funding, and often unlimited resources distinguish APTs from other threat groups. Moreover, APT threats aim to remain undetected in the compromised environment for an extended period and maintain their persistence. This characteristic applies even when the victim organization detects an APT's presence and attempts to eradicate the threat actor from their network.

APT attacks are targeted and carefully planned to infiltrate resources. As part of the attack chain, APT actors often leverage customized malware, employ detection evasion techniques, and exfiltrate data over a prolonged period.

An example of an APT threat actor is Cozy Bear, also called APT 29. According to the cybersecurity firm CrowdStrike, Cozy Bear is an "adversary of Russian origin, assessed as likely to be acting on behalf of the Foreign Intelligence Service of the Russian Federation."[4]

Organized Cybercrime

Over the last several years, we have witnessed an unprecedented rise in cybercrime, and we expect the trend to continue. Cybercrime refers to criminal activity leveraging computer systems for financial gains. A prime example of cybercrime is ransomware, a type of malware that encrypts data and specific system files and demands payment to provide a decryption key and unlock the data.

These days, we are dealing with a highly structured cybercrime ecosystem comprising functions resembling technology development, operations, finance, marketing, and sometimes even call centers. Moreover, cyber threat actors specialize, collaborate, and form affiliate networks and their relationships are often based on trust and brand reputation.

The shift to an as-a-service model gave rise to specializations, such as malware development, initial access brokers, ransomware operators, and money laundering services. Furthermore, the financial model includes purchasing access to networks from access brokers, profit sharing, payroll for staff, and affiliate commissions for successful ransomware deployment. Access brokers specialize in compromising and planting malware on corporate networks and selling that access on the dark web.

This phenomenon, further intensified by the increasing use of cryptocurrencies which offer anonymity and ease of cross-border

[4] Crowdstrike Adversary List, available here: https://adversary.crowdstrike.com/en-US/adversary/cozy-bear/.

transactions, has contributed to a massive wave of ransomware attacks in recent years. Coupled with geopolitical tensions and cyber criminals operating from jurisdictions outside the influence of Western governments, this has led to a catastrophic impact on their victims. The decentralized and often unregulated nature of cryptocurrencies has made it easier for threat actors to demand and receive ransoms, exacerbating the ransomware crisis.

Hacktivists

Hacktivists are threat actors who blend cyber hacking and activism to conduct damaging operations and draw attention to political, social, or religious causes. The common targets of hacktivists include corporations, governments, and other entities they perceive to be corrupt, greedy, abusing human rights, causing social injustice, or not aligned with their ideology.

Their tactics include DDoS attacks, website defacement, destructive malware, and data leaking.

In recent decades, one of the most prolific hacktivist groups has been Anonymous, responsible for attacks against governments, corporations, and religious institutions. One of their most famous attacks was "Operation Tunisia," where the group took down eight government websites in support of the Arab Spring Movement in the 2010s.[5]

Insider Threats

An insider threat is a threat that comes from within the organization and can include current and former employees, contractors, and business partners who have access to protected assets. Insider threats are particularly dangerous due to the level of access and trust insiders are given to perform their functions. They often have an intimate knowledge of the organization, including business processes, policies, controls, and valuable data.

5 Crowdstrike, "Hacktivism: Types and Examples," July 8, 2002. Available here: https://www.crowdstrike.com/cybersecurity-101/hacktivism/.

Insider threats can have different means and motives that often revolve around financial gain or espionage on behalf of a foreign intelligence agency. Moreover, disgruntled employees with grievances about their employer may also engage in insider threat activities.

It is worth emphasizing that insider threats are not always malicious. Employees and associates can cause harm due to neglect, careless behavior, or even manipulation.

Chapter 5

Preparing for a Cyber Crisis

Preparing for a crisis can be a complex undertaking that can take months, depending on the size and complexity of your business. However, adequate preparation can save precious hours during a significant cyber event, avoid unpleasant surprises, and accelerate the overall response effort.

This brief chapter outlines some fundamental guidance for organizations embarking on this journey who need help getting the process started on the right foot.

Establishing a Policy

Establishing a crisis response capability starts with a policy. A policy is a foundational component of crisis response and includes the following benefits:

- Demonstrates senior leadership's commitment to establishing a program and dedicating resources to make it successful
- Sets a strategic direction for capability development
- Defines the principles and high-level actions for the program

You can enact a dedicated crisis response policy that exclusively sets the principles and rules governing crisis response or include a crisis response requirement in a broader enterprise-level policy.

We recommend the first approach, especially for larger enterprises, to ensure that crisis response receives the necessary attention and resources to be successful. The latter approach typically works for small and medium-sized businesses (SMBs) that may not have the same resources to create a dedicated program as large corporations. Regardless of the approach, we strongly encourage you to consider the following when enacting a policy:

- Create a mission statement.
- Assign ownership and overall responsibility for the program.
- Establish scope. A scope example may include a specific geographic region for independent subsidiaries or the entire enterprise.
- Establish a statement of authority to empower the team to respond to crises on behalf of the enterprise.
- Identify critical functions and determine the program's applicability to those functions.

Ensure you create a policy jointly with critical stakeholders who will form the Crisis Response Team or consult them throughout the process. We have observed that the most successful crisis response teams unite their members around common objectives. Each stakeholder has a unique perspective, and including their needs in the policy and the consequent program will allow you to start crisis management planning on the right foot.

Developing a Plan

A crisis is a complex and often unpredictable event that can hit your organization like a meteor crashing through the Earth's atmosphere, leaving you in the public spotlight until you get the situation under control and recover from the event. Therefore, having a crisis response plan is critical during such events. You must take swift and constructive actions to stabilize the situation, focus on critical priorities, and organize the response.

After establishing a Crisis Response Policy, we recommend working with department and business unit leaders to create a Crisis Response Plan, also called a Crisis Management Plan. If you lack in-house skills and resources to develop a plan, we recommend partnering with an external consulting firm with expertise and a proven track record. The firm will bring a framework, industry knowledge, and best practices. However, you will still have to make resources and key stakeholders available and work closely with the firm to ensure the final deliverables are tailored and actionable for your organization. Depending on the organization's size, stakeholder alignment, distribution of resources, and other organizational factors, developing a Crisis Response Plan can take several weeks to several months. This includes socializing the plan with vital stakeholders, testing it through exercises, and formal project sign-off.

A practical and actionable plan includes several elements. We briefly outline them below. However, we discuss the specific details in their respective sections of the SONAR framework.

- An introduction outlining the purpose, scope, and executive sponsor of the plan, and a reference to an appropriate policy
- Clearly outlined crisis parameters and plan activation criteria
- A Crisis Response Team definition, including a chain of command
- A high-level response process, including a workflow diagram
- Roles and responsibilities for stakeholders participating in the process
- A communication plan outline
- Logistics for on-site and remote responders
- An emergency contact list
- Scenarios outlining response requirements for specific events
- Post-crisis activities, including root cause analysis and lessons learned requirements

A word of caution! Unless you create a plan for compliance purposes, keep it succinct, focused, cohesive, and concise. The purpose of the plan is to guide a response to a crisis. If your plan is not actionable, then it will be of no use during an actual emergency. For example, if the body of your plan exceeds 60 pages, you will need to ask yourself whether responders can quickly locate information and put it into action.

What If You Already Have a Crisis Response Plan?

Often, organizations already have Crisis Response Plans for more traditional events, such as natural disasters, and ask us if they need a separate plan to address cyber crisis events. Another question we frequently encounter is the difference between those two types of plans.

Cyber crisis response is an extension of traditional crisis management. Crisis response is about managing a crisis from a strategic perspective, ensuring the organization recovers as soon as possible, and effectively managing its impact and the response perception from an internal and external perspective. As we often say, a crisis is a crisis, regardless of the root cause.

Depending on the scenario, the tactical activities will significantly differ. However, from a business and executive perspective, you employ the same functions and processes to handle the crisis. The only difference is how you handle the specific intricacies of a cyber crisis, and this is what this book is all about. We do not teach you about the fundamentals of managing a crisis. Instead, we assume you are familiar with crisis management and want to augment that knowledge with how to handle crisis events caused by a significant cyberattack.

Suppose you already have a Crisis Response Plan, and everyone within your organization is familiar with their roles and responsibilities and trained in their domain. In that case, you are already in a good place. Your next step is to extend the plan with cyber-specific scenarios, such as an unauthorized data disclosure or destructive cyberattack. Note that we neither use the term "breach" nor recommend using it. We explain the rationale behind this choice in the Organize section of this book.

However, if you start from scratch, we recommend developing a Crisis Response Plan with cyber-specific scenarios and extending it with other scenarios as required. The reason for starting with cyber scenarios is that, in our experience, cyberattacks are more likely than natural disasters to impact your business negatively.

If you are unsure where to start, consider partnering with a firm with a proven track record of responding to cyber crisis events and a consulting arm that can assist with cyber crisis response planning.

Establishing Relationships with External Vendors

Managing a cyber crisis is a complex undertaking that often requires external support. Many organizations hire external experts to augment internal capabilities. External experts bring industry expertise, assets, and experience acquired through numerous client engagements. For example, outside counsel with expertise in cyber can assist with navigating potential legal issues caused by a crisis event and minimize the risk of litigation. Depending on the size and nature of the relationship, there are several ways to establish relationships with external partners, including:

- Retainer agreements
- Service agreements
- Non-contractual agreements and arrangements
- Strategic partnerships

Cybersecurity is a hot market, and many organizations attempt to capitalize on the opportunity to grow their business in this space without adequate investments in acquiring the necessary skills and resources. During crisis response engagements, we have encountered organizations advising our clients without the required expertise and a proven track record of success in the cyber domain. For this reason, it is essential to evaluate prospective partners and service providers before entering into a contractual relationship. We recommend the following evaluation considerations:

- **Proven Track Record of Success** – Ensuring that a potential partner has a proven track record of success, mature capabilities, expertise, and industry experience to deliver on their promises is vital. The capabilities include assets, methodologies, and delivery processes. Determining if the firm stays abreast of new industry developments is essential.

- **Service Portfolio** – Service offerings vary significantly from firm to firm, even if those firms operate in the same industry and are of similar size. Larger organizations tend to have a more comprehensive service portfolio, whereas boutique firms focus on specific services. For example, a large legal firm may offer a wide range of legal advice and services. In contrast, a smaller firm may focus on data privacy laws and regulations, such as GDPR in the European Union.

- **Geographic Presence** – Large enterprises may prefer to partner with a service provider with a global footprint or presence in multiple locations. In contrast, boutique firms often cater to a specific market or operate within a confined geographic location. Understand whether you need global or regionalized services before entering into an agreement with a service provider.

- **Skills and Experience** – In our experience, the skills and expertise of professionals can vary from firm to firm. Be sure to find out about the background, skills, experience, and industry expertise of professionals who will provide services to your organization. For example, we have come across PR firms that had expertise in traditional crisis management but could not handle a cyber crisis effectively.

- **Cost** – Often, firms that provide specialized skills and services come with a hefty price tag. As you build your crisis management program, the cost can add up very quickly. For this reason, perform a cost-benefit analysis of hiring in-house personnel versus an external firm. Furthermore, even firms with similar capabilities and industry experience can significantly differ in pricing.

Hiring an external firm to augment your internal capabilities does not automatically lead to success. You need to establish and foster a relationship with the firm to ensure they can provide optimal support during an actual crisis. The following paragraphs offer proven guidance based on our consulting experience.

Examples of external firms that can augment internal crisis management capabilities include:

- Public Relations (PR) firm
- Outside counsel
- Digital forensics and incident response (DFIR) firm
- Insurance vendor
- Breach coach services
- Expert negotiation firm for cyber extortion events
- Disaster recovery firm, especially a firm that has extensive expertise in DR following cyberattacks

Practice, Practice, Practice!

How do you get to Carnegie Hall? Practice, practice, practice! Having a well-drafted Crisis Response Plan collecting dust on a shelf waiting for a crisis is not enough. Effective crisis response requires regular practice so the Crisis Response Team can build muscle memory, and their responses become automatic. Furthermore, we have observed that crisis responders who regularly undergo crisis response training better control stress and remain rational during significant events.

One key point we want to emphasize at the outset of this book is that a crisis is a fluid and dynamic state of affairs. Preparation and practice are key! You cannot script a response for every situation. No amount of reading and scripting can replace practice and experience.

You practice crisis response through regular and realistic exercises. Practicing crisis response is like an inoculation. It exposes you to a significant event, helping you build immunity without experiencing an actual catastrophic event. Crisis exercises are simulations exposing your Crisis Response Team to probable scenarios in a safe, controlled, and often informal environment.

At one end of the spectrum, discussion-based tabletop exercises allow participants to walk through the Crisis Response Plan and discuss how they would respond in their functional areas. At the other end of the spectrum are highly immersive scenarios with audio-visual elements and gamification techniques that resemble more realistic scenarios. Those exercises are often delivered in specially designed cyber ranges.

Regardless of which options you choose, there are several benefits to conducting regular exercises, including:

- Building muscle memory and emotional resiliency
- Familiarizing participants with their roles and responsibilities
- Identifying opportunities for improvement in the process
- Increased collaboration and appreciation of everyone's roles in the process

Moreover, an effective scenario should cover all the Crisis Response Plan components and the SONAR framework. We recommend conducting an exercise at least once a year.

Section 2

Stabilize

"It is not the strongest species that survive, nor the most intelligent, but the one most responsive to change."

~ English naturalist and biologist Charles Darwin

Introduction

The lead author for this section is Christopher Scott, with significant input from and in collaboration with Andrew Gorecki.

At the heart of crisis response, the preliminary Stabilize phase within the SONAR framework forms the foundation upon which all ensuing steps rest. However, the daunting task is identifying the best course of action through this intense, high-pressure stage. Who should we include in the process? What's our plan of action? How do we navigate our teams through this turbulent time laden with uncertainty?

Every crisis, as seen through the eyes of a Global Chief Information Security Officer (CISO) and business leaders, presents its unique set of challenges. Different risk profiles, operational obstacles, personnel, and external factors influence each crisis. Striking a balance between these variables while keeping a sharp focus on the organization's security is no small task.

When confronted with multiple risks and pressures, quickly identifying and responding to the most critical issues is of utmost importance. How do we adapt our priorities as the landscape evolves? How do we make informed decisions to restore stability in a crisis-ridden environment? Above all, how does a senior leader successfully maneuver through this intricate landscape, minimize primary risks to the organization, and guide the team towards effective remediation, coming out stronger at the end?

The situation becomes even more intricate when contemplating potential legal exposures and the possible impact on the organization's reputation. Amid a whirlwind of questions demanding immediate answers, and various stakeholders looking for these answers, effectively prioritizing becomes the key to successful recovery and continuous operations.

The Stabilize phase of the SONAR framework aids in this process. It guides you to focus on the most urgent matters, devise strategies to respond to critical questions, and understand how to proceed even when some queries remain unresolved. As a CISO, this phase empowers you with the tools and perspectives to shepherd your organization through the tempest and toward a safer destination.

Chapter 6

The Crisis Emerges

Let's visualize a common scenario: it's late Thursday afternoon, and your team looks forward to a well-deserved three-day weekend. Suddenly, a security alert signals suspicious outbound communications amidst the pre-holiday cheer. The world of cybersecurity is filled with such incidents—threat actors keenly understand that long weekends provide an ideal window for their clandestine activities.

Is this alert something more severe? Does it rise to the level of an incident? Does this evolve into a crisis? What are the criteria or processes that help an organization determine this situation?

We define the transition from an alert to an incident and then to a crisis by the severity and potential impact of the threat. At this point of the process, the severity and impact are unknown. This is the moment where you rely upon your staff's expertise and the technology that you have deployed and configured. This melding of human intuition and contextualizing technology allows for better decisions early in the process.

The elevation from an alert to an incident would include verifying malicious activity. That may consist of detecting unauthorized access, evidence of data compromise, or signs of exfiltration. All crises are incidents, but not all incidents elevate to a crisis. Scenarios that involve the following are likely to become a crisis:

- An extensive data breach involving sensitive data
- A large-scale operational disruption
- Legal or regulatory issues
- Public relations concerns or substantial risk to reputation
- Severe financial implications or loss

In the scenario described, your team would now assess the alert's severity and decide whether it merits escalation. This is a test of your team's threat assessment capabilities. Is the technology deployed giving reliable alert levels? How will you use metrics to measure team performance and drive decisions? Will your team voice their concerns effectively? Are your team leads assertive enough to investigate the issue and seek a resolution? The questions are many, and the answers are critical.

Alert Levels and Alert Fatigue

Throughout our years of incident response work, technology has often failed to classify alerts so that a human can better understand them. In many cases, there is missing contextual information that does not allow for a more concrete decision. Alerts categorized as medium or lower risk may be dismissed in anticipation of the holiday. Yet, it's these dismissed alerts that often give birth to crises. "Alert fatigue" is a real issue, as the incessant flow of alerts can overwhelm even the most experienced teams. Implementing strategic, risk-based measures is essential for efficient management. As organizations have deployed more technology, the amount of data can become overwhelming. It is also important to consider how to take this amount of data and properly stitch the content into a cohesive representation of the risk to allow people to determine the impact adequately.

Metrics Drive Decisions

A critical element to bear in mind is the selection of metrics used to drive team performance. Metrics are invaluable tools for your security teams, aiding them in strengthening their defenses. Traditional IT operational metrics, such as the duration from alert ticket creation to closure, may not be the most suitable when handling security incidents. Therefore, ensure your team has enough time to evaluate an alert's potential threat accurately. For example, we have encountered situations where security analysts marked endpoint security alerts as false positives to avoid missing response metric targets, only for the organization to experience a catastrophic ransomware event within two days.

It's essential for metrics to align with your organization's ultimate goals. Therefore, security executives should work closely with the technical teams to identify what they hope to achieve and select metrics that directly support these objectives.

Voicing Concerns

This scenario has an alert before a long weekend. It is imperative that you have simulated situations like this and provide options for team members to express opinions on the issues raised. There will be times when these concerns are not valid, but having the discussion, even when everyone wants to head out for some well-deserved time off, is critical to the continued defense of the network. Focus efforts on teaching how to use communication channels, escalate when needed, involve subject matter experts, and especially have a plan for off-hours notifications.

Leadership Assertiveness

Accountable leaders make for an effective organization that leads to quicker resolution of incidents. Team leaders should be responsible for resolving security incidents, which should be fostered by clear support from the executive leadership. These leaders should feel that they can have open communication to share their thoughts and to help drive the team during all aspects of the security life cycle.

Preparing for the attack requires answers to the above questions. One of my favorite phrases is *shift left of boom*. In essence, we try to focus our efforts to stop the boom (incident/breach) from happening. It is not always possible, but preparing as best we can leads to the best outcomes when our proactive measures do not fully prevent an incident.

Welcoming the Crisis

Fast forward to the next morning. A call disrupts your serenity as you're peacefully sipping your morning beverage. Your operational monitoring systems report a series of malfunctions: systems are down, customers can't make purchases, security systems are not working correctly, and admin accounts are locked out. Suddenly, the realization dawns that the networks and systems under your watch are under attack.

Navigating a crisis is an intricate process that often leads to chaos, even for the best-prepared organizations. The focus during this period should not be on questioning past decisions but rather on swiftly stabilizing the environment and isolating issues as quickly and efficiently as possible.

Immediate Response Considerations

A leader's role during this period is critical. They must make definitive decisions based on the available evidence. An auditor, a lawyer, or a regulator will inevitably closely examine these early decisions, so accurately documenting what you learned and when is vital. This post-incident review process will involve technical staff, executives, and board members, ensuring everyone understands the sequence of events that led to the crisis.

Please note that the Organize section of this book contains a comprehensive discussion on the structure and interaction between stakeholders forming your Crisis Response Team. This section emphasizes key roles that are engaged at the onset of a crisis and can be considered as "first responders" before a broader Crisis Response Team is activated.

Timing and the Crisis

Understanding the business calendar and its implications is a pivotal aspect during the onset of a crisis. Factors such as impending financial reporting, peak sales periods, or key operational milestones can significantly influence the Crisis Manager's approach and response strategy.

Here's a structured approach to ensure that you effectively navigate the challenges:

- Business Calendar Assessment:
  - Thoroughly analyze the business calendar. Identify imminent events such as financial reporting dates, peak sales windows, or other operational milestones.
  - Recognize that these factors will be pivotal in shaping the crisis response strategy.

- Collaborative Insights:
  - Actively engage with leaders and representatives from various business units to gain insights into critical events and their timing.
  - For instance, be aware of fast-approaching deadlines, such as payroll submissions. It's essential to understand that irrespective of the crisis, employees anticipate timely compensation.
  - Delays in payroll can sow discontent and unrest. To pre-empt this, liaise with Board members and HR teams to communicate any potential hiccups. Transparent communication fosters trust and can minimize negative fallout.

- Customer Contractual Obligations:
  - Regularly interact with teams involved in customer relations and product delivery. They can provide vital insights into time-sensitive commitments.
  - Early communication with customers is essential if a crisis jeopardizes product or service delivery. This not only manages expectations but can also safeguard business relationships.
  - Given the criticality of contracts, involve individuals who are adept in contract management early in the crisis. They can guide on obligations, potential breaches, and renegotiations.

- Cross-Functional Collaboration:
  - Foster a culture where the technical and business sides of the organization collaborate seamlessly. This

integrated approach ensures a holistic crisis management strategy.

- Regularly convene cross-functional meetings to review potential risks, refine communication protocols, and reinforce the importance of collaborative crisis response.

The Crisis Manager's Role

In times of crisis, the role of the Crisis Manager, often the CISO, is paramount. Their responsibilities are multifaceted; it's not merely about making quick decisions but also ensuring clear communication, effective decision-making, and tapping the right personnel for an adept response. In the preliminary stages, the CISO, in collaboration with the CIO, must spearhead efforts to stabilize the environment swiftly. As the situation evolves, their role transforms into a more structured leadership, directing the response team toward an effective resolution.

The Crisis Manager should proactively communicate the areas of concern to business peers to better enable them to help assemble an effective team. Utilize terms like "We may be facing a crisis" or "I'm apprehensive about our operational resilience" to mobilize necessary resources. The foremost objective remains clear: secure the environment. In this endeavor, pinpointing the right individuals to involve is crucial, necessitating a concerted effort from both technical and business sectors.

Ensuring rapid stabilization hinges on the Crisis Manager's ability to discern key systems integral to core operations, pinpoint vital assets, and involve personnel with a comprehensive grasp of the business's functionalities. This process should be complemented by fostering a clear command chain with the operations team, guaranteeing efficient crisis response.

Confronting crises is an inevitable facet of business. A proactive Crisis Manager, reinforced by a synchronized team, can considerably mitigate its adverse impact. Their collective efforts ensure minimal disruptions, demanding the active participation of the technical cadre and the Board. Through unity and foresight, they can ensure the organization survives the turmoil and emerges more resilient and robust.

In the remaining chapters in the Stabilize section, we describe key considerations to "stop the bleeding" and initial containment to prevent its exacerbation and give your organization enough breathing space to create an action plan to investigate the event adequately, execute long-term containment and eradication measures, and recover your environments to an operational state.

Chapter 7

Understanding Your Distributed Environment

As our world advances technologically, companies find their workloads and assets distributed across numerous locations, including on-premises servers, cloud platforms, and a blend of both. Advanced applications operate across multiple cloud ecosystems, each presenting unique operational requirements, logging, and monitoring systems. Grasping the location of these assets, the individuals capable of managing them, available data for analysis, and supporting systems is vital when facing a crisis.

The following list provides the fundamental elements needed to stabilize the crisis and achieve initial containment:

- **Institutional Knowledge**: Expert generalists with broad system knowledge are crucial for swift decision-making.
- **Digital Resources and Location:** Awareness of computing asset locations and their management is necessary.
- **User, Application, and Administrative Profiles**: Recognizing account and access control capabilities are necessary to stabilize the environment rapidly.
- **Network Details**: Navigating and managing the complexities of various networked systems during a crisis is key, including business partner connectivity and connectivity between hybrid environments.
- **Security Instruments/Devices**: Familiarity with available security tools and their capabilities is essential.

We dive into each topic in the following sections.

The Need for Institutional Knowledge

Centralized knowledge is a linchpin in crisis management. However, many organizations still struggle with asset management. In our experience, organizations often learn the hard lesson about tracking assets and their configuration information following a cyber crisis event. If the systems storing essential information are offline or asset information is unavailable, individuals possessing this knowledge become indispensable. While specializations have taken precedence, generalists, with their broad range of skills and knowledge, are invaluable for making fast, critical decisions during a crisis. For this reason, identify and engage your expert generalists at the onset of a crisis. Then, leverage their knowledge to make crucial stabilization decisions and identify non-obvious risks, such as an impact on a downstream system or even a business partner, when executing initial containment activities.

Locating Digital Resources

The computing assets' location is as important as the assets themselves. Today's businesses utilize various platforms, such as Amazon Web Services, Google Cloud, or Microsoft Azure; data centers; and Software-as-a-Service (SaaS) applications. Even employee computers in various locations contribute to the complexity of asset management. Knowing where these assets are and possessing the expertise to manage them is crucial during a crisis. For example, analysts often must deploy analysis tools to compromised environments and acquire forensic images from systems heavily used by the Threat Actor. Having knowledge of the location of those systems and the ability to access them promptly can have a tremendous impact on the velocity of the response.

Understanding User, Application, and Administrative Profiles

As part of the response effort, you often must make changes to different account types, such as user profiles, application profiles, and administrative profiles. Knowing these accounts' location and potential impact enables more effective responses and precise actions. For example, making configuration changes and amending permissions for a highly privileged account running a business-critical application requires a different approach than resetting credentials for a non-privileged user.

Furthermore, familiarity with your access control mechanisms, including authentication and authorization capabilities within your identity platforms, is crucial to implementing initial containment measures while minimizing the risk of unintentional business impact resulting from those actions.

Navigating Network Details

Today's interconnected computing environments often spread assets across various networks. Understanding the complexities of securing and managing these systems during a crisis is crucial. Furthermore, with the popularity of microservices and distributed applications, a single system can be composed of assets hosted on multiple networks, some of which may be managed by third parties.

Asset management, perimeter controls, encrypted traffic, and physical locations play significant roles in the overall network security strategy and options to implement containment measures.

Security Tools and Platforms

A crisis response team must understand the available security tools and devices, including endpoint technology, network edge controls, cloud-based services, and personnel authorized to implement these controls. This knowledge is crucial in determining an initial containment approach and using the capabilities for analysis, long-term containment, and eradication. In our experience, many company employees are not familiar or comfortable with all the capabilities that come with their tools, especially features that are not used on a day-to-day basis. Consider engaging vendors to compensate for in-house knowledge gaps if that's the case.

For example, with the right endpoint tools and expertise, you may be able to isolate specific compromised systems instead of disconnecting an entire network segment to contain a malware outbreak. This approach can help you minimize business impact from a containment strategy to specific systems only.

Recognizing Dependencies

The crisis response team must understand the dependencies of various systems and applications. Collaboration with key business application owners to understand the connections and potential impacts of a system's loss can enable a more effective crisis response.

Maintaining an adequate inventory is paramount, particularly during crisis management efforts. The inventory could take many forms, but having one during a crisis is critical. Having the institutional knowledge of a generalist, knowing the locations of your digital resources, understanding user profiles, and recognizing the capabilities of various security instruments will significantly aid in navigating through a crisis.

With their vast knowledge, the generalist guides the team of subject matter experts (SMEs) to make quick changes, stabilizing an environment. The locations of digital resources play a significant role in managing a crisis. Knowing your user profiles can help identify abnormal behavior, signifying a possible breach. Understanding the details of your network and the available security instruments and devices will aid in ensuring the safety of your systems.

It's essential to remember that creating and maintaining these inventories requires regular reviews to ensure accuracy. This effort will undoubtedly pay dividends during a crisis and in identifying potential weaknesses in your defenses before an incident occurs. Ensuring that your incident response team has easy access to this information is also critical. The result will be a more resilient organization capable of effectively managing and overcoming crises.

The world of computing resources has evolved. We now deal with not just local networks but an expansive digital universe. When the Internet is the data center, locating your digital resources becomes more complex. Do you utilize Amazon Web Services, Google Cloud, Microsoft Azure, or a combination? Is there a physical data center? How about employee computers connecting from a variety of locations? Understanding the location of these resources and the expertise required to manage them is critical to crisis management.

Moreover, with the evolving complexity of data storage and the growth of centralized cloud storage, data is often replicated and stored in multiple places to suit various usage scenarios. As cyber threats increasingly involve potential data release, knowing where specific data resides and whether unauthorized entities have accessed it is critical to effective remediation.

Every situation calls for specific technologies and approaches for resolution. Does your team already have the requisite expertise? Do you rely on third-party resources for some aspects of management? How much information can you safely share with third-party entities during a crisis without jeopardizing your data's security? It's crucial to address these questions proactively before a crisis occurs.

Understanding user profiles, which you might overlook during a crisis, can also offer critical insights. Detailed user profiles may include normal user behavior patterns, such as data access habits, frequently used applications, and typical login times. Spotting deviations from these patterns can help identify potential breaches.

Application profiles are another integral part of your inventory. The profiles should cover what each application does, where it's hosted, who uses it, what data it uses, and how it communicates. This can be particularly useful in identifying abnormal behavior and understanding the impact of a potential breach.

Similar to user profiles, administrative profiles help you comprehend who has access to sensitive areas of your network and systems. These include IT staff and business users who have been granted administrative rights. Understanding who these individuals are, what they have access to, and their typical behavior can help you identify potential insider threats or compromised accounts.

Understanding your network topology, including all internal and external connections, is also vital. This includes details about your WAN, LAN, and any VPN connections. Knowing what connections should be in place can help you identify unauthorized connections during an incident.

Lastly, your security tools and devices are critical to your defense and response capabilities. This includes firewalls, IDS/IPS systems, endpoint security tools, and any other security tools you use. An inventory of these tools, their location, configuration, and the data they collect can be invaluable during an incident response.

In conclusion, identifying and understanding these dependencies can significantly improve your incident response capabilities. It can also help you identify potential weaknesses in your defenses before an incident occurs. However, creating and maintaining these inventories is not a one-time activity. It requires ongoing effort and regular reviews to ensure that they remain accurate and up-to-date. It's also important to consider how you will use this information during an incident and ensure that your incident response team has easy access to it. Preparedness is the key to efficient crisis management, and understanding your distributed environment is a significant part of that preparedness.

Chapter 8

Initial Containment Strategy

Securing a network under attack requires swift and calculated action. A well-crafted containment strategy can provide a stable base to minimize damage, isolate threats, and lay the groundwork for recovery. This strategy often hinges on isolating assets and accounts, which requires careful consideration of various factors and potential risks.

The following sections describe various isolation strategies you need to consider to prevent crisis exacerbation while minimizing business impact.

Data-Dependent Isolation

At the heart of every containment strategy lies the protection of critical data. When contemplating asset isolation, first scrutinize the nature of the data housed within. Asking key questions can illuminate the path forward:

- Is the data subject to regulatory control?
- Could the release of the data harm the company?
- Can the data be swiftly recovered if encrypted?
- Is the data crucial for backup and recovery?

Organizations must proactively reassess their backup strategies to address the evolving cyber threats effectively. Instead of broadly assigning administrator rights to backup users and servers, consider implementing isolated backups with stringent controls. Specifically, grant backup accounts access to production systems but prevent production systems from accessing backup accounts. Adopting this strategy minimizes data loss risks and speeds up the recovery process during the Remediation phase of The SONAR Method.

Time and Event-Based Isolation

To maximize the effectiveness of isolation and safeguard the organization's bottom line, adhere to the following steps:

- Prioritize understanding of the organization's key business events and financial reporting timelines.
- Avoid implementing major operational changes during these critical periods.
- Integrate the security team's strategy with the financial and business operations calendar to prevent disruptions.
- Establish mandatory quarterly meetings with finance and sales teams.
- Use these meetings to evaluate risks, refine decision-making processes, and enhance organizational readiness and resilience.

Location-Based Isolation

Location-specific assets can become focal points for the containment strategy during the Stabilization phase. As we mentioned in the previous chapter, understanding the assets' location—a home office, a remote site, or a coffee shop—can aid in isolating specific network sections.

Further questions to guide this process could include:

- Can entire offices or Virtual Local Area Networks (VLANs) be isolated?
- Can you separate affected and unaffected assets?
- What technologies are available at each location?

Comprehension of network design and the technology at each site is crucial to developing a robust location-based isolation strategy.

Asset Impact-Based Isolation

Not all assets bear the same weight. The isolation of those integral to customer-facing business operations can present increased risks. To understand the potential impact, ask:

- Does the asset relate to a core business process?
- Is the asset key to company communication?
- Will a data loss on this asset be detrimental to the business?
- Will the asset's isolation affect external customers or internal users more severely?
- Would the isolation impact manufacturing systems or safety systems?
- How easily can an impacted asset be isolated?
- When an asset is isolated do security tools fail to operate correctly?

To effectively prepare for potential threats:

- Initiate collaboration with business divisions well in advance.
- Together, identify and list all critical assets.
- Rank these assets based on their importance and potential impact.
- Develop a preemptive action plan for each prioritized asset to address potential threats.

Account Impact-Based Isolation

Compromised accounts can be a threat actor's gateway for lateral movement within the network, credential collection, and data exfiltration. Successful isolation of all user accounts, service/application accounts, and administrative accounts can prevent a minor incident from escalating into a significant breach.

To enhance your organization's ability to isolate based on accounts, follow these steps:

- Conduct a thorough audit of all existing accounts and their associated permissions.
- Identify and list any accounts with default administrator access.
- Develop a plan to modify or revoke unnecessary administrator privileges from these accounts.

- Implement a policy to prevent default administrator access for all future accounts.
- Regularly review and update account permissions to ensure security best practices are maintained.

Backup Strategy Assessment

In light of escalating cyber threats, reassessing backup strategies is prudent. Traditional methods granting backup servers and users wide-ranging administrative access across the network may no longer suffice. A more isolated setup with strict controls can limit the avenues available to a threat actor. A possible tactic is to permit backup accounts to access production systems, but not the reverse. This approach reduces data loss risks and accelerates the recovery process during the Remediation phase of The SONAR Method.

Understanding Network Infrastructure

A thorough comprehension of your network layout and the technologies available in each area is paramount for effectively implementing location-based isolation strategies. With this knowledge, you can make informed decisions regarding which assets to isolate and the potential ramifications of those decisions. Keeping this information up to date and readily accessible is critical to preparing for and efficiently responding to a crisis.

Assessing the Impact of Isolation

Deciding whether to isolate an asset requires understanding its significance to your business operations. This involves identifying systems vital to business functions, such as operations, customer applications, and payroll. Furthermore, awareness of your service level agreements (SLAs) can inform your decisions, helping to minimize business disruption while effectively containing the threat.

Account-Level Isolation

The capability to isolate accounts individually can be a potent component of your containment strategy. This demands an understanding of the accounts within your system and their permissions. Reassessing and potentially revising your architectural design to minimize the risk of a single compromised account leading to a system-wide breach is essential. This might involve eliminating default administrator access to all systems and implementing stricter access controls. Regular review and account design updates can significantly enhance your containment strategy.

Collaboration and Trust Building

Decisions about isolation can profoundly impact various business operations. This necessitates the creation of trust and understanding between the cybersecurity team and the rest of the business. Regular meetings with crucial departments, such as finance, operations, manufacturing, and sales, can ensure that your containment strategy considers their unique requirements and vital operational periods. Moreover, these discussions can aid in creating a comprehensive risk and decision-making framework, providing invaluable guidance during a crisis.

To conclude, formulating an effective containment strategy is complex but essential, encompassing numerous considerations and involving various stakeholders. The emphasis should be on early preparation, regular collaboration, a comprehensive understanding of your systems, and continuous reassessment in the face of evolving cyber threats. This approach can help your organization navigate network stabilization successfully and lay the groundwork for efficient recovery.

Chapter 9

Perception and Reality

The need for a cohesive crisis response strategy has become more apparent as the modern cyber landscape continues to evolve. This chapter delves into the complexities of navigating a crisis, from stabilization to organization, highlighting the importance of cross-functional collaboration, strong leadership, trust building, and strategic transitions. The goal is to provide a comprehensive guide for effectively navigating the critical stages of a crisis.

1. Harmonizing Security and IT Operations

The first step towards effective crisis management is harmonizing Security and IT operations. A synchronized relationship between these two critical teams forms the bedrock for swift and effective responses to security incidents. This synergy stems from a culture of open communication, shared objectives, and mutual understanding of each team's roles and responsibilities.

Aligning strategies and maintaining a constructive dialogue with the company's CIO can enhance operational resilience. This alliance can expedite stabilization, even amidst a complex crisis. To nurture this relationship, you must address potential hurdles such as internal politics, blame culture, and divergent operational goals. When Security and IT operations harmonize their efforts, they can efficiently navigate the SONAR phases, enhancing the organization's overall security posture.

2. Crisis Leadership

In the early stages of a crisis, decisive and strong leadership is paramount when pressure mounts and uncertainties loom. The leader should set clear and concise goals, foster a culture of focusing on facts rather than speculation, and streamline decision-making processes. This might require limiting the number of decision-makers in favor of a decisive leadership style.

However, this approach may be necessary during high-stress situations to stabilize the situation and ensure team cohesion. Effective crisis leadership, characterized by decisiveness, clarity, and direction, can mitigate the impact of a crisis and set the stage for successful resolution.

3. Cultivating Trust

The cornerstone of successful crisis leadership is trust, and building this trust during normal operations is critical. Transparency in decision-making processes and acknowledgment of the team's effort can foster a sense of ownership and encourage open communication. This reserve of trust can then be called upon during a crisis, enabling leaders to make swift decisions without extensive questioning or resistance.

Trust building is not just about crisis preparedness; it's about cultivating an organizational culture where team members feel valued, heard, and trusted. This trust can be invaluable in high-pressure situations, supporting efficient and effective crisis management.

4. Transitioning from Stabilization

The Stabilization phase, aimed at securing internal systems to maintain business continuity and prevent further threat proliferation, eventually transitions into the Organize phase. This critical transition requires an assessment of the situation: Have all known impacted business functions been evaluated and stabilized? Is the crisis containment sufficient to allow other areas to operate within acceptable risk parameters? What critical information should you share with the Incident Response (IR) team?

Addressing these questions ensures readiness to transition to the Organize phase. It's about gauging the situation accurately, ensuring a smooth transition, and setting the stage for the next steps in crisis resolution.

5. Maintaining Continuity of Stabilization

Even as the focus shifts to the Organize phase, elements of the Stabilization phase remain relevant throughout the crisis. As new information surfaces, or if the threat actor tries to infiltrate other business operations, you may need to reapply strategies from the Stabilization phase continuously.

This continuity underlines the significance of maintaining a robust, flexible, and resilient security posture throughout the crisis management process. Preparedness to reapply stabilization measures ensures the organization can respond promptly to evolving threats and minimize potential damage.

Wrapping Up

Navigating a crisis is no simple task. It demands harmony between critical teams like Security and IT operations, strong leadership under pressure, a foundation of trust within the team, and a strategic approach to transitioning between phases of crisis management.

Leadership and Team Dynamics

Strong leadership that fosters clear communication and decisiveness can significantly reduce confusion and uncertainty, facilitating a more effective response to crises. Moreover, leaders should strive to earn and maintain the trust of their team members. This trust can help ensure swift decision-making in crises, as team members will likely feel more confident about their leader's judgments and less likely to question or push back against their decisions.

Additionally, it's important to foster strong relationships and synergies between the Security and IT operations teams. Their alignment is crucial for efficient responses to security incidents. Any friction or misalignment between these teams can impede the organization's ability to stabilize a crisis rapidly and can exacerbate risks.

Stabilization and Transition

During the Stabilization phase, the objective is to quickly solidify internal systems to maintain business operations and prevent the further spread of a threat. However, the focus eventually shifts to the Organize phase, which involves coordinating efforts, prioritizing tasks, and developing a strategy to address the crisis. The key to this transition is ensuring all impacted business functions have been evaluated and stabilized and that you have contained the situation to a level where other areas can continue to operate within acceptable risk parameters.

Stabilization Continuity

Remember, elements of the Stabilization phase persist throughout the crisis. As you discover new information, or if the threat evolves, you must reapply stabilization strategies. This underscores the need for a robust, flexible, and resilient security posture that remains vigilant and adaptable throughout the crisis management process.

Managing a crisis requires technical expertise, effective team collaboration, proactive leadership, trust, and strategic planning. By recognizing the importance of these elements and integrating them into your crisis management strategy, your organization will be better prepared to navigate any crisis.

Summary

At the crux of crisis response, the initial Stabilize phase of the SONAR framework serves as the fundamental bedrock on which we based all subsequent steps. Yet, the formidable challenge lies in determining the best pathway through this demanding, high-stress phase. Who should participate in the process? What is our strategy? How do we guide our teams through this tempestuous period fraught with uncertainty?

Each crisis, viewed through a Global Chief Information Security Officer (CISO) lens, introduces its unique array of challenges. Varied risk profiles, operational barriers, team involvement, and external influences shape these challenges. Achieving a balance between these components while preserving an unwavering focus on the organization's security is indeed a significant undertaking.

In the face of numerous risks and pressures, the ability to identify and address the most critical issues rapidly becomes paramount. How do we modify our priorities as circumstances evolve? How do we make enlightened decisions to regain stability in an environment of crisis? How does a top-tier leader adeptly navigate this complex scenario, alleviate primary risks to the organization, and steer the team towards effective remediation, ultimately emerging more robust?

The scenario gains another layer of complexity when considering possible legal implications and the potential impact on the organization's reputation. Amidst the storm of questions demanding immediate answers and a variety of stakeholders seeking these answers, the capacity to effectively prioritize becomes a linchpin for successful recovery and sustained operations.

We engineered the Stabilize phase of the SONAR framework to assist in this process. It directs you to concentrate on the most critical issues, formulate strategies to address pressing questions, and comprehend how to progress even when some inquiries remain unanswered. As a CISO, this phase provides you with the necessary tools and perspectives in this ever-changing landscape of threats and vulnerabilities. The ability to stabilize effectively can mean the difference between a swift recovery and a prolonged struggle.

Lessons Learned

Here are the key lessons learned from the Stabilize phase of the framework:

Immediate Threat Assessment

Quick and clear judgment is critical in the early moments of a cyber threat. It's akin to sizing up a situation before diving into action. You need to determine the size and scope of the attack swiftly. Monitoring tools and network logs are invaluable in this respect, identifying where the attack is coming from and which areas are affected, and detecting Command and Control (C2) communications and beaconing activities. These logs can reveal the patterns of C2 traffic and beaconing signals, which are often hallmarks of advanced persistent threats. By analyzing these logs, you can uncover covert channels that threat actors use to control compromised systems and exfiltrate data, allowing for a more informed and effective response to the cyber threat. The decisions made now will shape how you handle everything that follows.

Identification of Core Systems and Assets

Once you have a clear picture, determining what's most important is the next step. Just as not every item in your home has the same value, not every system in an organization holds the same importance. Identify which systems are vital for daily operations and focus on them, especially if they're under threat. Make a list of digital assets, understand their importance to the business, and prioritize them accordingly. This ensures that you look after the most important assets first.

Deployment of Countermeasures

With a clear understanding of what's at stake, it's time to defend your systems. Imagine it's like setting up a game plan once you know the opponent's moves. Organizations should already have a set of actions in place for known threats. This could be cutting off specific systems, redirecting online traffic, or shutting down accounts that might have been hacked. But sometimes, the threat is unfamiliar. It's best to rely on tried-and-true strategies to keep things safe.

Monitoring and Adaptive Response

Once defenses are up, keeping a close eye on the situation is essential. Set up a system that watches over things and alerts you to any changes or issues. But remember, being flexible and ready to change tactics if needed is vital. If something isn't working, be prepared to try another strategy. Stay proactive, always looking for the best way forward.

Collaboration with External Entities

Sometimes, getting fresh eyes or some outside expertise can be invaluable. If you're stuck or facing an unfamiliar threat, consider contacting cybersecurity experts or specialized firms for help. In serious situations, getting law enforcement involved might even be necessary. There's no shame in asking for help when the stakes are high.

Documentation and Evidence Collection

When a cyber crisis hits us, we must look back and determine what occurred. It's not just about jotting down notes; it's about learning and preparing for what's next. You need to hang onto all the important stuff—your digital logs, emails, the times people got into your system, and any chats during the crisis. These pieces are like a puzzle; put them together, and you have a clear picture of what happened.

Keeping these digital footprints lets us dive into the threat actor's playbook. We can see where our defenses were weak and patch those holes. We can tell the whole story by lining up all this information, which is perfect for training our team and beefing up our security for the next round.

Plus, this isn't just about being smart with our security. There are rules and legal principles we must follow. We often must report these cyber incidents and show we've done our part to fix and reduce the damage. Having all this documented helps us with our legal obligations and makes the case for more resources to strengthen our cyber defenses.

In short, solid documentation and evidence collection are more than just record-keeping; they're about turning a challenging situation into a chance to learn and fortify our defenses. It's how we stay one step ahead in the cybersecurity game.

Internal Communication and Updates

Keeping everyone informed during a crisis is vital. Like letting your family know what's going on during a power outage, keeping key stakeholders updated ensures everyone's on the same page. Regular updates help with decision-making and ensure everyone pulls in the same direction. It's all about teamwork and making sure everyone knows the game plan.

Section 3

Organize

"Deciding what NOT to do is as important as deciding what to do."

~ Apple Co-Founder Steve Jobs

Introduction

The lead author for this section is Andrew Gorecki, with significant input from and in collaboration with Christopher Scott.

In the last section, we discussed how to stabilize the initial chaos when a crisis event occurs and get the situation under control. However, stopping the bleeding is just the first step in the response process. In this section, we dive into the Organize phase.

Crisis response is a complex undertaking that involves many moving parts, including investigation and remediation, crisis management, legal and data privacy considerations, internal and external communications, working with partners and vendors, and logistics. Executing and coordinating a response requires careful planning to ensure it is coherent and aligned with business priorities.

Three primary response groups with unique expertise and organizational knowledge form a Crisis Response Team: technical, business, and executive. You can manage the response complexity more effectively by breaking the response team into those groups and establishing communication and coordination.

We refer to those response groups as the Crisis Response Team. However, we recognize that naming conventions vary from organization to organization and are influenced by different standards or even industry-specific nomenclatures. Feel free to substitute or customize the conventions used in this book with terms specific to your organization or industry.

In this section, we explain how to organize a crisis response, including setting up technical and business teams, the role of executive management in the response process, crisis management and coordination, and response planning and execution. Finally, we conclude with an overview of breach response investigations and remediation and recovery considerations. We included this topic because investigation findings drive critical technical and business decisions, and it is essential to understand the process from a high-level perspective and appreciate its complexity.

Chapter 10

Establishing a Technical Team

A Technical Team is at the center of crisis response. It is responsible for data analysis, malware analysis and threat intelligence, containment and eradication, and system recovery. There is no one-size-fits-all model for establishing a Technical Team. The team size and composition depend on various factors, including the size of the organization, available resources, outsourcing arrangements with external vendors, and the extent of the cyber crisis.

Moreover, external vendors often augment technical responses. Those vendors often include existing outsourcing partners and firms you need to engage to assist with the response.

The following sections outline the functions that typically comprise a Technical Team.

Cybersecurity

The Cybersecurity function is at the center of the technical response. Several activities fall within its scope, including:

- System and network data analysis, including data generated by security tools such as Endpoint Detection and Response (EDR)
- Malware analysis
- Threat intelligence
- Containment and eradication
- Incident management, including coordination and communication between the stakeholders participating in the response process

- Analysis, including forensic examination of compromised systems, network data analysis, EDR telemetry analysis, and log analysis

Note that in smaller organizations or during a large-scale cyber event, an external Digital Forensics and Incident Response (DFIR) firm often handles system analysis, malware analysis, and threat intelligence. The firm may also provide guidance and advise on containment and eradication, as described later in this chapter.

In addition to its core response responsibilities, the Cybersecurity function also fulfills an advisory role to IT. For example, cybersecurity professionals often guide and advise IT about system hardening, attack surface reduction, and other security-related matters required to ensure the recovery of systems to an operational and secure state. An attack surface is the area of your technology stack exposed to potential unauthorized access and exploitation by a threat actor.

Information Technology

IT is another essential function within the Technical Team responsible for tool deployment, system configuration and hardening, restoration, and recovery.

The specific IT groups you need to include in the Technical Team depend on the nature and extent of the cyber crisis. For example, during a destructive cyberattack, your organization may activate the network, server, middleware, database, and application support groups to assist with the investigation and recovery. In contrast, you will likely activate only a subset of those groups during a data privacy event for support activities such as forensic data acquisition and containment.

Activities that fall within the responsibilities of IT usually include the following:

- Deploying security tools to support the investigation
- Executing containment measures in collaboration with cybersecurity where containment requires changes to existing systems
- Eradication tasks, such as system hardening, attack surface reduction, and patching vulnerabilities
- Restoring systems and data from backup
- Rebuilding systems when restoration from backup is not feasible

Operational Technology

The term Operational Technology (OT) refers to systems that control industrial equipment and infrastructure, such as programmable logic controllers, supervisory control and data acquisition systems (SCADA), and computer numerical control (CNC) tools. Those systems typically run industrial processes, including manufacturing, utilities, transportation, and lighting control and automation, among many others. Depending on your sector and type of business, they may fall within the scope of critical infrastructure.[6]

In most cases, OT environments are primarily designed and maintained with availability and resiliency as a key functional requirement. Moreover, many of those systems run on legacy hardware and software containing many vulnerabilities and typically have a weaker security posture compared to corporate networks. This is one of the reasons why cyberattacks against OT environments are common occurrences these days.

A successful cyberattack against systems supporting critical infrastructure can lead to health and safety concerns and cause an event at a local or national level. A notable example is the attack on

[6] Cybersecurity & Infrastructure Security Agency, Critical Infrastructure Sectors, https://www.cisa.gov/topics/critical-infrastructure-security-and-resilience/critical-infrastructure-sectors.

the Colonial Pipeline that forced the company to shut down its operations for several days, causing fears about fuel shortages.[7]

If your organization runs OT environments, we strongly recommend including the OT function in your Crisis Response Team and having contingency plans in place to deal with the impact caused by a potential cyberattack. We have encountered numerous situations where the victim organization believed their OT environments were "air-gapped" and not prone to cyberattacks. Unfortunately, those clients learned the hard way the need for crisis preparedness when destructive malware caused havoc in their OT environments.

Disaster Recovery

In most organizations, Disaster Recovery is a group within the IT department. However, Disaster Recovery deserves a dedicated discussion with the proliferation of destructive cyberattacks in recent years, including ransomware. Moreover, we have worked with organizations that placed Disaster Recovery in the Security department. One of the primary reasons for this choice was the high probability of a cyberattack leading to a crisis instead of an environmental event, such as a hurricane.

Historically, Disaster Recovery planning focuses on natural disasters such as hurricanes, flooding, power outages, and other environmental events. The principle behind this thinking was that when a natural event impacts one location, critical infrastructure and applications can temporarily run from a secondary location to ensure business continuity. However, destructive cyberattacks have shaken the fundamental architectural tenants of traditional Disaster Recovery approaches and forced many organizations to rethink how they approach this domain.

7 Cybersecurity & Infrastructure Security Agency, "The Attack on Colonial Pipeline: What We've Learned & What We've Done Over the Past Two Years," posted May 7, 2023, available here: https://www.cisa.gov/news-events/news/attack-colonial-pipeline-what-weve-learned-what-weve-done-over-past-two-years.

In recent years, Cyber Recovery has emerged as a technical discipline. Cyber Recovery aims to ensure organizations can survive catastrophic cyberattacks and continue business operations under adverse cyber conditions. The following paragraphs provide high-level guidance and cyber recovery considerations. However, an in-depth discussion is beyond the scope of this book, and we recommend further personal research and exploration of this domain.

This approach requires a business process-centric approach and a plan to orchestrate the recovery based on business priorities, including revenue, contractual obligations, health and safety concerns, and other critical factors. We discuss recovery in-depth later in this book. However, for this section, the process should include the following activities:

- Business priority management to ensure recovery prioritization when an event impacts multiple business functions and processes
- Technical management to ensure the organization identifies dependencies and recovery order and organizes the effort into workstreams
- Project management to track recovery activities and their status and ensure the necessary resource assignment to workstreams
- An end-to-end workflow of activities
- System and data recovery

We want to emphasize that conducting regular Business Impact Analysis (BIA), documenting system dependencies, and establishing recovery priorities as part of day-to-day operations is crucial to enabling the above functions. Discovering which systems support critical business functions and their dependencies during a crisis often prolongs the response. It is not the best use of resources when time is of the essence. We recommend conducting annual BIAs, at a minimum. Chapter 15, Remediation and Recovery Planning section further expands on this topic.

External Vendors and Outsourcing Partners

A cyberattack can impact multiple business areas, and during the most severe events, the response may require a heroic effort to resume business operations and have enterprise-wide consequences. As a result, it is rare for organizations to respond to a cyber crisis without the support of vendors and business partners. In this section, we briefly discuss the role of external vendors in the response process.

Incident Response Firm

We strongly recommend partnering with a reputable Digital Forensics and Incident Response (DFIR) firm to augment internal response capabilities during a cyber crisis. A reputable DFIR firm expands internal capabilities and brings the experience of past cases and specialized skills to the table. These skills include system and network data analysis, digital forensics, malware analysis, and cyber threat intelligence.

Moreover, DFIR firms often bring in the technology necessary to support the investigation at scale and provide advice regarding restoration and hardening. Experienced consultants can help you navigate the complexities of the technical response and avoid some of the pitfalls you would encounter when attempting to tackle the crisis alone.

When choosing a DFIR firm, ensure it has a proven track record of investigating large-scale breaches. Breach response is a hot topic, and in our experience, many organizations want to join the ride without mature capabilities and industry experience. Unfortunately, we have witnessed many investigations that went horribly wrong when inexperienced consultants stumbled through the investigative processes during a crisis.

Restoration Firm

During a destructive cyberattack, such as ransomware, we recommend partnering with a restoration firm to assist with recovering the impacted environments. This recommendation is especially applicable when you manage IT in-house and do not have sufficient resources to recover the affected systems and applications according to the timeline set by the business.

In traditional Disaster Recovery (DR) planning, data recovery and data restoration have distinct and precise meanings. However, in the context of cyber recovery, we use those terms interchangeably to mean restoring systems and data from backup and rebuilding systems where restoration is not feasible.

A reputable restoration firm can augment internal resources and bring specialized skills and experience in restoring complex IT environments following cyber events. Furthermore, such firms are often familiar with the breach investigation process and can effectively work alongside analysts and security personnel. This approach helps to preserve the necessary forensic data before system restoration and appropriately harden systems before moving them into the production environment.

The typical channels to engage restoration firms include retainer agreements, cyber insurance vendors, and DFIR firms.

Security Vendors

In addition to DFIR and restoration support, you will likely need assistance from other security vendors during a cyber crisis. In our experience, you may have to engage vendors to assist with any of the following activities:

- Vulnerability assessment
- Attack surface mapping
- Access control enhancements, including Active Directory hardening and reducing attack surface around privileged identities
- System hardening and implementing vendor best practices pertaining to security
- Security tool deployment, such as EDR

During a crisis, you have a limited time to implement tactical remediation measures to recover the impacted systems and applications to an operational and secure state. Tactical remediation refers to short-term measures to harden the impacted environment and address the weaknesses exploited by the threat actor before implementing longer-term solutions.

You will likely have to implement those measures under tremendous pressure from the business and in a limited timeframe. For this reason, partnering with reputable security vendors can accelerate the process and alleviate some stress on the internal security team.

Managed Security Service Provider

Suppose you leverage a Managed Security Service Provider (MSSP) for security tool management, monitoring, and response service as part of Security Operations. In that case, you can leverage the MSSP service to augment the response process. For example, in our experience, many MSSPs can assist with the following activities during a cyber breach:

- Build detections and analytics dashboards in tools, such as Security Information and Event Management (SIEM) and Endpoint Detection and Response
- Provide heightened vigilance and monitoring for any Indicators of Compromise (IOCs) and behaviors identified through the analysis process
- Undertake basic response actions when detections are triggered

Activating team members to work multiple shifts may work for the first few days. However, burning the midnight oil for several consecutive days without sufficient sleep can lead to mistakes and be counterproductive during a prolonged crisis. Including your MSSP in the response process is especially important if your security team cannot handle 24x7 monitoring and response during an active investigation.

Technology Outsourcing Partners

If your organization has existing relationships with strategic technology partners and vendors, leverage those relationships to augment internal capabilities and extend the Technical Team with additional staffing. For example, if your organization outsourced specific technology functions, such as infrastructure or application management, engage the partners to assist with the crisis response. Because outsourcing providers often build a resource bench, they may be able to deploy specialized skills within days or even hours. However, because of the likely sensitive nature of these matters, we recommend involving legal counsel in this process.

In addition to existing business relationships, you may have to engage external vendors ad hoc. For example, as we mentioned earlier, you may have to hire an external DFIR firm to assist with a forensic investigation. In our experience, the following third parties augment the Technical Response Task Force:

- DFIR firm to assist with breach investigation, containment, and eradication
- Technology vendors to assist with product expertise and extend internal capabilities
- Service vendors to provide resource support
- Outsourcing partners that manage technology and applications on behalf of the organization

Those vendors can assist with any of the activities described in the Information Technology section of this chapter.

We strongly advise you to engage your legal counsel when contracting technology partners. This advice especially applies to hiring a DFIR firm. In our experience, forensic investigations are often conducted at the direction of outside legal counsel to shield sensitive information from discovery and reduce legal risk in anticipation of litigation.

Key Takeaways

- Technical response is not the sole responsibility of the Security department. It requires a cross-functional effort involving various security and IT functions, augmented by security vendors and outsourcing partners.

- Do not tackle a cyber crisis alone. Instead, partner with a reputable DFIR firm and other security vendors to assist with analysis, containment, hardening and eradication, and restoration of the impacted systems and applications.
- Cyber recovery requires a business process-centric approach to recovery that includes infrastructure, applications, data, and dependencies between those components. Ensure you understand their dependencies as part of your preparedness effort to avoid painful and prolonged restoration following a significant cyber event.

Chapter 11

Establishing a Business Team

As described earlier in this book, a cyberattack can affect an organization in a significant way. For this reason, effective crisis management cannot focus entirely on technical response. Data privacy, financial, and brand reputation damage can impact the organization long-term, sometimes for years. A great example of this phenomenon is the Equifax data breach disclosed in September 2017.[8] In December 2022, more than five year after the breach, the Federal Trade Commission (FTC) was still handling settlement payments.

Crisis response must also include business-level capabilities to manage external and internal communications, data privacy and regulatory considerations, third-party notifications, and Human Resources-related matters, among other concerns. This is where a Business Team comes into play.

The following sections describe the business functions you will likely activate when responding to a cyber crisis.

Public Relations

If we could describe the role of Public Relations (PR) during a crisis response in a single phrase, it would be "brand reputation management." PR is the communication gateway to the external world during a crisis, and the quality of their work directly impacts how external parties perceive the crisis. A good PR strategy can lead to empathy toward your organization. In contrast, inadequate PR

8 Federal Trade Commission, Equifax Data Breach Settlement, available at https://www.ftc.gov/enforcement/cases-proceedings/refunds/equifax-data-breach-settlement.

can cause a negative perception, brand reputation damage, or lead to lawsuits. The following list provides the typical activities the PR function is responsible for during a crisis response:

- Drafting external and internal statements
- Designating and preparing a spokesperson for media interviews and external inquiries
- Monitoring social media sentiment
- Serving as the focal point for external inquiries

However, external communications are not the only PR responsibility. Internal Communications is a PR branch responsible for handling communication within the organization. In our experience, employee communication is equally, and sometimes even more important, during a cyber crisis. For example, PR may draft and disseminate internal communications when a significant event becomes public knowledge or provide employees with instructions and status updates while the business restoration is underway.

Your internal PR department does not work in isolation. For example, during a significant event, you may hire an outside PR firm specializing in responses to destructive cyber events and large consumer data breaches. Furthermore, PR professionals work closely with your legal counsel to ensure internal and external communications do not expose the organization to unnecessary legal risks, including class action lawsuits.

Legal and Data Privacy

While PR diligently works to minimize the reputational damage from a cyberattack, Legal plays a vital role from a counsel and data privacy standpoint.

The responsibility of legal counsel is to minimize the legal risk associated with a crisis event and prepare for potential litigation. The activities typically include.

- Protecting and maintaining information and communication confidentiality through protocols, such as the attorney-client privilege

- Engaging outside counsel to provide specialized legal assistance
- Guiding the Technical Team on digital evidence preservation
- Working with an electronic discovery (e-discovery) firm to assist with electronic evidence gathering to prepare for potential legal proceedings
- Reviewing internal and external communications prepared by PR
- Ensuring that necessary reporting occurs according to applicable legislation under regulatory rules and protocols

In many organizations, the Legal department also handles data privacy, which is primarily concerned with protecting Personally Identifiable Information (PII) and other personally sensitive information. When a forensic investigation reveals evidence of unauthorized access to such data, attorneys must evaluate the data privacy impact and notify external parties per applicable laws and regulations, if required.

Before further discussion, it is worth explaining the difference between a *system breach* and a *data breach*. We have observed that sometimes even seasoned professionals confuse these two terms. This can result in unforeseen legal consequences for your organization. A system breach occurs when a cyberattack results in unauthorized access to a computer system. On the other hand, a data breach occurs when a cyberattack causes unauthorized access to confidential data, regardless of whether the access is intentional or unintentional.

We want to emphasize that this definition applies to cyber breaches only. In the context of legal frameworks and regulations, a data breach can have a much broader definition beyond data disclosure by a malicious threat actor. For this reason, consult your legal counsel before defining this term in your crisis response plan.

In our experience, a best practice is to avoid the term *breach* during a crisis and replace it with *event* or another appropriate term advised by your legal counsel. It is up to qualified attorneys to determine if a data breach occurred.

To expand on this thought a bit, it has been our experience that people without legal training often feel compelled to use legal jargon when a more prudent approach is to leave that to the Legal team. Non-lawyers often misunderstand and misuse three important concepts. Attorney-client privilege is a legal privilege that protects communications between an attorney and their client. It is only invoked by an attorney. When doing so, the attorney is specific about what communications are taking place under privilege and how that privilege is asserted (e.g., using specific wording on emails or documents). The Work Product Doctrine protects an attorney's thoughts, impressions, conclusions, opinions, and legal research or theories they provide in anticipation of litigation. While this is not necessarily confidential, it is only used in anticipation of litigation. Finally, only a qualified attorney should declare a data breach. If you are not on the legal team, use these three terms in reference to the event only when and in the manner directed by an attorney.

Risk Management

Cyber breaches and crisis events often stem from known risks. Unfortunately, those risks were accepted or even intentionally ignored in many cases. We recommend including Risk Management in the Business Team to assist with reviewing and assessing the root causes of the crisis as part of the post-mortem analysis. In larger organizations, Risk Management may also invoke cyber liability insurance during a crisis and act as a liaison between the organization and the insurance provider. Let's briefly examine each of these roles.

With the proliferation of cyberattacks, many organizations purchase commercial cyber liability insurance to cover potential costs associated with damages caused by cyberattacks. Depending on the policy, it may cover a wide range of harms and expenses, such as hiring external vendors to assist with an investigation, legal fees, recovery costs, or even lost revenue.

In larger organizations, the Risk Management department is typically responsible for handling matters related to cyber liability insurance, often in close collaboration with legal counsel.

Risk Management also plays a vital role in post-crisis evaluation. Organizations with a mature crisis response process often analyze root causes and identify lessons learned following significant events. Those activities aim to improve the response process and address the security weaknesses and vulnerabilities that allowed those events to occur.

We have observed that security weaknesses and gaps identified during post-mortem analysis are often symptoms of more significant, systemic issues, such as inadequate governance or misalignment between business, IT, and Security. Therefore, a risk assessment is important following a cyber crisis event. Post-mortem activities are so essential that we dedicated an entire chapter to this topic in the Remediate section of this book.

Following root cause analysis, it is essential to identify remediation measures to address those weaknesses and minimize the risk of similar events occurring in the future. As part of this process, risk managers and senior leaders must review the proposed measures and determine if they will sufficiently and cost-effectively reduce risk.

Finance

An important reason why Finance is a vital member of the Business Team is materiality in financial disclosure. In the United States, publicly traded companies must disclose to the Securities and Exchange Commission (SEC) the impact of significant cyber events in their financial statements. Consequently, if your organization experiences a significant cyber event, your Chief Finance Officer (CFO) must assess if there is a substantial likelihood that the event would influence potential shareholder investment or voting decisions. If that is the case, the organization must disclose the impact in its financial statements.

The disclosure requirement is another area that warrants further explanation. The U.S. Securities and Exchange Commission keenly focuses on timely disclosures of "material" cybersecurity incidents to the investment community. In the *Cybersecurity Risk Management, Strategy, Governance, and Incident Disclosure* rule that took effect in December 2023, the SEC requires that registrants notify the investment community within four days of discovering a material cybersecurity incident by filing a Form 8-K disclosure. The disclosure must include the incident's details and likely impact on the registrant. The disclosure must note when the incident was discovered, whether the incident is ongoing (including impacts to operations), and a brief overview of the incident scope and if any data were compromised.

The Form 8-K disclosure is not a file-and-forget affair. Under the SEC's final rule, if material updates to the declared cybersecurity incident exist, registrants must update the investment community with an amended Form 8-K. Depending upon the national security context of the cybersecurity incident, registrants can request that the U.S. Attorney General authorize an initial 30-day delay (which may be extended for another 30 days should circumstances warrant).

In effect, the SEC requires registrants to be transparent and timely about their disclosures of cybersecurity incidents. This regulatory context is not limited to the SEC. The Office of Civil Rights within the Department of Health and Human Services is stepping up enforcement actions related to HIPAA Security Rule violations. Multiple regulatory authorities, including state-specific regulators, now prioritize cybersecurity.

The SEC declares information material if a reasonable person would consider it important when making an investment decision or if it would significantly affect existing publicly available information about a company. It expects companies to resolve doubts in the investor's favor. We recommend that you rely on your Legal team to make that determination.

Countries outside the United States may have similar requirements. For this reason, check with your CFO and legal counsel so see if there are any materiality considerations you should include in your crisis response planning if your organization operates outside the United States.

Furthermore, responding to a cyber crisis often requires resources and funding beyond your budget for the year. In our experience, organizations rapidly incur significant expenditures during a cyber crisis, including hiring external vendors and contractors, legal and PR fees, staff augmentation, and overtime expenses.

For this reason, consider including Finance in the Business Team and ensure the organization has a process to expedite expenditure approval. Otherwise, financial matters may unnecessarily delay the response and recovery process, leading to a prolonged business impact and loss of revenue.

Business Continuity

The previous chapter briefly covered Disaster Recovery as part of the discussion on the Technical Team. While Disaster Recovery focuses on restoring systems and data following a significant event, Business Continuity is primarily concerned with business contingency planning to ensure the organization can continue business operations during a disaster, including notable events caused by a cyberattack.

As part of Business Continuity Planning (BCP), many organizations conduct a Business Impact Analysis (BIA) to identify critical functions and processes. The BIA output feeds into Business Continuity and Disaster Recovery (BCDR) planning. BCP is essential during a cyber crisis because a destructive cyberattack may impact multiple business areas, and your leadership will have to identify and prioritize the recovery of critical business functions and processes. Chapter 15, Remediation and Recovery Planning, discusses this topic further.

Suppose a ransomware attack impacts the operations of multiple applications supporting business, manufacturing, and human resources (HR) processes. An adequate BCP prescribes what processes the organization must prioritize for recovery. Furthermore, a BCP includes contingency planning, such as manual process execution or operating from another site, even if it means operating at a reduced capacity. In contrast, a Disaster Recovery Plan prescribes how to restore those applications, including their dependencies and data.

Business Continuity is not only about technology. It also includes people, physical locations, manual workarounds during technology failures, partners, and other elements necessary to keep the business operational. For example, when a cyberattack impacts the operations of a customer order system at a manufacturing firm, the organization may implement a plan to collect orders manually via email or telephone to ensure the continuity of business operations.

Organizations with immature or poor BCP practices often experience prolonged recovery following a destructive cyberattack. For example, in one case, an organization severely impacted by a ransomware attack did not have systems mapped to business applications, and the engineers who built those applications were no longer with the organization. This gap led to excruciating and prolonged recovery, and even after the business resumption, the recovered applications experienced severe operational issues.

Line of Business Leaders

Most businesses exist to generate value for their shareholders and customers through products and services. Destructive cyberattacks can negatively impact business operations and the ability to deliver those products and services. For this reason, including Line of Business (LOB) leaders in the response process is essential.

They ultimately know their business areas and have the expertise to assess the impact of a cyberattack on their LOB and prioritize systems, applications, and data for recovery. Another reason for including LOB leaders in the Business Team is their ability to invoke and implement a Business Continuity Plan to ensure continuity of operations while recovery is underway.

When a cyberattack leads to health and safety issues or impacts employees' ability to perform work, LOB leaders are typically responsible for downstream employee communication through their management chain. This point is crucial if your organization decides to communicate verbally with employees instead of sending mass emails or posting messages on the internal corporate website.

Corporate Security

Corporate Security is another function that plays a vital role during a cyber crisis. In many organizations, Corporate Security acts as a liaison for law enforcement, and it may have relationships with agencies such as the Federal Bureau of Investigations (FBI) or other authorities if your organization operates outside the United States.

Other responsibilities often falling within the scope of Corporate Security include:

- Providing access to facilities for employees and contractors
- Securing surveillance video in cases of physical intrusions
- Seizing and securing physical assets during insider threat cases

For example, Corporate Security engages law enforcement and secures surveillance video when there is evidence of physical intrusion into a data center or office to gain unauthorized access to the network. It is important to note that such cases are rare. However, they do happen, so it is vital to include Corporate Security on the Business Team.

Business Relationship Management

Depending on the nature and extent of a cyberattack, a crisis can impede an ability to deliver products and services and impact a larger supply chain. For example, Hydro Norsk, one of the world's biggest aluminum producers, was hit by a ransomware attack in 2019 that affected its production capacity. As a result, aluminum prices globally rose by 1.5%.[9]

[9] "Aluminum giant Norsk Hydro experiences serious ransomware attack," TechGenix, March 2019, available here: https://techgenix.com/aluminum-giant-norsk-hydro-experiences-serious-ransomware-attack/.

Client representatives are often the first point of contact for the affected clients and business partners. For this reason, they must be involved in crisis response, either directly or indirectly. The organization will inevitably face external inquiries, and client representation must have appropriate messaging ready when their clients contact them.

Of course, this list of the various business and corporate functions you may want to include on your Business Team is not exhaustive and may vary from organization to organization. Your task as a leader is to critically evaluate which functions to include in the Business Team, identify their representatives, and work with them to determine their responsibilities in the response process.

External Parties

The previous chapter described how technology and security vendors augment internal capabilities within the Technical Team. The business-level response also requires external, specialized support. Depending on the nature of a crisis, you may want to engage one or more of the following external parties:

- Outside counsel to assist with navigating legal risks and matters pertaining to data privacy
- A PR firm to assist with external messaging and brand reputation management
- An Electronic discovery (e-discovery) firm when a cyberattack leads to unauthorized access to and exfiltration of data
- A Cyber liability insurance vendor to assist with matters relating to cyber insurance. We recommend engaging your insurance vendor in the early phases of a crisis regardless of whether the organization plans to make a claim.
- A breach coach to assist with managing the overall cyber crisis. Outside legal counsel, cyber insurance vendors, and cyber crisis management firms often provide this service.

Check with your outside counsel and cyber liability insurance vendor to determine whether their services include a breach coach.

Establishing solid relationships with external parties as part of crisis response planning is critical. We have encountered organizations that hired and replaced PR and Incident Response firms amid a crisis. This reactive approach delays the response and may harm the organization in the long term. We recommend including external vendors in annual crisis management exercises.

The Role of Executive Management in Crisis Response

Executive Management is the uppermost function in the crisis response process. It typically takes an active role during situations that severely impact the bottom line or even threaten the organization's existence. Examples of executive leaders that often actively participate in crisis response include:

- Chief Executive Officer (CEO)
- Chief Finance Officer (CFO)
- Chief Information Security Officer (CISO)
- Chief Operations Officer (COO)
- Chief Technology Officer (CTO)
- Business Unit Managers and Presidents
- Chief Legal Officer (CLO)
- Chief Privacy Officer (CPO)
- Chief Information Officer (CIO)
- Chief Human Resources Officer (CHRO)

During a cyber crisis, Executive Management provides an overall strategic direction and priorities for the response. For example, when a crisis causes an operational impact across different business units and functions, Executive Management often determines the order of prioritizes for recovery efforts when resources are limited based on factors such as revenue, health and safety concerns, and legal and regulatory obligations. Other Executive Management responsibilities during a crisis include:

- Handling regulatory matters
- Board-level communications
- Approving expenditures for resources
- Providing order of priorities
- Deconfliction of priorities
- Overcoming organizational silos
- Designating a spokesperson for media interviews

In our experience, executive leaders focus on strategic decision-making or crisis leadership, especially in larger organizations. For this reason, you must ensure that lower-level functions handling the crisis response provide timely and accurate information to enable executive leaders to make informed decisions regarding handling the crisis. We will discuss coordination and crisis management in the next chapter.

Before concluding this section, it is worth mentioning that conducting annual cyber crisis response exercises with Executive Management can help them rehearse and prepare for significant cyber events and familiarize them with their roles and responsibilities. Leaders often juggle multiple tasks, and their time is a scarce resource. In our experience, gamified crisis response exercises are of significantly higher value than reading a response plan alone.

Key Takeaways

- Business response requires a cross-functional effort and involvement from multiple business functions and LOBs. Identify all those functions in crisis response planning and ensure they are familiar with their roles and responsibilities.

- Partner with external vendors through retainer agreements to augment internal capabilities, including legal, PR, and breach coach services. Also, engage them early during a crisis to avoid irreversible mistakes that can affect the organization long-term.

- Engage and educate Executive Management on their role in crisis response. Moreover, consider annual crisis response exercises to ensure they are well-versed in the process.

Chapter 12

Response Coordination and Orchestration

Handling a cyber crisis is a complex undertaking that requires horizontal and vertical collaboration across the organization. The previous chapters focused on identifying the members of the Technical, Business, and Executive Management Teams. The next step is to create an organizational model for the response team to facilitate coordination and communication between all the stakeholders participating in the response process. An organizational model is also referred to as an operating model.

For a crisis response to be successful, there must be synergy between all the stakeholders participating in the response process. For this reason, you need to establish a coordination role within each team and establish a process to facilitate upstream and downstream communication between the various groups.

Suppose you are responding to a cyberattack where a threat actor gains access to highly confidential data subject to regulatory requirements. You convene a Technical Team, and after the initial containment, you instruct the team to acquire forensic data and perform an in-depth analysis of the compromised systems to determine what data the threat actor accessed, the method of access, and what vulnerabilities allowed the threat actor to gain access to that data.

The scenario above is just a part of the overall response process. You must also communicate the forensic findings upstream to the Business Team. This requirement is essential for Legal to identify the corresponding data privacy impact and perform the necessary regulatory notifications. For instance, if the intrusion impacts data associated with European Union citizens, the organization may be legally obligated to notify a supervisory authority in Europe within

72 hours of confirming unauthorized access to that data. Moreover, legal counsel may direct the team to conduct a forensic analysis.

Another example is a destructive cyberattack that impacts systems, applications, and data supporting core business processes and functions. With limited resources and competing priorities, the Business and Executive Management Teams must establish a business recovery order based on business priorities, such as revenue, contractual obligations, or regulatory requirements.

For the reasons outlined above, you need to create an organizational model for the combined teams, assign coordination roles to orchestrate the response, and assign roles and responsibilities to stakeholders participating in the process.

Defining an Organizational Model

An organizational model describes the structure of the combined teams and their interactions.

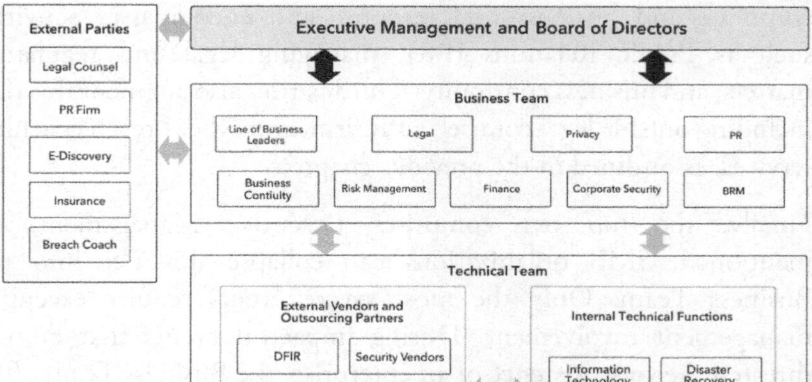

Figure 2 – Crisis Response Team Generic Model

Figure 2 provides a generic model that you can use as a basis for organizing a Crisis Response Team.

Vertical Scaling

Depending on the size and complexity of your organization, you can scale the model horizontally and vertically. For example, suppose your enterprise operates within the small- and medium-sized business (SMB) market. In such a case, you could collapse the Business and Executive Teams into a single entity by removing the top tier. However, large organizations with complex and global operations often require multiple layers of management and communication.

Not all cyber crises start with a big bang event. Organizations often detect small events that can indicate a more significant problem. For this reason, the response process usually starts with the Technical Team, which handles the initial analysis and containment. Only when an event escalates to a high severity or crisis level will the incident manager escalate the situation to senior management to activate a business-level response.

The middle tier comprises the Business Team, which focuses on corporate and business-level response and encompasses activities such as Public Relations (PR), managing legal and regulatory matters, and business continuity. Third parties also augment this tier, including outside legal counsel, a PR firm, and cyber breach coaching services, as outlined in the previous chapters.

Finally, the top tier comprises Executive Management. As mentioned, SMB organizations can collapse this tier into the Business Team. Only the most severe events require executive management involvement. During impactful events that do not threaten the very existence of an enterprise, the Business Team often informs and consults Executive Management but does not actively involve it in managing the event. In this model, Executive Management sets business priorities for the response and approves resources and expenditures.

To organize a crisis response, you must ensure synergy between technical and enterprise activities. Activities within the Technical and Business Teams are often interdependent. Consequently, you must ensure bi-directional information flow between them. For example, while forensic analysts may determine that a threat actor gained unauthorized access to systems handling highly confidential data, data privacy experts must determine whether the organization must notify regulators and other third parties. We will discuss coordination later in this chapter.

Horizontal Scaling

In addition to vertical scaling, you will likely need to scale your Crisis Response Team horizontally. You can achieve this task by sourcing skills externally and through existing vendor agreements.

Chapters 10 and 11 describe the roles of vendors during a crisis. You can leverage the vendors to achieve two types of scaling:

- Acquire specialized skills and capabilities such as Digital Forensics and Incident Response (DFIR) to fulfill roles lacking internally
- Extend existing skills and capabilities with additional resources to keep up with the additional workload caused by a crisis

Suppose destructive malware cripples your operations. In such a case, you will need support from a reputable DFIR vendor and additional hands-on keyboard resources to assist with and accelerate the restoration process.

An example of horizontally scaling the Business Team is hiring an external Public Relations (PR) firm and outside counsel.

It is worth noting that larger enterprises often have a dedicated Emergency Operations Center (EOC) or a similar function responsible for crisis management. The EOC brings together stakeholders representing the functions discussed below and coordinates the response activities. Moreover, an EOC is often responsible for developing and maintaining a crisis response plan, training key personnel annually, and ensuring the organization has the necessary resources and logistics to respond to a potential crisis.

Creating a structural model for your Crisis Response Team is not enough. You also need to designate roles responsible for coordinating and orchestrating the response. The following section discusses how to achieve this objective.

Coordination and Orchestration

Response coordination ensures that the different groups involved in the technical and business response work communicate effectively, share information, and work in an organized manner. Orchestration, conversely, unifies all the response activities into an end-to-end process and helps ensure alignment between technical and business activities.

For example, incident coordination can involve daily status update meetings and communication between various groups participating in the response process. In contrast, orchestration brings all the response elements together, including people, the technology they leverage, and processes specific to their functions. In other words, coordination is more communication-oriented, whereas orchestration focuses on the bigger picture and unifying all the elements.

Coordination and orchestration are essential to crisis response. On several occasions, we experienced crisis response efforts that were so disorganized and chaotic that the victim organizations could not stabilize the situation and outline and agree on an action plan. For example, we regularly encountered situations where fifty or more participants attended crisis update calls including technical personnel and leadership. Those in charge did not set a clear agenda and the blend of technical and management-level discussions led to chaos and a lack of alignment between the response functions.

The following paragraphs outline the roles involved in crisis coordination. If you work for a smaller organization, you can combine some of those roles into a single assignment, as described in the next section.

Identifying Coordination Roles

In our experience, strong leadership and communication skills are essential during a cyber crisis. We have observed that individuals with the right technical experience, people skills, and a wealth of institutional knowledge can drive response activities more effectively than project managers who merely execute the process.

We refer to those individuals as expert generalists. This term describes an individual with breadth and depth of skills across multiple disciplines who can articulate complex technical concepts in simple terms, often using storytelling, and guide stakeholders with diverse backgrounds and expertise with confidence and authority.

The following paragraphs describe typical crisis management roles that we recommend including as part of your Crisis Response Team. It is worth emphasizing that one person can wear multiple hats in smaller organizations. For example, we have worked with small hospitals and manufacturers where a single individual assumed the Incident Manager and Technical Lead roles. How you structure crisis coordination and orchestration depends on your organization's size and the crisis's scale.

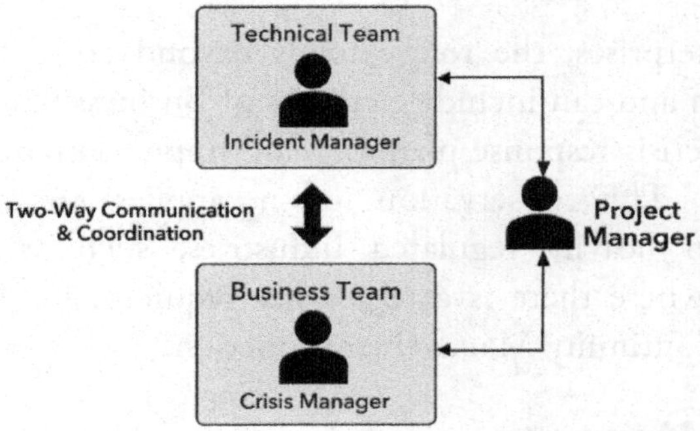

Figure 3 – Communication Model

Crisis Manager

The Crisis Manager is a senior manager or a member of the leadership team with the authority and the necessary resources to coordinate business-level response and provide direction to the groups participating in the response. In our experience, the Chief Information Security Officer (CISO) or Chief Information Officer (CIO) often assumes this role in smaller enterprises. In contrast, large organizations often have a dedicated Crisis Management function with a senior-level manager responsible for crisis planning and response.

Typical Crisis Manager responsibilities include:

- Coordinating enterprise-level response and working with other senior leaders to ensure the technical and business response activities are aligned with business priorities
- Providing strategic oversight and direction to the Crisis Response Team based on business priorities and direction provided by the Executive Management Team
- Updating Executive Management on the response status, issues, and required resources

In large enterprises, the role extends beyond crisis response and coordination and can include elements of Business Continuity, risk assessment, crisis response planning and implementation, and even compliance. This observation often applies to organizations operating in heavily regulated industries, such as banking or healthcare, where there is a regulatory requirement to establish a Crisis and Continuity Management function.

Incident Manager

While a Crisis Manager focuses on managing the overall crisis response, the Incident Manager role is responsible for activities within the Technical Team. Larger organizations typically have dedicated Incident Managers that handle security and operational incidents as part of day-to-day operations. During a crisis, one of those individuals usually takes on the role of a Major Incident

Manager. On the other hand, in smaller enterprises where technical personnel often wear multiple hats, a senior technical staff member often assumes this role.

An Incident Manager is normally responsible for the following tasks:

- Identify internal groups and vendors with skills required to respond to a crisis and assemble a Technical Team
- Oversee the technical response, including data analysis, containment, eradication, and restoration of the impacted systems
- Coordinate activities and communication between the groups involved in the technical response
- Provide regular status updates to the Business Team
- Ensure technical response is aligned with business priorities

Project Manager

The Incident Manager often requires assistance managing and tracking tasks, taking notes during meetings, and following up with technical teams on execution status. This requirement is especially applicable during large-scale and complex crises. The Project Manager's responsibilities often include:

- Working closely with the Incident Manager and other technical leads to develop an action plan in the early phases of the crisis
- Working with managers and technical leads to assign personnel to shifts
- Tracking task progress within each technical workstream
- Taking notes and documenting action items during meetings

Some organizations may assign a Scribe where project management is not required. For example, a Scribe is usually responsible for incident documentation but not tracking action items and tasks.

Other Significant Technical Roles

During complex cyber events involving multiple technical groups and workstreams, you will likely need to designate additional leads responsible for the investigation, recovery, and other necessary technical activities. Those leads will report to the Incident Manager and provide technical direction and leadership within their workstreams. We briefly describe these roles below.

The first role we want to discuss is that of Investigation Lead. An Investigation Lead is responsible for the overall investigation of a network intrusion and scoping the extent of the compromise. Investigating a complex intrusion often requires multiple analysts with forensic analysis, malware analysis, and threat intelligence skills who may work on parallel activities. This complexity warrants a dedicated lead.

The typical activities an Investigation Lead is responsible for include:

- Data collection, analysis, and scoping of the intrusion
- Preserving forensic evidence, especially during cases where your organization anticipates civil litigation
- Tracking and documenting important investigative information, including Indicators of Compromise (IOC), a list of compromised systems and user accounts, and other relevant information.
- Creating an intrusion timeline based on analysis findings
- Providing containment and eradication guidance based on analysis findings

Large enterprises may have skilled individuals to fulfill this role. However, in our experience, organizations typically source the capabilities described above through a Digital Forensics and Incident Response (DFIR) partner that provides an Investigation Lead. We will discuss this topic in the final chapter in this section.

Another critical role during complex cyber events is the Recovery Lead. In our experience, a dedicated Recovery Lead is required during a large-scale destructive attack that destroys multiple systems and data, leading to complex and often prolonged recovery.

A Recovery Lead works hand in hand with an Investigation Lead to ensure system recovery to an operational and secure state. This includes applying hardening and eradication measures as part of system restoration.

The typical Recovery Lead's responsibilities include:

- Activate the Disaster Recovery Plan (DRP) and convene a recovery team
- Plan and organize recovery efforts into work streams based on business priorities set by the Crisis Manager
- Identify system dependencies and establish a restoration order
- Oversee system hardening and eradication measures as part of the restoration effort
- Communicate restoration progress to the Incident Manager and Crisis Manager
- Manage contracts and external personnel providing staff augmentation and specialized skills

We want to mention that the final role within a Technical Team is the Technical Lead. While Incident Managers are expert generalists, they must rely on Subject Matter Experts (SMEs) with an in-depth understanding of specific technologies deployed within the enterprise. For example, during restoration following a ransomware attack, there is typically one Technical Lead for each IT group involved in the effort, such as Active Directory, server, middleware, application, and networking. A Technical Lead is usually responsible for the following:

- Provide technical direction to analysts, engineers, developers, and other technical personnel to achieve the objectives the Incident Manager and Recovery Lead set
- Provide input and technical expertise for planning and execution of tactical activities
- Oversee technical activities in their respective domains

Now that you are familiar with the roles that lead and coordinate a crisis response, it is time to cover other roles and responsibilities to ensure that everyone involved in the response is clear on their tasks and that ambiguity does not hamper the response.

Defining Roles and Responsibilities

At first, roles and responsibilities may seem self-evident to many Crisis Response Team members. However, our experience tells us that key stakeholders are unfamiliar with their roles and responsibilities during a cyber crisis in many organizations. We have frequently observed chaos and the inability to make decisions during a crisis caused by key personnel unfamiliar with their roles.

Clearly defined roles and responsibilities improve the effectiveness and efficiency of the response process and help build trust and ownership among responders. The time spent preparing for a crisis pays off by increasing response velocity and results in faster recovery.

The Importance of Roles and Responsibilities

A role is a position assumed by a Technical or Business Team member. A word of caution: do not confuse roles with people. A single person can assume one or more roles during a crisis. For example, in some situations, the same individual can act as both Incident Manager and Technical Lead.

In contrast, responsibilities refer to the tasks and activities a specific role fulfills. For example, a Data Privacy Officer evaluates forensic analysis investigation results to determine if unauthorized access to data subject to laws and regulations occurred.

As part of crisis response planning, document roles and responsibilities for critical members of the Technical and Business Teams, leveraging the definitions outlined in Chapters 10 and 11 as a starting point.

Establishing roles and responsibilities leads to several benefits, including:

- Removes ambiguity and provides clarity by establishing roles, assigning them specific responsibilities, and designating primary and secondary personnel who will assume those roles during a crisis event.

- Improved communication between responders. When responders are familiar with their roles and responsibilities, there are fewer occasions for miscommunication.
- Familiarity with roles and responsibilities saves time during a crisis because responders do not have to figure out who does what amid a tense and stressful situation.

Keeping roles and responsibilities succinct, clear, and concise is vital. Focus on what, not how, and document only the crisis management responsibilities. We have reviewed crisis management plans that were long, verbose, and written in convoluted language. Instead, use the technical writing style to make the documentation practical and actionable. For example, typical responsibilities for Public Relations (PR) may include:

- Draft internal and external statements
- Engage a PR firm on a retainer
- Respond to media inquiries
- Monitor social media for sentiment regarding the event
- Assist Executive Management with preparation for interviews with the media and communication with external stakeholders

As you can see, the responsibilities focus on what tasks PR must execute, assuming the PR department has the necessary processes, procedures, and resources to fulfill those tasks.

RACI Chart

As discussed earlier in this book, you may partially or fully activate the functions within the Technical and Business Teams depending on the nature and scale of the crisis. Furthermore, each team often consists of mandatory and optional members. For example, Corporate Security is essential during environmental events or active shooter scenarios. However, it may have a limited role during a crisis caused by a cyberattack.

In addition to documenting responsibilities, a RACI chart is an excellent tool to provide clarity to crisis responders and ensure the right level of involvement. For example, you may not need to inform a Data Privacy Officer (DPO) about the ongoing response to a Distributed Denial-of-Service (DDoS) attack. However, that person will likely be responsible and accountable for assessing the data privacy impact and notifying regulators when a threat actor gains unauthorized access to highly confidential information.

Here is an explanation of the RACI assignment:

- **Responsible** – a role that performs a specific task. For example, an analyst may be responsible for log analysis and forensic analysis of compromised systems.

- **Accountable** – a role owning the task. For example, a Chief Information Security Officer (CISO) is typically accountable for an incident investigation but delegates the execution responsibility to an Incident Manager.

- **Consulted** – a role providing input or advice but not actively participating in a task. For example, legal counsel may advise technical personnel about forensic data preservation requirements but is not actively involved in acquiring and preserving that data.

- **Informed** – a role that needs to know about decisions or actions but does not provide input or actively participate in a task. For example, you may need to inform your Chief Executive Officer (CEO) about the recovery status of the impacted environment but they will not likely provide input or participate in the recovery operation.

RACI is especially applicable for scenarios where only partial team activation is required.

Key Takeaways

- As part of crisis response planning, identify coordination roles and create a model depicting how communication flows between the various stakeholders involved in the response process.

- Ensure the personnel you assign to fulfill the roles described in this chapter have expertise in their functional areas and excellent communication and organization skills. Organizational knowledge is also a requirement.
- Depending on the nature and scale of a crisis, activate only the required roles and combine their responsibilities where needed.
- Document roles and responsibilities and create a RACI matrix for the Crisis Response Team.

Chapter 13

Planning and Execution

The previous chapters focused on the structural constructs necessary to enable effective crisis response. However, establishing a Crisis Response Team and assigning coordination roles to that team is not enough. You must also create a response process and have a mechanism to break the response into manageable workstreams, schedule work, and manage resources.

Execution is everything. There are few situations where this statement is more applicable than crisis management. Managing a crisis requires the parallel execution of multiple activities with close coordination and communication between workstreams and minimal planning time. This is especially applicable when a destructive cyber-attack halts an organization.

Planning and execution require a divide-and-conquer approach with parallel execution workstreams that focus on several activities, including:

- Intrusion investigation and containment
- Restoration of systems and data
- Managing legal and regulatory matters
- Brand reputation and stakeholder management
- Business resumption

Managing all the activities without a plan is like embarking on a long journey without directions. Of course, you may eventually arrive there. However, the process will likely take longer, with precious resources wasted along the way, not to mention a significant amount of stress incurred by everyone involved. We have witnessed situations where poor planning led to personnel working long hours in a heroic effort to restore business operations for as much as six weeks.

Unfortunately, this inadequate planning and poor management led to burnout and the loss of skilled and experienced employees.

Creating a Plan

After the initial chaos subsides and the situation stabilizes, it is time to create an action plan to address the crisis event. During a large-scale event, creating separate plans for the technical and business workstreams is important as they each have a different focus. In our experience, mixing a technical response with enterprise-level activities often leads to confusion and chaos.

This section focuses on the bigger picture and creating a plan encompassing crisis response milestones. Later in this chapter, the authors show you how to employ a divide-and-conquer approach and create workstreams to achieve those milestones.

It is also a good practice to assign dedicated project managers to assist with creating and managing the plan. Crisis response is often a significant and dynamic undertaking that requires changes as new information becomes available. For this reason, it requires a role dedicated to coordination. Here are some considerations for creating a response plan.

1. Identify core response areas to address as separate units of work and establish milestones for those areas. Furthermore, for each milestone, identify tasks and document their description, owners, status, desired outcomes, dependencies, and contingencies.
2. For tightly coupled milestones or tasks that have dependencies and require close coordination, consider creating a runbook describing their sequence in the order of dependency, allocated time, and roles responsible for fulfilling them.
3. Document vital roles, responsibilities, and backup personnel.
4. Document risks and mitigation measures or contingency plans for each milestone.

Furthermore, some response areas have dependencies and prerequisites to consider as part of your plan. For example, before executing long-term containment and eradication and restoring systems to an operational state, the following prerequisites must be in place:

- A comprehensive understanding of the threat actor footprint in the compromised network
- An inventory of assets for remediation, including network infrastructure, systems, applications, and data
- A list of compromised accounts
- Hardening requirements for systems and applications
- A list of indicators of compromise (IOC) for blocking and monitoring

Resource Management and Scheduling

During large-scale destructive cyberattacks, recovery may take several days or even weeks. For example, we have witnessed cyberattacks that significantly impacted business operations for up to six weeks. Moreover, those events typically require recovery efforts with around-the-clock shift work. For this reason, resource scheduling is critical to crisis response.

In our experience, organizations face two primary challenges related to resource scheduling: time and capacity. These two variables are related to each other. Increasing capacity can often reduce the time it takes to respond and recover from a crisis. However, increasing resource capacity alone will not accelerate the response. The phenomenon is explained later in this section.

During a large-scale event, we recommend creating a resourcing plan in the early stages of the crisis. The plan should include a roster with start and end times and allow personnel enough time to rest. In our experience, the initial phases of crisis response are demanding, require long hours, and cause significant stress. These demands lead to rapid burnout and cannot be sustained for weeks. Appropriate resource management and scheduling allow personnel to rest and avoid burnout.

Another critical consideration is the appropriate distribution and allocation of resources to workstreams. It is a good idea to create cross-functional squads with complementary skills, such as network, system and database administration, middleware, and application support, and assign those squads to specific workstreams or activities. Creating silos and managing activities using the waterfall approach that passes tasks between isolated functions is highly ineffective. A waterfall model is a project management approach that breaks activities into linear and sequential phases. For example, we have encountered organizations that assigned technical personnel to work on recovery activities during a night shift without assigning personnel to those shifts with knowledge of how systems were architected and the necessary context to restore them adequately. As you can imagine, senior management was frustrated that the night shift responders were unproductive. The moral of this story is that you need to plan work and allocate resources to that work wisely. This is why we mentioned earlier that more resources do not necessarily translate into quicker outcomes. You must allocate resources wisely and manage them appropriately for their work to be as accretive as expected.

During a crisis, you may hire external contractors to increase capacity and provide specialized skills to augment the response process. Resource management must consider what skills contractors bring to the table, their ability to work autonomously, and the hours or shifts they are willing to work. Furthermore, contractors will require access to facilities, systems, and other organizational resources. For this reason, you will likely have to shortcut the normal onboarding process to ensure that external personnel can start supporting recovery as soon as possible.

A word of caution. You will still have to pair contractors with internal personnel to ensure they can understand systems and business context. For example, we have worked with organizations whose senior management hired external contractors to assist with the recovery of systems impacted by ransomware. However, their work required understanding the technical architecture of the systems they were tasked with recovering. Left alone with system credentials and no supervision, those contractors could not make tangible progress.

Activity Workflow

As the old saying goes, a picture is worth a thousand words. During a crisis, time is of the essence. You have to manage conflicting priorities, and no one has the time to read lengthy documents, often written in cryptic language.

To alleviate this problem, consider creating a workflow diagram with swim lanes depicting the response process. As part of each swim lane, you can capture the steps necessary to analyze a breach, determine and execute the required containment and eradication measures, and recover systems to an operational state.

In our experience, diagrams are an invaluable communication tool that allows technical and business audiences to quickly get on the same page.

Logistics

Logistics is another essential but often overlooked aspect of crisis response. This point applies especially to destructive cyberattacks that may require key personnel to work long and unsocial hours to recover business operations.

We recommend designating a role responsible for logistics. Because time is often a precious resource during a crisis, you want to ensure that your most skilled personnel concentrate on vital tasks instead of ordering food or making travel arrangements. In our experience, a project manager, administrative assistant, or another person with organizational knowledge is well suited to fulfill a Logistics Coordinator role.

One of the immediate tasks a Logistics Coordinator can assist with is travel arrangements and accommodation. For example, key employees and Subject Matter Experts (SMEs) may have to travel to the location where the Crisis Response Team has established a command center or to facilities impacted by an event. Assist those employees with travel arrangements and book hotel rooms to minimize time spent on administrative tasks.

You also need to ensure that vital personnel and contractors obtain access to facilities and systems promptly. Moreover, you must ensure the contractor onboarding process is speedy and smooth. We have witnessed situations where organizations hired contractors who had to wait a few days for onboarding and system access. During a crisis, you need to cut through the corporate bureaucracy and ensure everyone has the means to fulfill their roles and responsibilities.

Finally, provide food, drinks, and other refreshments. It is easy to forget about food amid a crisis. However, arranging breakfast, lunch, and dinner catering is essential for personnel working long and often unsocial hours. This consideration is another time-saver and something that employees will greatly appreciate.

Communication

One of the most critical aspects of crisis response is communication. Effective crisis communication is required to ensure that the response effort does not result in communication silos and that everyone works toward the same goals.

We recommend daily status updates within the Technical and Business Teams. You will likely require a twice-daily cadence in the initial crisis phases, especially if teams work shifts or are distributed across different time zones. Then, as business operations and a sense of normality resume, you can change the cadence to once a day and eliminate weekend updates, as appropriate.

Earlier chapters discussed incident coordination and the need to facilitate horizontal and vertical communication flow between the stakeholders involved in the response process. Tooling is another essential aspect of crisis communication. Destructive cyberattacks can negatively impact communication systems like email and video conferencing. For this reason, as part of crisis response planning, you must ensure your organization has the necessary tools to communicate effectively during a crisis.

During a crisis, you must ensure everyone has the means to communicate, even if this involves using personal email accounts and temporarily subscribing to a third-party tool with a corporate credit card. Also, do not forget about employee communication. If a cyberattack impacts emails and other primary communication systems, subscribe to a third-party emergency system to ensure you can send text or voice messages to employees and other critical personnel.

Furthermore, we recommend leveraging an instant messaging platform to ensure responders can communicate asynchronously with one another without the need to wait for a call.

However, before using out-of-band communication, engage your legal counsel to discuss legal and confidentiality considerations and how that may impact legal doctrines, such as the attorney-client privilege. This applies especially to data breaches where communication systems often remain operational, and going out-of-band may not be necessary. It can lead to legal discovery of sensitive information.

Divide and Conquer

Responding to a crisis can be an overwhelming task. In our experience, even the most resilient professionals can experience an emotional meltdown caused by extraordinary stress and pressure to restore business operations during a catastrophic cyber event. Decomposing the response into smaller components helps to manage the complexity of crisis response and alleviates the burden on responders. This is where the divide-and-conquer approach comes into play.

Divide and conquer refers to decomposing a large and complex problem into smaller manageable components to address separately and then combining the individual outcomes into an overall solution. The following paragraphs describe how you can apply this approach to crisis response.

- First, establish and enforce the coordination model described earlier in this section. It is often enticing to take shortcuts under pressure, invite everyone to a single video conferencing room, and keep it open for prolonged periods. However, we have observed that this approach leads to confusion.

Furthermore, mixing business response with technical discussions creates chaos and delays response. For this reason, separate technical, business, and executive responses into dedicated workstreams.

- Set expectations regarding hours and effort with key personnel from the onset of a crisis response. Stress and emotions are going to run high over the next several weeks. Responders must know what to expect, even if the message implies long hours, stress, and many unknowns. Moreover, personal issues may also arise. For example, we have worked with clients who missed weddings, family birthdays, and other important events due to a cyber crisis. We have observed that leaders sometimes overlook this aspect of the response. Rewarding the responders verbally and financially for their heroic recovery efforts is also essential. In our experience, a crisis often leads to staff turnover due to burnout and feeling unappreciated. Shaking hands and telling everyone they did a great job is insufficient to retain employees and compensate for the burnout, stress, and time lost with their families.
- For each team, schedule an update cadence. We recommend starting with updates twice daily and adjusting as you stabilize the situation and resume business operations. Moreover, keep the meetings succinct and focused on status updates and action items within each workstream and agree on the next steps. Also, everyone must join prepared to maximize the time and effectiveness of the meetings.
- Within each team, identify workstreams and assign Workstream Leads. There are many moving parts within technical and business responses. Breaking the work into workstreams will allow you to manage the complexity and accelerate task execution. Workstream Leads responsible for activity execution are accountable to the Technical and Business Team Leads. They also provide updates during status calls.

- Plan activities within each workstream. The plan does not have to be overly formal and verbose. A simple bullet list and role assignment for each activity are sometimes sufficient. Responding to a crisis with chaos is not a good idea. Instead, get organized and use resources and time wisely.

- Ensure that you prioritize resources. Workstream Leads within the Technical and Business Teams must work with managers to ensure personnel with the required skills are available. For example, the lead will need networking, operating system, middleware, database, and application support resources for a workstream focused on recovering a specific application or environment. Those resources may report to different managers. For this reason, as part of the Crisis Response Team, we recommend establishing a resource management function.

- Assign a Project Manager to each task force. In the most difficult situation, you will likely need multiple Project Managers. Workstream Leads and Task Force Coordinators are often simultaneously focused on execution and managing various activities. Assigning a Project Manager to assist with documentation, tracking action items, and preparing status updates can accelerate the response effort. The authors recommend identifying project managers with a solid technical background who can understand technical tasks and their complexities. In our experience, when they are under pressure technical personnel often get frustrated explaining technical concepts to non-technical project managers. Furthermore, this can introduce management overhead and defeat the purpose of involving a Project Manager in the first place.

Now that you know the importance of decomposing a crisis into manageable components, we are ready to discuss how to organize work into workstreams.

Organizing Work into Workstreams

Crisis response requires adequate organization. However, the response process must be flexible enough to adapt to changing circumstances. Modularizing crisis response and organizing work units into workstreams allow organizations to be agile at scale. In principle, there is no limit to the number of workstreams that can run in parallel. However, in practical terms, this approach is constrained by the available resources.

In crisis response, a workstream is a set of tasks executed to accomplish a specific activity. For example, an investigation workstream typically includes forensic data acquisition, data analysis, malware analysis, threat intelligence enrichment, and documenting investigative findings. We highly recommend organizing technical and business responses into workstreams to facilitate efficiency and agility.

Assigning a lead to each workstream is crucial. Consider assigning a senior staff member with expertise in the domain the workstream addresses. Following the previous example, a good candidate for the intrusion investigation workstream is a senior member of the cybersecurity department, ideally with a background in incident investigations.

Another consideration is workstream duration. Some workstreams may be short-lived, whereas others will last through and beyond the crisis. For example, data privacy and PR workstreams persist during the response and often months after resuming business operations. In contrast, technical workstreams focused on system and data restoration tend to be short-lived. Once a temporary workstream achieves its objectives, re-allocate resources to another workstream. Moreover, execute workstreams in parallel as long as the necessary resources are available to accelerate the response. For example, we recommend organizing the restoration of different systems and data simultaneously as long as you can identify and manage system dependencies.

As mentioned in the previous paragraph, dependencies are an additional consideration when organizing activities into workstreams. This point is essential for system restoration. The Technical Team Lead must understand system dependencies before prioritizing systems for recovery. For instance, if a business application depends on directory services and a domain name system (DNS), the recovery team must restore those systems first; otherwise, the application will not function as expected.

The following list outlines a battle-tested procedure for organizing activities into workstreams. It focuses on technical workstreams for demonstration purposes. However, the procedure is equally applicable to enterprise response.

1. Identify core response areas to address as separate units of work; for instance, forensic analysis, remediation, system hardening, and recovery.

2. Analyze each identified area and determine if further decomposition is required. A perfect example is system recovery which may require multiple work streams focused on restoring specific technologies and data. Some system recovery workstreams can run in parallel if the enterprise has the necessary resources.

3. Prioritize which areas to address first. For example, forensic analysis typically takes precedence over remediation when a crisis does not cause an operational impact.

4. Organize each unit of work into a dedicated workstream. For example, you can organize system recovery into the following workstreams: directory services, enterprise resource planning (ERP), and payroll system.

5. Assign a Workstream Lead and personnel with the skills necessary to execute the work.

6. Identify workstream dependencies. For example, if the ERP system mentioned above depends on directory services, prioritize restoring systems that support directory services.

7. Create a plan. At the workstream level, the plan should be concise and provide a sense of direction, and there is no need

for verbose plans that include contingency planning. Depending on the workstream complexity, several bullet points might be sufficient.

8. Execute tasks within the workstream and report on progress.

9. When the work is completed, tear down the workstream and allocate resources to another workstream on the priority list.

Key Takeaways

- Create a Crisis Response Plan that addresses Technical and Business response domains.
- Ensure that you understand and validate dependencies for system remediation and restoration.
- During a complex and large-scale event, manage resources and appropriately schedule work.
- Ensure the Crisis Response Team has the necessary tools to communicate. Additionally, ensure regular communication cadence and status updates.
- Do not forget logistics, including accommodations, travel arrangements, and food.
- Decompose crisis response into smaller components to manage the response complexity and alleviate the burden on responders.
- Organize the response into workstreams focused on specific activities.

Chapter 14

Breach Investigation

Investigating a cyber breach causing a cyber crisis is a complex process that can take up to several weeks depending on the sophistication level of the threat actor, the compromise scope, and the threat actor's dwell time on the network. The outcome also underpins many other crisis response activities, including containment, eradication, recovery, regulatory notification requirements, and even legal processes.

The purpose of this chapter is not to make you a technical expert in threat investigations. Instead, we want to ensure you understand the overall process and can effectively leverage this knowledge when making business-level decisions regarding a crisis response.

This topic is so essential to crisis response that we have dedicated an entire chapter to discussing conducting an effective investigation and clarifying some common misconceptions.

This chapter primarily focuses on the process to identify and scope a network intrusion. In other parts of this book, we discuss containment, eradication, and recovery. Figure 4 below outlines the process.

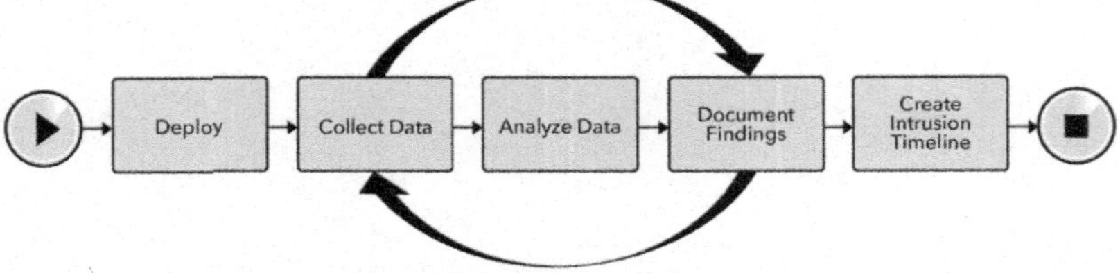

Figure 4 – Process to Identify and Scope a Network Intrusion

The Importance of Conducting an Investigation

We frequently encounter organizations rushing to complete investigations and restore business operations without conducting a comprehensive intrusion analysis. We recognize the impact system and application downtime causes on business operations and the downstream impact on customers, business partners, and often the general public. At the same time, concluding an investigation without understanding the complete intrusion timeline is often counterproductive. Scoping an intrusion is critical to fully contain the event, eradicate the threat, and establish a recovery point based on the earliest evidence of unauthorized access to the network.

First, you must determine the scope and impact of a cyberattack to inform the business response, including notifications to employees, customers, and business partners, prepare for potential litigation, and notify regulators in appropriate jurisdictions. Of course, this list is incomplete, and you must work with your legal counsel and senior leadership to determine post-breach obligations. For example, suppose a threat actor gains access to data subject to data privacy laws and regulations. In that case, you must identify and evaluate the data accessed and potentially exfiltrated by the threat actor to inform the business-level response. The crux of the matter is that you must conduct a thorough investigation to enable business-level decisions based on facts, not speculations or assumptions regarding the attack.

Secondly, thorough intrusion analysis allows you to identify the compromised systems, user accounts, malware, and other artifacts to determine appropriate containment and eradication steps. As part of the attack lifecycle, threat actors often compromise multiple systems and establish persistence through malware to ensure they can retain access to the network. For example, when investigating espionage cases by nation-state actors, we have observed that they often attempt to re-compromise the network after eradication to continue their operations. Therefore, a comprehensive investigation is necessary to inform containment and eradication steps and ensure you recover the impacted systems and applications to a secure state.

Now that you understand the importance of intrusion analysis, let's explain the typical process organizations go through during a large-scale cyber event.

Technology Considerations

During a large-scale investigation, your organization must be able to collect security data at scale, sometimes from tens of thousands of systems. In the early days of cyber investigations, the process heavily relied on analyzing forensic images of compromised systems. However, with the proliferation of cyber threats and the need to minimize operational impact resulting from downtime, this approach alone is no longer appropriate for most enterprises. Moreover, traditional forensic analysis approaches do not scale well when a threat actor compromises multiple systems as part of the attack lifecycle.

The evolution of Endpoint Detection and Response (EDR) technologies made combing traditional analysis with large-scale data collection possible. An EDR solution captures and analyzes a rich set of system-level events for evidence of malicious activity and other suspicious behavior. It aggregates the data and alerts into a centralized repository for further analytics and threat intelligence enrichment. Moreover, analysts can leverage the EDR capabilities to analyze, contain and remediate compromised systems remotely.

You can leverage EDR and other at-scale data collection technologies in the following ways during a cyber crisis:

- Analyze system and network data collected as part of day-to-day operations. This approach accelerates the analysis process. However, your organization must have the technology deployed before a breach. Furthermore, the major drawback of this approach is that EDR data retention policies are relatively short because of the large volumes of data collected by the technology.
- Leverage the EDR to deploy bespoke scripts to collect historical forensic artifacts necessary to establish the

compromise scope. This step is critical because threat actors may dwell on the compromised network for weeks or even months. By the time the victim organization detects an intrusion, historical events may no longer be available due to a data retention policy.

- Many EDR solutions can also block specific behaviors associated with threat actor activity and you can leverage this as part of your containment and eradication strategy. These capabilities include system isolation, blocking malware execution and network connectivity to attacker infrastructure, and other behaviors associated with cyber threats.

A word of caution. When you decide to sever network access during a destructive attack to contain the event, ensure that EDR and other security tools can communicate with their cloud back-ends. Otherwise, you may be unable to use those tools for further containment and investigation.

In our experience, many organizations still lack modern threat detection and response technologies, or those technologies have limited deployment. In such cases, when we respond to large-scale cyber events, the first step is to deploy an EDR technology to endpoints to facilitate data collection, analysis, and containment.

The process often involves the following steps:

- Engage an EDR vendor and provision the technology. If you hire a Digital Forensics and Incident Response (DFIR) firm to assist with the investigation, the firm can recommend a preferred and supported technology and facilitate this step on your behalf.
- Obtain a software package from the DFIR firm and use a software deployment tool to deploy the package to your systems at scale. On the surface, this step seems to be straightforward. However, in our experience, many organizations struggle to promptly deploy software agents at scale. There are several reasons for this, such as unsupported

legacy operating systems, poor asset management and control over IT environments, slow network connection for deployment to remote locations, or a lack of appropriate tools.

As part of crisis response planning, we recommend ensuring that your organization can collect system-level events at scale or at least rapidly deploy appropriate technology to end-user and server endpoints.

The Investigation Process

The threat analysis process often follows a lifecycle model, as Figure 4 depicts. This point especially applies to investigating large-scale events with evidence of lateral movement and foothold across numerous systems. Moreover, some activities may require several iterations until you reach diminishing returns related to new findings. We describe this phenomenon later in this section.

The following sections describe each phase of the lifecycle model.

Collect Data

The first step in the process is data collection. Analysts are typically interested in the following types of data:

- Security data generated as part of day-to-day operations, including audit events, security alerts, event logs generated by systems and applications, and telemetry generated by endpoint and network security tools.
- Historical forensic data required for in-depth analysis of compromised systems. This data includes historical forensic artifacts collected through specialized software packages and forensic images of system memory and disk volumes. Historical data acquisition requires specialized skills and tools and can include activities such as disk volume imaging, volatile memory (aka RAM) imaging, running tools to collect specific system artifacts, or even cloning an entire virtual machine.

In recent years, the industry has been increasingly shifting to data collection and analysis through tools such as EDR and relying on digital forensics only for deep-dive analysis of systems of particular interest, such as Patient 0. A Patient 0 is the first system a threat actor compromises before establishing a foothold and moving laterally within the network. In other words, leveraging collection at scale allows analysts to focus on the bigger picture and identify the tip of the iceberg. In contrast, digital forensics enables them to see and analyze the entire iceberg. The approaches complement each other and allow analysts to accelerate an investigation while gaining deeper visibility into systems of interest.

You can localize data collection or have an enterprise-wide scope. For example, when a cyberattack impacts only a specific environment or application, or your organization detected an incident in the early phases of the attack lifecycle before lateral movement, you can limit data collection to particular systems or environments and expand it later on as required.

When evidence shows that a threat actor established a foothold and moved laterally within the network, we strongly encourage you to collect data enterprise-wide. Today's intrusion investigation approaches heavily rely on statistical analysis and data analytics, making the analysis process scalable with little extra effort from analysts. For this reason, it is worth casting a wide net for data collection to gain assurance about the compromise scope. Note that evidence implies event logs, system and network telemetry, security alerts, and forensic artifacts produced during system operation, such as registry entries and file system metadata.

Another essential component of data collection is data preservation, especially if there is a reasonable expectation that a cyber breach may lead to civil litigation or even a class action lawsuit. Data preservation refers to securing and storing data in a forensically sound state that protects against alteration or destruction. Depending on the type and source of the data, preservation may include the following steps:

- Isolating compromised systems from the network and preserving their state. Preservation refers to retaining the current system condition, including events and data, and minimizing changes during the acquisition process that can hinder forensic analysis.

- Collecting forensic images, logs, and telemetry in a secure vault for long-term storage
- Calculating cryptographic hashes for data integrity purposes
- Documenting a chain of custody for physical assets, for example, when sending compromised end-user workstations to a remote forensic lab

You can preserve and store data on external hard drives in a secure physical vault. An alternative solution is to create a virtual vault in a file share or cloud object storage. The latter approach requires a strict access control protocol and auditing to prevent accidental deletion or alteration of the data and prove its authenticity.

Finally, regardless of the acquisition method, you need to ensure that the acquisition and analysis protocol is legally defensible and can withstand any spoliation claims. Data spoliation occurs when forensic evidence is altered or destroyed intentionally or through negligence.

You can build a defensible protocol by leveraging industry standards, taking the necessary steps to ensure data integrity, and producing comprehensive documentation for each acquisition method. Note that the National Institute of Justice (NIJ) provides legal guidance for forensic experts on data acquisition.[10] If you reside in a country outside the United States, consult your organization's attorneys for guidance specific to your jurisdiction.

As a final word for data collection, we recognize that not every cyber event may lead to a material impact. Business priorities such as

[10] National Institute of Justice (NIJ), Law 101: Legal Guide for the Forensic Expert, available at https://nij.ojp.gov/nij-hosted-online-training-courses/law-101-legal-guide-forensic-expert/pretrial/pretrial-rules-evidence#:~:text=The%20Federal%20Rules%20of%20Evidence,an%20issue%20in%20a%20case.

restoring operations or keeping systems running during a cyberattack often precede matters such as forensic data preservation or an in-depth analysis. We advocate for balancing business needs and ensuring cyber events are investigated thoroughly. Therefore, working with legal counsel and business stakeholders to establish a risk-based response protocol is critical in cyber crisis response preparedness.

Analyze Data

Large-scale breach analysis is a complex process that spans multiple domains, including log analysis, digital forensics, cyber threat intelligence, and malware analysis. That is one of the reasons why we recommend establishing a relationship with a DFIR firm with a proven track record of investigating large-scale breaches to assist with this task, as described in Chapter 11.

As described earlier, we strongly advocate conducting a comprehensive analysis of your environments when there is evidence of lateral movement within the network or the threat actor has multiple entry points into the network. The analysis typically consists of the activities outlined below.

- **Analysis of the collected data** – involves reviewing alerts and looking for suspicious events and outliers indicative of attacker activity, correlating events of interest, and "stitching together" findings into a timeline to visualize how the attack progressed. This process often consists of statistical analysis, analytics, and human analysis. As described earlier in this chapter, the data can come from endpoint and network security tools, event logs generated in day-to-day operations, forensic images of compromised systems, and data collected through EDR and custom scripts.

- **Cyber threat intelligence** – augments the analysis process by contextualizing findings and data points of interest with threat research. This approach directs analysts by correlating and extending analysis with data related to similar past attacks. Where sufficient high-fidelity artifacts relating to threat actor activity are available, threat analysts can also attribute the attack to a specific threat group. However, this becomes increasingly difficult as threat actors frequently leverage off-the-shelf tools, share many commonalities, and leverage the as-a-service model by collaborating with other threat actors.

- **Malware analysis** – threat actors often leverage malware and other tools to compromise a network, establish persistent access to systems, and exfiltrate data. As part of the analysis process, analysts often extract malware from compromised systems and analyze it to determine its purpose and extract indicators of compromise (IOCs). An IOC constitutes evidence of potential attacker activity. Malware analysis requires specialized and niche skills. Also, malware analysis is integral to cyber threat intelligence and can provide rich information about a specific threat actor.

Threat actors often rely on in-memory attacks and utilize the tools they find in their compromised environments to blend with normal network activities. We refer to this approach as "living off the land." This is another reason why deploying an EDR solution as part of day-to-day operations is crucial for system compromise detection and analysis.

As depicted in Figure 4 data analysis is an iterative process. Analysts iterate through the collection and analysis lifecycle until there are diminishing returns related to new findings. For example, suppose you identify malware on a specific system and scan the network for evidence of that malware on other endpoints. If you find other compromised systems, analyze them for additional attacker activity and leverage any new findings for further scanning and analysis. This process continues until you reach diminishing returns.

It is important to note that the data required to answer investigative questions might not exist in many cases. There are several reasons for this, including:

- Short data retention policies set in security tools
- Short log retention policies configured in systems and applications
- Data is inadvertently destroyed during incident containment
- Forensic data is overwritten in the course of system operation
- A threat actor employs anti-forensics tactics such as clearing log files

In such cases, it is essential to document that specific data of interest was unavailable and the reasons for its absence.

Document Findings

As analysts collect and analyze data, they produce findings related to compromised systems and user accounts, malware and attacker tools, and forensic artifacts serving as evidence of attacker activity. Therefore, we strongly recommend recording and maintaining all those findings and artifacts in a centralized repository for the following reasons:

- You will need this information to produce a timeline of threat actor activity and an investigation report for senior management and legal counsel

- Analysts working on different data sets need access to the most up-to-date repository of findings to leverage as part of the analysis process

- Law enforcement may request this information

- You need the information to build detection logic, alerts, and dashboards for monitoring

During a minor incident, you can use a Word document or a simple spreadsheet to keep track of this information. However, this approach does not scale during large-scale breach investigations.

Many Security Orchestration, Automation, and Response (SOAR) platforms include a feature for recording and cross-referencing investigative findings with threat intelligence. We highly recommend deploying a SOAR and creating templates for tracking investigative information as part of crisis response preparedness. However, suppose your organization does not have the budget or resources to deploy a SOAR. In that case, you can create an Excel template with separate tabs to track incident information, such as compromised user accounts, systems for remediation, and malware.

No matter what approach you take to recording and maintaining investigative findings, you need to ensure the information is complete, accurate, relevant to the case, and updated as analysts identify new artifacts related to threat actor activity. Moreover, ensure that entries with temporal characteristics have a timestamp field recorded in the Universal Coordinated Time (UTC) leveraging the ISO 8601 format. During investigations spanning international boundaries, we have observed that analysts and clients can easily get confused by different time formats and conventions used in their respective countries. For this reason, using the ISO 8601 timestamp format is essential.

Finally, investigative findings are often very sensitive and can expose the organization to unnecessary legal risks if not guarded appropriately. For this reason, we recommend tightly controlling access to this information and granting permission to access it on a need-to-know basis.

Document an Intrusion Timeline

As mentioned earlier, one of the objectives during a large-scale breach is determining the scope and timeframe of threat actor activity in the compromised environment. Many data types collected and analyzed during a breach investigation have temporal characteristics, including filesystem activity, audit logs, and system and application events.

Reconstructing an intrusion timeline is a powerful analysis technique that chronologically arranges findings related to attacker activity.

Timeline analysis is a potent tool during large-scale investigations. To arrive at a timeline of threat actor activity, analysts often create timelines for individual compromised systems and then combine them into a single master timeline that paints a chronological picture of how the attack unfolded.

A well-constructed timeline helps to visualize the attack progression and is invaluable for reporting and communicating investigative findings to senior management. In our experience, a timeline with a concise and coherent narrative in plain English helps senior management to understand the extent of a breach without getting entangled in the details or complexities of the investigation.

Threat Hunting

The last topic we want to cover in this chapter is threat hunting. In our experience, it is one of the most misunderstood and misused terms in cybersecurity. Threat hunting proactively identifies previously unknown or ongoing non-remediated threats.

Although threat hunting is primarily a proactive approach to threat detection, we decided to briefly discuss it because clients frequently inquire about this topic and ask us how to leverage it in their organizations.

In our experience, threat hunting is part art and part science that combines a framework, endpoint and network security technologies, cyber threat intelligence, and human analysis skills and experience. Moreover, there are two broad approaches to threat hunting: data-driven and threat intelligence-driven.

During data-driven threat hunting, you collect historical system and network data across your IT environments and leverage techniques, such as statistical analysis and analytics augmented by human analysis, to identify outliers in the data set that may indicate malicious activity. Then, you "stitch together" data points of interest by correlating events across disparate systems and looking for cause-and-effect relationships. In other words, data-driven threat hunting can be compared to looking for the proverbial needle in a haystack by identifying statistical outliers.

In contrast, during intelligence-driven threat hunting, you leverage tools such as EDR, Network Detect and Response (NDR), and Security Information and Event Management (SIEM) to scan your environments for IOCs associated with a specific threat actor, malware, or even a campaign. In other words, you first form a hypothesis relating to a potential cyberattack and then leverage threat intelligence to prove or refute that hypothesis.

You may be wondering why we included threat hunting in the discussion if it is primarily a proactive threat detection approach. The primary reason is that you can leverage many breach analysis methods in threat hunting. Furthermore, threat hunting is indispensable when there is minimal information about a breach, and you need to either work with a hypothesis or look for the proverbial needle in a haystack.

For example, sometimes analysts have one or two indicators of compromise and may have to leverage an intelligence-driven approach to examine their environments for additional indicators of threat actor activity before transitioning into a breach response mode and activating the Crisis Response Team.

We have also worked with organizations that received a Common Point of Purchase (CPP) notification from a payment card brand. A CPP notification is a notice to a payment card processor that their Point of Purchase was the last location where the payment cards had been used before fraudulent purchases occurred at other merchant locations. This is often indicative of a cyber breach. Without a "smoking gun," we leveraged data-driven hunting, collected data from payment systems, and analyzed it for evidence of unauthorized access to unravel the mystery.

If you want to learn more about breach investigations and responses, we encourage you to read *Cyber Breach Response That Actually Works. Organizational Approach to Managing Residual Risk*, authored by Andrew Gorecki and published by Wiley & Sons in July 2020.

Key Takeaways

- Be sure to conduct a comprehensive investigation as part of a cyber crisis response. An incomplete understanding of the compromise scope may lead to partial containment and eradication, and the threat actor eventually re-compromising the network.

- Data collection and analysis is an iterative process. Iterate through the data acquisition and analysis lifecycle until reaching diminishing returns related to new findings.
- Enrich and contextualize forensic findings with cyber threat intelligence to identify all possible Indicators of Compromise (IOCs).

Chapter 15

Remediation and Recovery Planning

Remediation and recovery are critical steps in crisis response planning. Many breaches occur because of vulnerabilities and weaknesses in systems and applications and inadequate detection and response capabilities. Furthermore, these two domains go hand-in-hand. Recovery without remediation is like rebuilding a house on quicksand. Inadequately remediated systems provide a threat actor with an easy way to return to the network following eradication. In such cases, it is often a matter of time before another breach occurs.

This chapter covers high-level considerations for planning remediation and recovery. Then, in the Remediate section, we dive into the more technical aspects of this topic.

Understanding Remediation

The term remediation is often a source of confusion in crisis response. This book describes remediation as a two-step process: breach remediation, also referred to as tactical remediation, and post-breach remediation (a.k.a strategic remediation). Throughout this book, we will stick to the terms breach and post-breach remediation.

Breach remediation encompasses activities necessary to fully contain an event and eradicate the threat actor from the compromised environment. Furthermore, breach remediation includes system hardening and other tactical security enhancements to ensure you recover your environments to an operational and secure state.

In contrast, post-breach remediation refers to the long-term planning and measures you can implement after business resumption to minimize the risk of similar events occurring in the future. For example, during a root cause analysis, you might establish that a threat actor exploited a vulnerability in an Internet-exposed system to gain initial access to the network. Consequently, a post-breach remediation project would aim to develop a vulnerability management program to ensure you minimize the risk of future exploitations. We dedicate an entire chapter to this topic in the Remediate section.

Breach remediation planning includes technical preparation, low-level planning, and business considerations. For example, you do not want to execute long-term containment, eradication, and hardening activities on a day when your payroll or another business-critical process runs unless retaining your job is not a high priority. Moreover, even during a destructive cyberattack that is negatively impacting business operations, remediation must consider the business and requires planning to ensure you recover systems to an operational and secure state.

The planning process can be complex, and you must prioritize what activities to execute as part of tactical remediation versus what weaknesses you will need to address as part of post-breach remediation.

Understanding Cyber Recovery

While remediation aims to secure and regain control of your environments, recovery focuses on restoring systems and data to resume business operations. However, you must ensure there is synergy between these functions. We have observed that it is only a matter of time before an organization experiences another significant event when recovery is disjointed and executed without remediation considerations.

The old mantra goes, "You cannot protect what you don't know." Our spin on the mantra is "You cannot recover what you don't understand." Therefore, identifying business-critical functions and processes that support your organization's mission is an essential first step to building cyber recovery capabilities. The next step is understanding the applications, data, infrastructure, and core enterprise services supporting those processes.

We often refer to this concept as a Minimum Viable Company (MVC). An MVC is a set of functions, processes, people, data, and technologies necessary to fulfill an organization's mission, sell products, and provide customer service.

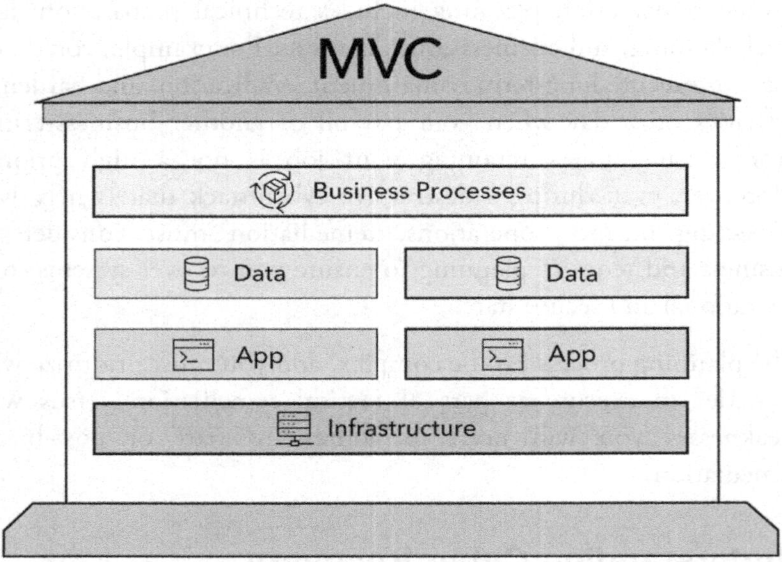

Figure 5 – Minimum Viable Company

Starting a cyber recovery project by establishing an MVC has a significant benefit. It forces your organization to shift thinking away from a system or application-centric approach and focus on business process recovery planning. One of the reasons traditional Disaster Recovery (DR) can fail during a catastrophic cyber event is a system-centric approach that does not consider an end-to-end business process and dependencies between the applications, infrastructure, and data supporting that process.

If your organization is serious about efficient recovery following a catastrophic cyber event, you must move away from a system-centric approach to recovering an entire business process.

We want to emphasize that the concept of MVC cannot be achieved as part of crisis response planning alone. Instead, it requires a more comprehensive approach, moving away from manual DR towards increasing resiliency and automating recovery, and a top-down enterprise approach with support and oversight from Senior Leadership. We highly recommend approaching cyber recovery as part of a broader cyber resiliency program.

Have Traditional DR Approaches Failed Us?

Traditional DR approaches focus on minimizing business disruption and data loss resulting from disasters, including hurricanes, floods, power cuts, and other similar unforeseen circumstances. Your DR team has likely established resiliency metrics such as Recovery Time Objective (RTO) and Recovery Point Objective (RPO) based on the criticality of your applications and the supporting infrastructure. Establishing those metrics helps to ensure you can recover the impacted technology in a reasonable timeframe while minimizing potential data loss.

You may use various technical approaches to facilitate DR. These include backups, taking regular snapshots of your virtual machines, data replication to a remote location, or even hosting applications in two data centers and load-balancing network traffic between them. In recent years, we have even observed increased interest in tape backups.

However, from a cybersecurity perspective, this approach has a fundamental shortcoming. When you architect systems and applications for resiliency, you assume that backups of those applications will be available in a remote location. Unfortunately, ransomware and other destructive cyberattacks challenged this assumption. This why it is crucial to consider immutable storage solutions to ensure a threat actor cannot destroy backups prior to deploying destructive malware.

As part of a typical attack lifecycle, a ransomware operator must progress through several stages before deploying destructive malware, including initial compromise, foothold and persistence, privilege escalation, and lateral movement.

Arguably, privilege escalation is at the heart of a cyberattack. A ransomware operator with unrestricted access to a domain and the proverbial keys to the kingdom can inflict catastrophic damage to systems. This ability has broad implications for traditional DR, including:

- Not only are elevated privileges often sufficient to deploy ransomware to many systems, but they also allow a threat actor to delete backup copies of your systems and data before the deployment.
- Suppose you run a hot DR site. If systems in the primary and disaster recovery sites are part of the same domain, a threat actor can also deploy ransomware to your secondary site.
- Ransomware often has an enterprise-wide impact, whereas traditional disaster recovery plans and capabilities focus on recovering individual systems and do not consider business recovery and orchestration.

We have witnessed numerous cases where a threat actor deleted the backup before deploying ransomware, rendering recovery impossible and forcing the victim organizations to pay a ransom.

Cyber recovery aims to address those challenges by providing principles and architectural approaches that help organizations preserve critical data, applications, and infrastructure to ensure survivability and accelerate recovery during a business-impact cyber event.

Business Considerations

Remediation and recovery planning must take into account business considerations. The requirement to remediate and recover the affected systems is obvious during destructive events that impact business operations. However, data privacy events that do not negatively impact business operations still require remediation that can temporarily impact business operations. As a result, executive-level communication and buy-in are essential.

Executive Buy-In

We recommend socializing the plan with Executive Management and obtaining their buy-in as part of remediation planning. As part of the plan, it is essential that you clearly articulate the need for remediation, key activities and their outcome, and their potential impact on business operations. For example, remediation activities may temporarily impact the availability of systems supporting business functions. Sometimes, you may even disconnect specific network segments from the Internet to ensure the threat actor cannot access those systems before eradication. This is another reason why executive communication and setting expectations with the business are essential.

Business Disruption

As outlined in the previous section, breach remediation can disrupt business operations. Disruption is sometimes unavoidable, especially if a threat actor gains a significant footprint in the network, compromises highly privileged credentials, and deploys malware to multiple systems. At this point, the risk of further impact, such as data exfiltration or ransomware deployment, is high enough to opt for disruptive remediation to protect the enterprise.

For example, we have worked with organizations willing to temporarily halt business operations and manufacturing processes to prevent potential ransomware deployment. In those cases, accelerated and disruptive containment and eradication were necessary because those organizations had very little confidence in their backup systems and the ability to recover operations after a destructive attack.

As part of the preparation, you must perform rapid planning to manage crisis aspects, such as external statements and public relations, internal employee considerations, and activating business continuity plans.

Execution Timing

Our experience shows there is no ideal time to execute a remediation plan. For this reason, you must work with Executive Management and the business to determine a window with the least impact on business operations. For example, executing remediation on the day your organization runs the payroll process is not a great idea unless you want to deal with unhappy employees.

At the same time, it is also vital to clearly articulate to the business the risk and impact of delaying remediation. Having an active threat on the network can lead to unforeseen consequences, and the leadership must understand the potential outcomes and accept the risk before delaying remediation or opting for partial remediation only.

Additional Expenditure

We discussed the importance of including Finance as part of the Business Team earlier in this section. As we mentioned, organizations rapidly incur significant expenditures during a crisis response. Remediation is no exception. For example, expenditures for hiring contractors and procuring technologies are essential considerations. Consequently, you must secure the necessary budget and resources as part of remediation planning to ensure the effort is successful.

Technology Considerations

In addition to business considerations, there are several technical considerations you have to take into account. Many organizations evolve their IT environments organically following mergers and acquisitions and business growth. As a result, technical debt accumulates over time, and your environment may have inconsistent security controls and posture. The following paragraphs outline some of the considerations.

Upgrading Legacy Technologies

We regularly come across organizations running legacy systems no longer supported by vendors or relying on older insecure protocols.

Technical debt is a serious problem for many enterprises and cyberattacks amplify this issue. Unfortunately, sometimes it takes a cyber crisis for an organization to consider upgrading legacy platforms and migrating to more secure protocols, even if those activities temporarily disrupt business operations.

Furthermore, you may have to upgrade older platforms to install tools that run on supported systems. For example, some EDR tools do not run on older Windows systems. You may not only have to upgrade systems and protocols as part of a containment and eradication strategy but also to enable incident monitoring, detection, and early response. We further explore this topic in the Remediate and Recover section.

Technology Deployment

As we mentioned earlier in this section, you may have to deploy tools and systems to enhance the security posture of your network before executing a containment and eradication plan. For example, you will need to deploy an EDR technology to facilitate analysis at scale and collect system data to support threat monitoring and containment. Another tool you may need to deploy is a Privileged Access Manager (PAM) solution to vault privileged accounts and rotate credentials to ensure the threat actor cannot easily compromise privileged credentials to access critical assets.

Communications

Arguably, Crisis Communications are as important as the technical activities executed during the Remediate phase. Therefore, we highly encourage you to engage your Crisis Communications team to prepare internal and external messaging even if you do not expect remediation to cause an outage of systems. We explore this topic in the Articulate section of this book. However, to organize remediation and recovery, consider the following communication requirements:

- Employee communication for situations where an outage prevents them from accessing the corporate network or impacts manufacturing processes

- Holding statements for your website and messaging for social media
- Communication for business partners and other entities that may be affected by the event
- A script for the call center. Consider recording an automated message if you expect a high volume of calls.

Moreover, determine how you are going to disseminate the messages. For example, most organizations use email for employee communications. However, if remediation results in an email outage, we recommend arranging for an alternative communication tool, such as a third-party mass notification system via text messaging.

Getting Vendor Support

Remediation and recovery are complex undertakings that require specialized skills and niche expertise. In most cases we have responded to, organizations needed vendor support with remediation planning and execution. This support included both advisory and hands-on keyboard support.

You can leverage existing vendor relationships to support the remediation effort, especially if your organization has outsourced technology and application management to an external firm. However, we have noted that even technology outsourcing firms do not possess all the skills and experience required to assist with incident containment and threat eradication. For example, we have observed that system administrators are well-versed in system configuration and management but often do not possess the skills to harden and secure systems following a cyberattack.

We recommend external support for the following activities:

- Remediation planning – You will need assistance creating a remediation plan based on the findings during forensic analysis. Analysts determine how the threat actor operated in the compromised environment as part of the response effort. The findings feed into the remediation plan and directly influence the containment and eradication activities you must execute.

- Support with Microsoft technologies – As part of your containment strategy, you must reset domain and service account credentials. This activity can disrupt system and application operations and requires careful planning. For example, you may need to reset the credentials for the Kerberos Service Account, which provides encryption material for authentication across your Windows domains. If not planned carefully, this activity can have a significant operational impact on your applications.

- Restoring and rebuilding systems – You must rebuild and restore multiple systems accessed by the threat actors. In our experience, internal teams do not have the capacity to execute this activity quickly. For this reason, you may have to hire contractors to support this effort.

- Application vendors to assist with re-installing complex, distributed applications. For example, suppose you must rebuild servers running an enterprise resource planning (ERP) application. You will likely need to engage the vendor to assist with installing and configuring the application.

- Networking support if your internal information technology department does not have advanced networking skills, especially in complex configurations and troubleshooting.

The above list provides some common use cases we have encountered when responding to crisis events. Ensure that you carefully evaluate your support requirements and engage the necessary external support.

Managing Workstreams

We often compare remediation to a data center migration in a condensed timeframe. Dividing the remediation plan into discrete workstreams will help manage the complexity and enforce ownership and accountability for specific parts of the plan.

As we highlighted in Chapter 13, a workstream is a set of tasks executed together to accomplish a specific activity. As part of remediation planning, you organized tasks into work streams and identified dependencies between them or even particular tasks.

The following list provides considerations for executing the plan through workstreams:

- During preparation, meet with managers leading technical groups to identify workstreams for execution. We recommend identifying workstreams by grouping related tasks or focusing on technical functions. Examples include Active Directory, networking, security tools, and restoration.
- Assign a lead to each workstream. We recommend assigning a senior staff member with expertise in the domain the workstream addresses. The leader is responsible for technical direction to personnel, task execution, and providing status updates to the Command Center.
- Ensure you understand dependencies between tasks and workstreams. A lack of dependency consideration may delay remediation or even impede the effort. For example, performing password resets for the compromised domain is a good practice before enrolling users in multi-factor (MFA) authentication.
- At the workstream level, create an execution playbook in the order of dependency. The playbook should contain specific tasks, execution timing, milestones, roles responsible for their execution, and success criteria.
- Moreover, ensure technical groups test configuration changes, tools, and other technical changes before remediation. Execution should be the focus during a remediation window. For example, figuring out how to configure or harden a server during a remediation window indicates inadequate preparation.

Key Takeaways

- Understand the difference between traditional DR and cyber recovery and ensure you know what applications, systems, and data support business-critical processes.
- Work closely with the Business Team to gain executive buy-in for remediation and determine an optimal execution timing and a security budget for resources and tools.
- Where possible and appropriate, consider upgrading legacy technologies to reduce technical debt.
- Include hardening, security posture enhancements, and attack surface reduction in your remediation effort.
- Proactively prepare internal and external messaging even if you do not expect remediation to cause an operational outage.
- Organize remediation into workstreams by grouping related tasks or focusing on technical functions. Also, identify dependencies between tasks and individual workstreams and create a playbook to execute them in the order of dependency.

Summary

In this section, we explained how to organize a crisis response. First, we covered topics such as establishing a Crisis Response Team and discussed the role of Executive Management in the response process. As the next step, we described how to coordinate crisis response and design a response model that enables effective vertical and horizontal communication between all stakeholders involved in the response. Then, we provided practical advice on response planning and decomposing a crisis response into workstreams to make it more manageable. Finally, this section concluded with a discussion on the importance of a comprehensive breach investigation and its role in driving technical and business decisions.

Key Takeaways

- A Technical Team is responsible for activities that include an intrusion investigation, containment, eradication, and system recovery. When establishing the team structure and capabilities, consider the size of the organization, available resources, and external support requirements.

- Cyberattacks often lead to operational, data privacy, financial, and reputational impacts to manage from a business perspective to prevent long-term consequences, such as brand reputation damage and loss of customers. A Business Team is responsible for handling such matters.

- Clearly defined roles and responsibilities improve the effectiveness and efficiency of the response process. They also help improve communication, build trust and ownership among responders, and accelerate recovery time.

- Managing a crisis is a complex undertaking that requires the parallel execution of multiple activities with close coordination and communication between workstreams and minimal planning time. Therefore, creating a plan that considers resource planning, communication, decomposing work into manageable chunks, and orchestrating the response process is critical to effective crisis response.

- A breach investigation is a critical element of a crisis response that underpins other response activities, including containment, eradication, recovery, regulatory notification requirements, and even legal processes. Conduct a comprehensive investigation to effectively scope the compromise and eradicate the threat actor from the network as part of the response process.

Next Steps

- Establish a cross-functional Crisis Response Team comprising technical, business, and executive-level stakeholders.

- Establish coordination roles, document responsibilities, and develop a communication plan to facilitate horizontal and vertical communication within the team.

- Enact a crisis response process, including a workflow diagram with swim lanes, activity descriptions, and role assignments.

- Conduct a BIA, identify system and business process dependencies, and establish a recovery order.

- Plan logistics and organize complex tasks into workstreams.

- Educate technical and business stakeholders on the importance of a thorough breach investigation. Interactive crisis response exercises are an excellent means to put key stakeholders through a crisis simulation in a safe environment.

Section 4

Negotiate

"One of the best ways to persuade others is to listen to them."

~ U.S. Secretary of State, 1961-1969 Dean Rusk

Introduction

The lead author for this section is Christopher Scott, with significant input from and in collaboration with Andrew Gorecki.

In the vital Negotiate section, we address the crucial art of setting priorities during a cyber crisis from the perspective of a Crisis Manager. Amidst a storm of pressing issues, how do you decide which to address first? This involves negotiations between various business leaders, each armed with their own agendas and priorities.

- **Risk-Based Decisions:** This chapter demystifies risk assessment and management in the cyber realm. As a Crisis Manager, discover practical strategies to harness risk evaluations for immediate action, striking a balance between security concerns and business continuity.

- **Empowering the Expert:** The significance of tapping into the specific expertise within your teams during a crisis cannot be overstated. Unearth effective techniques to fully utilize your cybersecurity experts in the decision-making process.

- **Business Priorities:** Cybersecurity efforts must align with broader business objectives. Explore the art of crisis management without losing sight of the organization's strategic goals, ensuring stakeholder trust and preserving your company's reputation during tumultuous times.

- **Technical Priorities:** Delve into the technological intricacies of a crisis, from swift response tactics to maintaining system integrity and ensuring a seamless service recovery.

Leading with precision and decisiveness during high-pressure situations is an art. The Negotiate section offers you the tools and insights to skillfully balance risk, business continuity, and technological needs. By the end, you'll be primed to discuss the severity of the crisis and its potential business impact with key stakeholders. Though trade-offs are inevitable, the collective decisions made here will invariably serve the organization's best interests.

Chapter 16

Risk-Based Decisions

Today's business landscape is littered with multiple priorities, and determining which ones are top priorities becomes even more challenging during a cyber crisis. Here, we delve into the art of aligning leadership via negotiation, understanding the intricacies of the infrastructure, and the role of threat intelligence in guiding decisions.

During a crisis, executive leadership alignment is crucial. The remediation process is complex, and diverging views can extend timelines, elevating business risks. Moreover, departments often operate in silos, unaware of how their individual systems tie into the broader infrastructure. Recognizing this interconnectedness is vital for understanding why you must prioritize certain areas over others.

Who are the members of this process, and what are their motivations?

Not all hands on deck are part of the negotiation process. It's about bringing the leadership of distinct areas to a consensus on remediation priorities. Participants often arrive with a protective mindset toward their respective domains. It falls upon the crisis leader to navigate this maze of interests and guide the team toward a unified recovery plan.

How does a crisis leader get agreement with such a diverse set of opinions?

Within this process, leadership is critical to bringing so many individuals together to agree on the most important items to resolve and the priority that exists. In our experience, this requires strong leadership skills in explaining the reasoning behind the priorities and also the empathy to understand the situation the business leaders are in. By showing your understanding of how their business areas operate, it becomes much easier to work through these issues with them. It is imperative not to dismiss their concerns, and this is one of the times that slowing down the process can have immense value. As the crisis continues, there are many stresses, and people may feel that leaders are not hearing them. Taking a moment to pause and thoroughly listen to the concerns can pay dividends to the success of the recovery in the long run. Imagine how much more receptive these leaders will be if they know you have taken the time to listen to them and understand their situation. We all want to be heard, and not dismissing someone shows that you care. Here is a list of some key tactics that you can utilize to find agreement with these business leaders:

- **Communicate effectively:** Communication is key during a cyber crisis, and cyber crisis leaders should keep business leaders informed of the situation, including progress, challenges, and roadblocks. You can accomplish this via a war room set up expressly for the crisis response. By keeping everyone on the same page, it's easier to find common ground and work towards a common goal.

- **Prioritize recovery efforts:** Cyber crisis leaders should work with business leaders to prioritize recovery efforts based on the impact on the business and the hierarchical structure of the business systems. By identifying the most critical systems and data and focusing on their recovery first, it's easier to demonstrate progress and build trust with business leaders. The most critical systems and data can also shift during the crisis.

- **Use data to support decisions:** When making decisions, cyber crisis leaders should use data to support their recommendations and clearly show why they chose a particular option for the recovery. By presenting data clearly and concisely, it's easier to persuade business leaders to support a specific course of action. Emotions can run high during a crisis. Data and facts help to alleviate these emotions and bring teams back to focusing on the overall goal.

- **Collaborate and compromise:** Cyber crisis leaders should be willing to collaborate and compromise with business leaders to find solutions that meet everyone's needs. Needs are different than desires. The key to this is being willing to listen and understand their needs and clearly articulate the goals of each recovery step. By working together and finding common ground, it's easier to move forward and recover from the cyber crisis as a team.

What do negotiations look like?

Delving deeper into the negotiation process, infuse your negotiations with threat intelligence. By understanding potential threat actor moves, targeted data, and their likely reactions to remediation efforts, the team can coalesce against a shared adversary. This unity against an external entity can foster internal alignment. If there's data or a system at immediate risk, and if the threat actor's modus operandi indicates potential data destruction or encryption, swift action via the stabilize team, even amid these business negotiations, can mitigate harm and underscore a commitment to data protection.

Although this is a chapter on internal negotiations between business owners, it is also necessary to discuss external negotiations with a threat actor. The critical use case is extortion-based attacks like ransomware.

Understanding the Implications of Extortion-Based Attacks

In an extortion-based attack, the negotiation dynamics are fluid and can evolve rapidly. An active attacker is unyielding in their pursuit of data theft and encryption. If your efforts in the stabilization phase fall short, your negotiations may extend beyond internal leadership to include direct interactions with the attacker.

Engaging with attackers isn't a course of action we advocate. Paying to retrieve data is anathema to our principles. However, the stark realities of business can sometimes leave few palatable choices. The legal landscape surrounding these negotiations is intricate and continually evolving. Before wading into such treacherous waters, consult external legal counsel. Note that some law firms offer breach coach services to help you navigate the intricacies of responding to a cyber crisis and navigating legal challenges stemming from such an event.

Here are some crucial considerations during this ordeal:

- **Situation Assessment:** Grasp the breadth and depth of the attack. This encompasses identifying compromised systems and data, pinpointing the entry methods employed by attackers, and discerning the ransomware variant.

- **Law Enforcement Collaboration:** It's imperative to notify law enforcement at the earliest opportunity. Their insights might shed light on the attacker's identity and modus operandi. They can be pivotal allies during this testing time.

- **Cybersecurity Expertise:** Collaborate with a cybersecurity firm specializing in these attacks. Their role extends beyond assessment. They provide intelligence on the attackers, aid in data recovery, and, if necessary, spearhead negotiations. Their engagement via your legal team ensures that all actions taken are within the confines of the law.

- **Recovery Assessment:** Before acquiescing to an attacker's demands, evaluate the possibility of restoring your data without resorting to a ransom payment. Recovery methods range from decryption tools to leveraging backups. This route, albeit challenging, is always preferable.

- **Data Valuation:** Appraise the worth of the encrypted data. This involves gauging the monetary and operational implications. If data loss is surmountable through recreation or alternative recovery means, bypassing the ransom might be a strategically sound decision.

- **Decryption Time Estimation:** Decrypting data is a resource-intensive endeavor, both computationally and temporally. The road to full recovery might be longer than anticipated. During this interim, formulating alternative operational strategies is essential.

Caution on Negotiating with Designated Entities

In today's geopolitical climate, it's essential to recognize that some of these cyber-extortionists may be linked to, or are themselves, entities classified as "terrorist organizations" by the Department of Homeland Security and other international agencies. Engaging with these groups, even under duress, can have significant legal implications. Beyond legal consequences, there are ethical considerations, as funds transferred might be used to finance further illicit activities. It is of paramount importance that you are aware of the broader implications and potential consequences of any negotiation.

In this context, it is crucial to consider the Office of Foreign Assets Control (OFAC) regulations. For example, if a cyber-extortionist is identified as a Specially Designated National (SDN) or operates from a sanctioned country, any transaction or negotiation with them could violate OFAC restrictions.[11] This means that even in cases where a cyber-attack severely impacts your operations, paying a ransom or engaging in any form of financial transaction with such entities might inadvertently lead to breaching U.S. sanctions. This poses legal risks and could result in substantial fines and reputational damage. Therefore, it's essential to conduct thorough due diligence and consult with legal experts familiar with OFAC regulations before deciding to respond to cyber extortion threats.

[11] The Specially Designated Nationals And Blocked Persons List (SDN) Human Readable Lists can be found here: https://ofac.treasury.gov/specially-designated-nationals-and-blocked-persons-list-sdn-human-readable-lists.

Remember, every situation is unique. While this guide provides a roadmap, tailor your response to the nuances of the specific challenge and work with external legal counsel in these matters.

In recent times, the threat of ransomware has evolved. Not only do malicious actors encrypt valuable data and hold it for ransom, but they increasingly threaten to release sensitive or proprietary information to the public or the highest bidder. This dual-threat approach compounds the situation's complexity and often escalates the pressure on the victimized entity to pay the ransom.

Expanding on the approaches to an extortion-based attack:

- **Two-Fold Ransomware Extortion:** Attackers not only encrypt your data, rendering it inaccessible, but they may also exfiltrate it. Even if you retrieve your data via backups or decryption tools, the attacker could threaten its public exposure as leverage in negotiations.

- **Situation Assessment:** Beyond understanding the affected systems and data, you must determine if any data was stolen. If so, what type? Personal Health Information (PHI)? Personally Identifiable Information (PII)? Intellectual property? Controlled Unclassified Information (CUI)? Confidential communications? Recognizing the nature of the exposed data will help gauge the repercussions of its potential release.

- **Engage Expertise for Dual Threats:** When retaining a cybersecurity firm, ensure they have experience not just with ransomware decryption but also with handling data exposure threats. They should guide on how to trace data breaches, assess the veracity of the attacker's claims, and advise on how to mitigate potential data leaks.

- **Public Relations Considerations:** If there's a threat of public data release, involve your PR team or an external crisis communication agency. Crafting a transparent, timely communication strategy for stakeholders, clients, and the general public becomes imperative.

- **Data Valuation with Exposure in Mind:** Evaluating the worth of your data isn't just about its operational value. Consider the ramifications of public exposure. Could it lead to lawsuits? Regulatory fines? Irreparable brand damage? This might influence your decision to negotiate or take other action.

- **Legal Implications of Data Exposure:** Laws like the General Data Protection Regulation (GDPR) in Europe and the SEC's *Cybersecurity Risk Management, Strategy, Governance, and Incident Disclosure* rule mandate timely disclosures of data breaches. If the threat actor's claim of data theft is genuine, consult your legal counsel about obligatory notifications and potential consequences.

By integrating these considerations into your response strategy, you'll be better equipped to address the multifaceted challenges presented by modern ransomware attacks. With encryption and data exposure both in play, it emphasizes the importance of a holistic, informed, and agile approach to cyber threats.

The Internal Process

Now, let's focus back on the internal process. If your business has been affected by ransomware, encrypted data is effectively destroyed data. Approaching the situation as destroyed or lost data can help move the process along. Many disaster plans are designed to recover the business from disasters where the data and systems have been destroyed. In this case, the systems still exist, but the data is lost. Utilizing these plans can help accelerate the agreement with leaders, and many of these agreed-upon recovery processes will work for this situation.

During the negotiation process, some business leaders may press for the complete isolation of the system from the attacker. Completely shutting down might seem a practical step, but it could inadvertently fulfill the attacker's goal. Here's a closer look at strategies a CISO might employ:

- **The Self-Inflicted Shutdown Paradox:** When faced with danger, our instinct often propels us towards immediate safety measures. Shutting down systems may feel like the quickest way to prevent further harm. However, by doing so, we amplify the damage and may extend the recovery time. It's essential to weigh the potential risk of an ongoing attack against the definite disruption of a complete shutdown.

- **Gradual Segmentation Over Full Shutdown:** Think of a building with various sections. If one section is compromised, it makes sense to isolate it while ensuring the other sections remain operational. Similarly, by segmenting networks, we can confine the breach, allowing unaffected parts to function smoothly. This tactic minimizes the overall operational disruption, ensuring only the infected segments are offline.

- **Continuous Monitoring and Real-Time Analysis:** Cybersecurity isn't just about building walls but also keeping a vigilant watch. Monitoring tools don't just act as alarms; they can offer insights into the attack pattern. By understanding the nature of the breach in real time, countermeasures can be more specific and effective, reducing the need for a blanket shutdown that affects all operations.

- **Decentralized Systems:** Putting all our digital eggs in one basket is risky. If that central system is compromised, everything grinds to a halt. By decentralizing system architectures, we spread the risk. Should one part face a breach, others can still function, ensuring that a single point of failure doesn't paralyze the entire organization.

- **Cloud Resilience:** A multi-cloud strategy is akin to having various escape routes in a building. If one exit is blocked, others offer a way out. Similarly, if one cloud environment is compromised, you can shift operations to another. Such resilience ensures continuity, denying the attacker the satisfaction of causing extended downtime.

By comprehending and executing these strategies, a CISO can ensure that even amid a cyber onslaught, the organization remains agile and resilient, resisting the urge to unintentionally play into the hands of the attackers.

Chapter 17

Empowering the Expert in Negotiations

The scarcity of technical expertise is a significant challenge many organizations face, and this shortage becomes acute during a crisis. So, how do we empower our experts, not only to lead but also to negotiate and collaborate effectively during these times?

Leveraging Authority in Negotiations

In any crisis negotiation, the room is often filled with stakeholders representing diverse interests. While the expertise of the generalist is undeniable, their authority must be understood, recognized, and endorsed by the broader leadership team to ensure effective decision-making.

1. **Setting Expectations:** Before diving into specifics, begin with a discussion on the value the expert generalist brings to the table. Highlight their multifaceted knowledge, ability to understand the technical intricacies of the crisis, and the potential business implications.

2. **Defining Boundaries:** While the expert generalist should have the autonomy to make swift decisions, it's equally important to define the limits of this autonomy. Outline what decisions fall under their purview and which ones require collaborative agreement.

3. **Addressing Concerns:** Key stakeholders might have reservations about granting extensive authority to the expert generalist, especially if it pertains to areas they oversee. It's crucial to provide a platform where these concerns can be voiced, understood, and addressed.

4. **Balancing Authority with Collaboration:** Emphasize that while the expert generalist is endowed with decision-making authority, it doesn't negate the collaborative essence of crisis management. Decisions made will always consider the collective interests of all stakeholders.
5. **Highlighting Past Successes:** If the expert generalist or similar roles have previously navigated challenges successfully, cite these instances. Demonstrating a track record can instill confidence among stakeholders.
6. **Continuous Review:** Assure the room that the authority granted is not set in stone. As the crisis evolves and as new information emerges, there would be periodic reviews to ensure that the decision-making framework remains effective and relevant.
7. **Achieving Consensus:** The ultimate goal is to ensure all key stakeholders are aligned. Utilize a consensus-building approach, where each stakeholder acknowledges the role and authority of the expert generalist, ensuring a unified front as the crisis unfolds.

In essence, while the expertise of the generalist is a valuable asset during a crisis, it's the collective agreement and trust from all stakeholders that truly empowers them to lead negotiations effectively. This shared understanding ensures that the negotiation process is not only swift but also collaborative and inclusive, addressing the concerns and priorities of all parties involved.

Role Assignment

Assigning experts to relevant roles ensures they can bridge the gap between technical nuances and overarching business objectives. This balance is pivotal during negotiations, where understanding the implications of technical decisions on the business landscape can lead to more informed and holistic choices.

Crisis Communication Protocols

Establishing sound crisis communication protocols provides a structure for conveying crucial information. Clear and efficient communication channels are pivotal for effective crisis management. Note that we explore the topic of crisis communications in depth in the Articulate section.

Continuous Modification of Authority

Given the fluid nature of cyber crises, the authority conferred upon experts may need dynamic adjustments. During negotiations, understanding the evolving risks and adjusting authority levels promptly ensures that decisions are made swiftly and in the organization's best interests.

Providing Business Context

Lastly, it is crucial to remember that while experts tackle technical challenges, they must do so within the business context. Facilitating communication between business leaders and technical experts enables the integration of changing business concerns into the remediation process.

Collaboration and Process

Expert Collaboration

The next step involves creating a conducive environment for experts to collaborate seamlessly, free from noise and unnecessary distractions. Our experience suggests many ways to achieve this.

1. **Diverse Expertise:** Remember that all of your team members have unique experiences and expertise. There will be operating system experts, database designers who understand the intricacies of data relationships, as well as analysts who pride themselves on knowledge of data flow and integrity. Make sure to understand the nuances and appreciate the team members and how they fit into the bigger view of the crisis.

2. **Dedicated Space:** A good, focused workspace is crucial. Be it a conference room or a digital space, it should be equipped appropriately so our experts can get down to business without any hitches.
3. **Staying on Track:** While it's good to explore different angles, it's essential to have a roadmap. It helps keep the conversation relevant and ensures we tackle the most pressing issues first.
4. **Promoting Open Communication:** Encourage everyone to speak their minds. Sometimes, it's the unconventional viewpoint that provides the most clarity.
5. **Limiting Distractions:** While everyone's input is valuable, non-essential communications can wait. It's best to keep interruptions to a minimum during important discussions.
6. **Making the Most of Modern Tools:** Use the tools at your disposal to share information efficiently. A well-crafted chart or graph can sometimes convey more than a lengthy discussion.
7. **Feedback Is Gold:** Always be open to feedback about the collaboration process. It's how you refine your approach and get better with each challenge.
8. **Addressing Disagreements Head-On:** Differences in opinion are natural. When they arise, face them squarely and work towards a common understanding.
9. **Continuous Improvement:** Every once in a while, consider workshops or training sessions to sharpen collaboration skills. As with any craft, practice makes perfect.

When it comes to expert collaboration during negotiations, it's not just about having the right folks in the room. It's about ensuring they're equipped, focused, and aligned to make decisions that safeguard our organization's interests.

Structured Decision-Making Process

Every team benefits from a solid game plan. That's why a predefined decision-making structure is invaluable. It doesn't just provide a roadmap; it states what information is crucial for decision-making. And when we're in those moments where information seems scarce, which happens often in crises, our plan will guide folks on how to navigate those murky waters, ensuring decisions are made with the best available insight. In our experience, utilizing a RACI matrix has had great success by maintaining the expected involvement level of experts while reducing overlaps and gaps. We have also found that mind mapping can be helpful for note taking and organization.

Limit External Distractions

In crisis management, focus is key. While input is valuable, we need to stick to the essentials. If a meeting, email, or any piece of information doesn't directly aid in addressing the crisis at hand, it might just be adding noise. By reducing these distractions, we ensure that our experts can concentrate on crafting solutions without getting bogged down.

System and Data Access

In a crisis, speed and access go hand in hand. By giving our experts the access they need to relevant systems and data, we empower them to act swiftly and decisively. But caution is paramount. We always need to weigh the advantages of access against any potential security risks. Ideally, these specifics should be ironed out well in advance, so when clouds gather, we're not left scrambling.

Scribe Inclusion

Accuracy matters, especially when the stakes are high. By including a dedicated Scribe in the process, we ensure that every decision and pivotal discussion is captured. This not only provides a record but allows our experts to immerse themselves fully in problem-solving, knowing that the details are being meticulously documented.

Approval Levels and Processes

Navigating a crisis requires agility, but that doesn't mean bypassing protocol. By establishing clear approval processes, both technical and business-oriented, we ensure decisions are vetted and aligned with organizational objectives. Whether it is technical experts determining the severity of a situation or business stakeholders weighing in on operational impacts, having a structured approval process ensures clarity and accountability.

Regarding technical approval, this could include a hierarchy of experts authorized to approve various decisions based on their knowledge, expertise, and the severity of the crisis. On the other hand, the business approval process should involve the relevant stakeholders who can approve decisions that impact business operations. This may include the Change Control Board (CCB), or in some cases, management may suspend the CCB to allow for quicker recovery options. Risks associated with the current situation drive these decisions.

To summarize, empowering technical experts during a crisis involves a multifaceted approach, blending authority delegation, communication strategies, structured processes, and various tools. Implementing these strategies can help your organization effectively navigate a crisis, enabling a rapid response and efficient recovery.

Refer to the Organize section of this book for guidance on how to establish the processes discussed above.

Key Takeaways

The key takeaways for empowering technical experts during a crisis are:

- **Granting Authority:** Give experts the authority to make swift decisions within clearly defined boundaries, allowing them to contain and mitigate the impact of the crisis.

- **Role Assignment:** Properly assign experts to relevant roles and responsibilities to optimize their decision-making autonomy and expedite the recovery process.
- **Crisis Communication Protocols:** Establish effective crisis communication channels to convey crucial information efficiently and maintain clear coordination.
- **Continuous Modification of Authority:** Regularly review and adjust the authority granted to experts based on evolving risks and needs during the response.
- **Providing Business Context:** Facilitate communication between technical experts and business leaders to integrate changing business concerns into the remediation process.
- **Expert Collaboration:** Create an environment conducive to seamless collaboration among experts by limiting distractions and unnecessary meetings.
- **Structured Decision-Making Process:** Establish a predefined decision-making process that outlines necessary information and guidelines for scarce data situations during crises.
- **System and Data Access:** Consider providing elevated access to relevant systems and data depending on the risks and requirements.
- **Scribe Inclusion:** Include a Scribe to take detailed notes during meetings and decisions, allowing experts to focus on their tasks and reducing distractions.
- **Approval Levels and Processes:** Establish clear approval levels for both technical and business decisions to ensure experts' voices are heard and crisis response remains efficient.

By implementing these strategies, organizations can effectively navigate crises, enabling rapid response and efficient recovery with the help of their technical experts.

Chapter 18

Business Priorities

Understanding the importance of negotiating and managing business priorities during a cyber crisis response is critical for any organization. As a Crisis Manager, the responsibility to orchestrate a structured, coherent approach to address the complexities and urgencies of cyber crisis management falls to you. This chapter will explore how to negotiate and balance these priorities within a cyber crisis context.

Setting the Business Priorities

Identifying business priorities ahead of a cyber crisis, when decision-making is not clouded by the stress of an active attack, is crucial. Organizations should conduct an analysis of their business functions, processes, and resources to pinpoint the most critical aspects. These could encompass maintaining customer trust, ensuring data integrity, minimizing downtime, protecting intellectual property, and safeguarding employee safety. Understanding these priorities serves as a strong foundation for decision-making during a cyber crisis response.

However, the chaotic nature of crises often means that actual priorities might deviate from pre-planned ones, making negotiation across business operations a critical part of the process. Quick assessment of the cyber crisis' impact on these priorities, considering risks and potential consequences for business operations, allows for effective prioritization and resource allocation during the crisis. Factors to consider include revenue loss, safety of connected systems, customer dissatisfaction, reputational damage, regulatory fines, and operational costs.

Balancing short-term and long-term priorities is crucial during a cyber crisis response. Short-term priorities might encompass quickly restoring disrupted services, containing the breach, and managing the immediate impact on customers and employees. Conversely, long-term priorities might involve implementing robust cybersecurity measures, investing in employee training, and fostering a security-conscious culture. This balance ensures immediate concerns are addressed while setting a foundation for future resilience.

Role of the Crisis Manager

As the Crisis Manager, your role in navigating this balance and making decisions is paramount. You must employ a standard, flexible, and scalable approach to managing cyber crises. This involves establishing a clear organizational structure defining roles, responsibilities, and reporting lines, as discussed in the Organize section of this book. Furthermore, facilitating effective communication during a cyber crisis response is vital. These channels, such as regular meetings, conference calls, secure messaging platforms, and centralized incident management tools, enable information sharing, collaboration, and decision-making among stakeholders.

Stakeholder Engagement and Alignment

Successful negotiation of business priorities requires active engagement from all relevant stakeholders. The delicate balance is to encourage collaboration, express concerns, and contribute expertise, while resolving the cyber crisis within a critical timeframe. Ensuring that all stakeholders contribute to the decision-making process can lead to effective negotiation of business priorities.

One of the main challenges in negotiating business priorities during a cyber crisis is aligning crisis response goals with the organization's overall recovery objectives. As a crisis manager, defining specific objectives for each functional area (e.g., containment, recovery, investigation, communication) in collaboration with trusted experts and linking them to the organization's key business priorities can help overcome this hurdle.

Principles for Negotiating Business Priorities

Transparency and openness are essential for successful negotiation of business priorities during a cyber crisis. Ensuring that stakeholders have access to accurate, up-to-date information about known risks and the incident's impact fosters trust, enables better decision-making, and creates a collaborative environment.

Inclusivity and collaboration are also critical. By involving business process owners in the decision-making process, the Crisis Manager ensures that a range of perspectives, expertise, and concerns are considered. This collaborative approach fosters a sense of shared ownership, leading to more balanced decisions reflecting the organization's overall interests.

In a cyber crisis, resources are often scarce, and decisions must be made quickly, often with incomplete information. As such, prioritizing and triaging business priorities to focus on the most pressing issues is a necessity. This requires identifying the most critical assets, processes, and functions, assessing their significance to the organization, and determining the order in which they should be addressed. With a systematic approach to prioritization and triage, a Crisis Manager can efficiently and effectively allocate resources.

In the face of a rapidly evolving cyber crisis, flexibility and adaptability are crucial. As new discoveries arise, threats escalate, or new vulnerabilities emerge, business priorities must be adjustable. This might involve reassessing priorities, adjusting response strategies, and reallocating resources as necessary. Maintaining this flexibility amidst dynamic and uncertain risks is vital for an effective remediation process.

Facilitating Effective Negotiation

If an impact analysis process exists, using it during a cyber crisis is a valuable tool to assess potential organizational consequences. Focus on time-sensitive operations, estimate disruption costs, and prioritize recovery efforts. If this process doesn't exist or isn't accessible, you can substitute it with collaboration between business process owners and technical experts. Determine the best path forward in the least possible time, understanding that decisions may not be perfect, but indecisiveness can be even more detrimental.

Consider developing a priority matrix to visualize tasks, objectives, or resources based on their urgency and importance. This can aid business stakeholders in understanding the larger recovery and remediation picture, accelerate stakeholder discussions, clarify the importance of different business priorities, and build consensus on resource allocation.

Leverage your external relationships during a cyber crisis. Strong relationships with external partners such as law enforcement, cybersecurity firms, and industry peers can bolster an organization's resilience during a cyber crisis. These partnerships can provide access to valuable resources, expertise, and intelligence, thereby enabling organizations to respond more quickly to a cyber crisis. They can also help in negotiating business priorities by providing another realm of technical expertise, providing context, and accelerating decisions.

Effective negotiation of business priorities during a cyber crisis is an iterative process centered on collaboration with business process owners, a thorough understanding of the organization's key functions, a structured process, and open communication channels. As discussed in this chapter, by applying these core principles and leading business process owners in negotiations, organizations can enhance their response to cyber threats and ensure the continuity of business operations in the face of a cyber crisis.

Key Takeaways

Reflecting on this chapter, the following items are the most important takeaways to consider in managing a cyber crisis:

- The need to understand and manage business priorities during a cyber crisis is paramount. These priorities, identified ahead of the crisis, may encompass customer trust, data integrity, downtime, intellectual property, and employee safety.

- Rapid assessment and negotiation of priorities during a crisis are crucial for effective decision-making and resource allocation. This can involve deviating from pre-planned priorities due to the volatile nature of crises.

- Balancing short-term and long-term priorities is key. Short-term objectives might include service restoration and breach containment, while long-term goals could involve cybersecurity improvements, employee training, and fostering a security-conscious culture.

- The Crisis Manager's role is critical in steering the organization through the crisis. This includes setting clear roles and responsibilities, facilitating effective communication, and maintaining the overall direction of crisis response.

- Engaging all relevant stakeholders is necessary for successful negotiation of business priorities. This fosters collaboration, gathers various perspectives, and contributes to efficient decision-making.

- Transparency and openness, inclusivity and collaboration, prioritization and triage, as well as flexibility and adaptability are crucial principles for negotiating business priorities during a crisis.

- Utilize existing business impact analysis processes or collaborate closely with business and technical experts to determine the best path forward during a crisis. Decisiveness, even if imperfect, is better than indecision.

- Consider developing a priority matrix to visualize tasks or objectives based on their urgency and importance. This can facilitate stakeholder discussions and consensus-building on priority areas.
- Leverage external relationships for additional support during a crisis. Partnerships with law enforcement, cybersecurity firms, and industry peers can provide valuable resources and intelligence.
- Effectively negotiating business priorities during a cyber crisis is an iterative, collaborative process. With a structured approach and open communication, organizations can enhance their response and ensure business continuity amidst cyber threats.

Chapter 19

Technical Priorities

Negotiating Technical Priorities during a Cyber Crisis Response

We just finished discussing the business priority process, and now we will explore the various factors, techniques, and considerations that a Crisis Manager should take into account when negotiating technical priorities during a cyber crisis response. The overall goal is to find the best way to balance both the technical and business requirements and establish a clear set of priorities while effectively communicating them to the incident response team to ensure a swift and efficient recovery from a cyber crisis.

Start by Identifying Critical Assets and Services

Let's delve deeper into the process of identifying critical assets and services during a cyber crisis. This identification serves as the technical foundation for establishing restoration priorities and directing response efforts. It also serves as a sounding board for the business process owners and their priorities discussed in the previous chapter.

We start by identifying critical assets in the organization. These are the hardware, software, data, and other resources that are vital to the organization's functioning and success. Identifying these assets requires a comprehensive understanding of the organization's infrastructure and systems. This is where the experts that have been brought into the process really shine. They have a unique ability to meld the business process priorities with the technical priorities and understand how each area is affected. Many times, the way this is accomplished is via inventory, classification, and dependency mapping. However, during a cyber crisis this information is often not available, or it has not been consistently kept up to date. As the Crisis Manager, you need to allow for the experts to communicate these technical priorities to business leaders. Create a place for them to record the known systems and their importance to the business.

Some of the items that should be recorded include the organization's key business services and functions. Focus should be on services that are revenue generating, operational for the business, and compliance and regulatory services. Revenue generating services are those services that directly contribute to a revenue stream and in many cases are targeted directly by attackers during a cyber crisis. Operational services are focused on the day-to-day functioning of the organization. These may be considered in the IT area of the business.

Compliance and regulatory services are designed to maintain compliance with legal and regulatory requirements.

A critical component of crisis response is understanding that many assets and services are interdependent. Rarely is this interdependency tested, and the failure or compromise of one can lead to cascading effects throughout the organization. The technical experts understand these interdependencies and can adjust the recovery priorities based upon this understanding. These include the relationship between assets, services, and functions and the potential cascade effect a cyber-attack can have. They can also properly prioritize the restoration of assets and services that have the greatest impact on other areas of the organization to minimize the risk of cascading effects and accelerate the remediation efforts.

By quickly identifying critical assets and services, as well as understanding their interdependencies, a Crisis Manager can effectively collaborate with technical experts to establish technical restoration priorities during a cyber crisis response. This understanding allows the response team to focus on the most critical aspects of the organization, helping to ensure a timely and effective recovery.

Prioritization Guidelines

During typical business operations, there can be robust prioritization frameworks for allocating resources. During a cyber crisis we find that guidelines tend to keep us on track. Guidelines focus on efficiently allocating resources and directing incident response efforts during a cyber crisis. This section outlines key factors and considerations for establishing prioritization guidelines that balance risk management and time sensitivity.

In a cyber crisis, time indeed serves as a relentless, often unforgiving factor, and organizations frequently grapple with finite resources. Here, we delve into three critical considerations when negotiating restoration efforts: Time-critical assets and services, resource availability, and resource trade-offs.

- **Time-critical Assets and Services:** Every organization has assets and services that are integral to its day-to-day operations. Some of these may be time-critical, requiring immediate attention in the event of a cyber crisis due to their time-sensitive nature. These could be systems that support key functions like customer services, production processes, or business-critical operations. Furthermore, systems underpinning functions that have strict service level agreements (SLAs) or regulatory deadlines must be promptly restored to avoid contractual penalties or non-compliance with regulations. This necessitates the identification of these assets and services well ahead of a potential crisis. The Crisis Manager must ensure that a detailed inventory of these assets and services is kept up to date, outlining their functions, the potential impacts of their disruption, and the stipulated time within which they should be restored to normal operation.
- **Resource Availability:** The restoration of operations during a cyber crisis is highly dependent on the availability of resources, both human and technological. Personnel are needed for different aspects of the response, including technical response teams, decision-makers, and communication teams. Equipment required might range

from hardware to software and specialized tools for detection, analysis, and recovery. Additionally, external support might be needed, in the form of specialized cyber incident response services, vendors, or even law enforcement. The Crisis Manager must accurately assess the resources required for each restoration task, including the time and skill set needed for each task. These assessments will form the basis for the allocation and prioritization of resources.

- **Resource Trade-offs:** In managing a cyber crisis, it is a reality that there will be competing needs for limited resources. This situation necessitates the careful negotiation of resource trade-offs. A Crisis Manager must be able to weigh the costs and benefits of reallocating resources from lower-priority tasks to higher-priority ones. This process involves an in-depth understanding of the organization's business priorities, the cyber threat landscape, and the implications of delaying or accelerating specific tasks. The decision-making process here is not linear but dynamic, requiring constant reassessment of priorities as the situation evolves. It requires collaboration between business leaders, IT professionals, and cyber crisis management teams to make informed decisions. Trade-offs might also involve deciding between short-term fixes and long-term solutions, considering not just the immediate crisis but also the organization's long-term cyber resilience.

Implementing Technical Restoration Priorities

Once the Crisis Manager has established and continuously adapted restoration priorities, the next step is to implement those priorities effectively. This section provides guidance on resource allocation and management, setting clear objectives and milestones, and developing contingency plans and fallback strategies.

Resource Allocation and Management

Effective allocation and management of resources are indispensable to the successful implementation of restoration priorities. This involves a strategic balance of deploying available resources to address the immediate impact and potential progression of a cyber crisis. Let's take a closer look at each aspect of this crucial process.

- **Allocation of Resources:** Allocating resources in a cyber crisis is not merely a distribution process; it requires a careful strategy, insightful decision-making, and a keen understanding of the incident's implications. Subject Matter Experts (SMEs), personnel, and equipment should be assigned to each restoration task based on its priority level as defined by the SMEs. SMEs, armed with their expert knowledge and insights, can accurately determine the impact and risk levels of different aspects of the cyber crisis, helping define which tasks need immediate attention and which can be deferred. The Crisis Manager must ensure that resource allocation aligns with these priorities, making sure that high-priority tasks are adequately resourced. This could include assigning experienced personnel, providing necessary equipment, or deploying specialist teams, such as digital forensics or malware analysis units.

- **Coordination of Efforts:** A cyber crisis is a multi-faceted challenge. Different teams work on different tasks simultaneously, and these tasks often interlink and impact one another. It's crucial to ensure that teams are aware of their interdependencies and coordinate their efforts to avoid duplication or conflicts that might delay restoration. A team working on system restoration, for example, needs to coordinate with the incident analysis team to ensure the threat has been fully eliminated before attempting system recovery. Similarly, the team handling internal and external communications must be synced with all other teams to ensure accurate and consistent messaging. The Crisis Manager is key to orchestrating this complex interplay of tasks, facilitating communication, and ensuring a unified and coordinated approach.

- **Monitoring Resource Usage:** Continuous tracking of resource usage is another key aspect of resource management. Just as the cyber crisis evolves, so too should resource allocation. By monitoring the usage of resources, the Crisis Manager can make informed decisions about adjusting allocations as needed, based on the progress of restoration efforts and changes in priorities. This could involve reassigning personnel from tasks that are nearing completion to others that are lagging, or reallocating equipment from non-critical tasks to critical ones. It might also involve identifying the need for additional resources, such as bringing in external experts or procuring additional tools or equipment. This dynamic approach to resource management ensures the organization remains responsive and adaptable in the face of a rapidly changing cyber crisis.

Establishing Clear Objectives and Milestones

Setting explicit objectives and milestones plays an integral role in keeping the incident response team focused, cohesive, and in sync with the overarching response strategy. Let's delve deeper into the importance of defining objectives, setting milestones, and monitoring progress during a cyber crisis response.

- **Define Objectives:** Clear objectives provide a definitive roadmap that guides the efforts of each team member, aligning their individual tasks with the larger mission. The objectives for each restoration task should be Specific, Measurable, Achievable, Relevant, and Time-bound (SMART). This means they should directly address the task at hand (Specific), have some quantifiable or qualifiable element to evaluate success (Measurable), be realistically attainable given the available resources and circumstances (Achievable), align with the larger goals of the organization and incident response (Relevant), and have an established timeline for completion (Time-bound). Ensuring that each task aligns with overall restoration priorities enables the team to make meaningful contributions to the broader recovery effort and helps prevent misdirected efforts or wasted resources. As the Crisis Manager, you are responsible for guiding the creation of these SMART objectives and ensuring they align with the strategic priorities of the organization.

- **Set Milestones:** Even with clear objectives in place, the magnitude of restoring operations post-cyberattack can be overwhelming. Breaking down larger objectives into smaller, more manageable milestones can help teams navigate the process more efficiently and maintain momentum. These milestones serve as markers along the restoration journey, giving teams intermediate goals to aim for and providing a sense of accomplishment when achieved. Milestones also help in demarcating phases of the recovery process, enabling a structured and phased approach to restoration efforts. For instance, a milestone could be the successful removal of a certain type of malware, or the restoration of a specific critical system.

- **Monitor Progress:** Continual monitoring of progress against objectives and milestones is essential to maintain the pace of recovery efforts and ensure their alignment with the overall response strategy. Regular assessments should be conducted to track the progress of each restoration task, comparing actual achievements with planned objectives and milestones. This involves analyzing both the quality of the work completed and the timeline, to ensure that tasks are not just being completed, but completed well and on schedule. If progress is slower than expected, or if tasks are consistently missing their milestones, this may indicate a need to adjust priorities or allocate additional resources. Such active monitoring allows the Crisis Manager to proactively address potential delays or issues, ensuring the restoration efforts remain on track.

Contingency Planning and Fallback Strategies

Developing robust contingency plans and fallback strategies is an indispensable element of any effective cyber crisis response. The unpredictable nature of cyber threats necessitates readiness for unexpected challenges and the ability to adapt quickly. This includes anticipating roadblocks, formulating alternative action plans, and implementing fallback strategies in the face of setbacks. Let's explore these elements in more detail.

- **Identify Potential Roadblocks:** One of the first steps in developing a contingency plan is identifying possible roadblocks that could occur during the restoration process. This involves conducting a thorough risk assessment that considers a range of potential scenarios, such as unexpected resource constraints, unforeseen technical difficulties, evolving threat landscapes, or even human factors like errors or miscommunications. This proactive approach helps the Crisis Manager to foresee challenges and prepare for them in advance, rather than reacting on the fly when issues arise. Consider all facets of the organization, from the technical infrastructure to human elements and external dependencies.
- **Develop Contingency Plans**: Once potential roadblocks are identified, create alternative courses of action that can be deployed to overcome or mitigate these obstacles. Contingency plans provide a pre-established roadmap that can guide the organization in the event of a disruption to the primary restoration strategy. These plans should be practical, achievable, and well-documented so they can be implemented effectively when needed. Each plan should include details such as the specific situations in which it would be activated, the roles and responsibilities of team members, the resources required, and the steps to be taken to execute the plan.
- **Implement Fallback Strategies:** Fallback strategies are a last resort when primary restoration efforts fail or encounter insurmountable obstacles. They are designed to minimize the

impact of a failure and ensure continuity of critical operations. This could involve activating backup systems, switching to manual processes, or engaging external support. Fallback strategies should be pre-defined, well-tested, and ready to be deployed quickly in order to minimize downtime and disruption. They are critical for maintaining resilience in the face of adversity.

By effectively identifying potential roadblocks, developing contingency plans, and implementing fallback strategies, the Crisis Manager strengthens the organization's resilience during a cyber crisis. This level of preparedness not only supports technical restoration priorities but also guides the organization towards a swift and effective recovery from a cyber crisis. With contingency planning and fallback strategies in place, the organization is equipped to adapt and respond to a shifting threat landscape, reducing the overall impact of the crisis and helping to ensure a smoother return to normal operations.

In conclusion, the ability to effectively negotiate technical restoration priorities during a cyber crisis response is an essential skill for a Crisis Manager. By applying a structured prioritization framework, engaging with key stakeholders, and continuously adapting to the evolving threat landscape, the Crisis Manager can help guide the incident response team towards a successful resolution. This chapter provides guidance on the critical steps and best practices involved in this process, with the ultimate goal of minimizing the impact and downtime resulting from a cyber crisis.

Key Takeaways

- **Identifying Critical Assets and Services:** During a cyber crisis, it's crucial to identify and prioritize critical assets and services that are essential for the organization's functioning and success. Expert input and comprehensive understanding of the organization's infrastructure are key in this process.

- **Interdependency of Assets and Services:** Recognize that assets and services are often interdependent, and the compromise of one can lead to cascading effects throughout the organization. Prioritize restoration based on their impact on other areas to minimize risks and speed up recovery.

- **Prioritization Guidelines:** In a cyber crisis, time is critical, and resources are limited. Develop prioritization guidelines that balance risk management and time sensitivity. Consider time-critical assets, resource availability, and resource trade-offs when allocating resources.

- **Implementing Technical Restoration Priorities:** Implement restoration priorities effectively by strategically allocating and managing resources, setting clear objectives and milestones, and developing contingency plans and fallback strategies.

- **Resource Allocation and Management:** Efficiently allocate resources based on priority levels defined by Subject Matter Experts (SMEs) and ensure coordination among teams to avoid conflicts and delays.

- **Setting Clear Objectives and Milestones:** Define SMART objectives and set milestones to keep the incident response team focused, cohesive, and aligned with the overall response strategy. Monitor progress to stay on track.

- **Contingency Planning and Fallback Strategies:** Prepare for potential roadblocks by identifying risks and developing contingency plans and fallback strategies. These plans provide alternative action paths in case the primary restoration efforts encounter difficulties.

- **Strengthening Resilience:** The Crisis Manager's role is crucial in guiding the incident response team towards resilience and an effective recovery from a cyber crisis. Adapt to the evolving threat landscape and continuously refine restoration priorities to minimize downtime and impact.

Summary

In a cyber crisis, the Crisis Manager plays an instrumental role in effectively balancing business and technical priorities, enabling a swift and efficient recovery. This requires a keen understanding of the organization's key priorities, the ability to conduct a thorough risk assessment, and a deft hand at negotiation to align stakeholders on a path forward.

Successful negotiation rests on a foundation of open and effective communication, collaborative decision-making, and respectful consideration of diverse perspectives and priorities. The Crisis Manager serves as a unifying force, guiding the negotiation process with a clear vision and understanding of the overarching business goals and technical challenges at hand.

Resource allocation is a delicate balancing act that requires thoughtful consideration of time-critical assets and services, resource availability, and necessary trade-offs. It involves assigning resources based on priority level, coordinating efforts to avoid duplication or conflicts, and continuously monitoring resource usage to adjust allocations as the situation evolves.

Setting clear objectives and milestones based on SMART principles guides restoration efforts, keeping the team focused and motivated while enabling effective tracking of progress. Regular assessments against these objectives and milestones further ensure that resources and strategies are aligned with changing circumstances.

Finally, the value of contingency planning and fallback strategies cannot be overstated. Anticipating potential roadblocks, developing alternative plans, and being ready with fallback strategies fosters resilience and ensures continuity of operations, even when faced with unexpected setbacks.

The task of negotiation during a cyber crisis is challenging but with the strategies discussed in this chapter, a Crisis Manager can successfully guide an organization through the complexities of a crisis, minimizing impact and paving the way for a resilient future. As we close this chapter, remember that negotiation in a crisis is an art—an art that blends understanding, communication, resource management, and resilience into a cohesive strategy that keeps the organization operational and strong in the face of cyber threats.

Section 5

Articulate

"If the tongue had not been framed for articulation, man would still be a beast in the forest."

~ American philosopher and poet Ralph Waldo Emerson

Introduction

The lead author for this section is Andrew Gorecki, with significant input from and in collaboration with Christopher Scott.

In the Negotiate phase, you sat down with other leaders behind closed doors and agreed on concrete actions to control the crisis. If your organization has a formal and tested Crisis Response Plan that everyone understands, the meeting likely took a few hours before the team sprang into action. Otherwise, figuring out a game plan and negotiating among leaders likely required several hours or even a few days in the worst-case scenario.

Now it is vital to put the plan into action and execute the tasks. As part of the Articulate phase, you must communicate decisions and actions to internal stakeholders, provide them with clear direction, articulate roles and responsibilities, and ensure everyone is marching in the same direction. Furthermore, you must also communicate with external stakeholders where appropriate. Otherwise, a negative perception will amplify the crisis and cause your organization a Public Relations nightmare.

Crisis response deals with the reality of a rapidly unfolding cyber event that can seriously hurt your organization in the long term. In addition, internal and external communication failures can make the crisis worse and damage your brand reputation. For this reason, the Crisis Communications team plays a critical role in this process, and a significant portion of the Articulate phase revolves around this function.

This section of the book introduces you to the fundamental concepts of crisis communications and brand reputation management. As part of the discussion, we will outline the difference between internal and external relations, communication strategies, and the Dos and Don'ts of crisis communications. Finally, we will briefly discuss executive leadership's role in this process.

Before we dive into the content, please note that we come from a cybersecurity background with a specific focus on breach response and remediation. We base the guidance in the Articulate section of the book on our experience in the trenches of crisis response. However, we also advise you to augment our advice by partnering with a Public Relations (PR) firm with a proven track record of managing cyber-related crisis communications. Let's dive into the first chapter!

Chapter 20

Understanding the Fundamentals of Crisis Communications

As we mentioned at the beginning of this book, crisis response deals with the reality of an unfolding cyber event that can seriously harm your brand reputation, impact business operations, lead to financial loss, or create regulatory headaches stemming from unauthorized access to data.

Crisis communications are one of the elements of a successful crisis response that deals with managing the perception of that reality and how your organization deals with the event by shaping internal and external opinions. However, a good crisis communication strategy goes beyond that. It helps to communicate vital information to employees and contractors, ensures that business partners understand how the crisis impacts their business, and facilitates positive communication with the general public and other stakeholders with an active interest in the crisis.

Not All Crisis Communications Are Equal

In his book *Crisis Communications: The Definitive Guide to Managing the Message*,[12] Steve Fink distinguishes two types of crises from a communications perspective: *oppositional* and *non-oppositional.*

An *oppositional crisis* occurs when your stakeholders and the general public believe the crisis is your fault. This may be due to neglect or deliberate choice, and your organization is perceived as the villain. An oppositional crisis is your worst nightmare. You are on the

[12] Steve Fink, *Crisis Communications: The Definitive Guide to Managing the Message*, McGraw Hill, 1st edition (March 5, 2013).

defensive from the start and must react to the situation instead of controlling the message from the event's outset.

On the other hand, a *non-oppositional* crisis occurs when your stakeholders and the general public are sympathetic toward you. They often believe you are the victim of an internal or external phenomenon you cannot control and could not have predicted, and your stakeholders want you to succeed.

When a cyberattack becomes public knowledge, you want to ensure your stakeholders perceive you as the victim, not as an organization that neglected its cybersecurity or did not protect its customer data adequately. In other words, you want to deal with a non-oppositional crisis. For this reason, your communications strategy must be flawless from the get-go. By considering the guidance provided in this section, you can ensure your crisis communications are not an afterthought shadowed by restoration priorities and legal concerns. We highly recommend that your PR team work closely with your outside legal counsel. An effective crisis communications strategy must also ensure external statements do not expose the organization to unnecessary legal risks.

What Is Corporate Communications?

Communication failures often precede a crisis and, in some situations, can make an already hot situation even worse. With poorly managed communications, a cyber event can spiral out of control. Moreover, the media, bloggers, and social media influencers looking for a sensation to keep their audiences and followers engaged can magnify the crisis exponentially if you do not control the message from the outset. In addition, poorly managed communications can harm shareholder value and give ammunition to firms specializing in class action lawsuits.

Crisis communications require trained and experienced professionals to communicate with internal and external stakeholders during a crisis. This is where Corporate Communications comes into play. The role of Corporate Communications is to communicate with internal and external stakeholders, shape the perception of a crisis, and protect brand reputation during a crisis.

Your Crisis Response Team may be doing a stellar job of containing a cyber breach, restoring business operations, and minimizing the impact on the affected parties. Still, poor communication can ruin the effort and cause long-term reputation damage if the world perceives the situation differently. Unfortunately, it is an immutable law that when reality faces perception, perception typically wins.

Corporate Communications are the gateway to your stakeholders and should be activated as soon as you observe crisis precursors. It is better to err on the side of caution and engage Corporate Communications early on. This approach will help you avoid unpleasant surprises. In our experience, it is better to be safe than sorry and stand down Corporate Communications when they are not needed.

Internal versus External Communication

Corporate Communications are responsible for managing internal and external messaging and information dissemination. While both branches have similar focus and goals, they have subtle differences, including audience, formality, and communication means.

Internal communication focuses on disseminating crisis-related information to employees and handling internal inquiries. This information can include communication between managers and employees, widespread messaging across the organization, or information flow within a specific department or business unit. Depending on the crisis scope, it can include emails, video conference calls, or even in-person meetings.

The purpose of internal crisis communication is to ensure employees understand the impact, how the organization is handling it, and clearly understand expectations of them.

In contrast, external communication involves exchanging information outside the organization to shape public perception and provide vital information to business partners, regulators, the general public, and other necessary external stakeholders. Communication includes social media posts, public announcements, press releases, and interviews.

It is essential to mention that not all cyber events become public knowledge or even widespread internal knowledge. However, having a sound and comprehensive crisis communications strategy will help you shape the perception among the general public and ensure that employees, business partners, and regulators understand the crisis impact, how the organization is handling it, and the efforts to restore business operations.

This consideration is particularly vital in the age of social media, where an army of bloggers, journalists, and social media influencers are like snipers watching every step you take and ready to target you. In other words, you no longer have the luxury of taking days or even hours to prepare crisis response messaging and manage the perception.

The Phases of Crisis Communications

In his book, Steve Finke outlines three distinct crisis communications phases: *identify*, *isolate*, and *manage*. Let's briefly discuss each phase in the context of responding to a cyber crisis.

Identify – First, you need to recognize a crisis. In the first part of this book, we discussed defining crisis parameters specific to your organization. Not all cyber crisis events manifest themselves in a big bang event, such as an operational outage caused by a ransomware attack. For this reason, you must be vigilant and always monitor events and precursors that may be early indicators of a crisis, such as an external notification about an active exploit.

Isolate – Once you recognize a crisis or its early indicators, you must isolate and assess the situation. In other words, you must dedicate personnel to the assessment and ensure they are not distracted by day-to-day duties. Crisis response requires an all-hands-on-deck approach, and you must postpone any non-critical activities until a steady state is achieved.

Manage – This is the phase when you actively manage crisis communications by leveraging some of the strategies and tools outlined in this section.

Crisis Communications in the Social Media Age

We live in a constant social media cycle where opinions and negative messages can spread in the blink of an eye. Social media is the proverbial double-edged sword during a crisis. Its power cannot be overstated. But, if not used properly, anyone looking for sensation can use it to spread rumors and misinformation at the speed of light and put your Crisis Communications team on the defensive.

In traditional journalism, reporters often check facts and verify information with their sources before publishing a story. However, this rule does not apply to social media. The world of social media is like the Wild West. Anyone with access to a computer and the Internet can say and share anything, whether true or not.

For this reason, you want to be proactive and control the message instead of being on the defensive and reacting to ill-informed opinions that are not rooted in facts and do not consider the well-being of your organization. In other words, social media must be part of your crisis communications strategy.

Social media can be pivotal in shaping the perception of the crisis, and your Corporate Communications team can facilitate it without leaving the corporate office or their house if they work remotely. Social media monitoring is crucial to this process. You must continuously monitor and leverage the digital world to proactively communicate with your stakeholders while also playing ball with the traditional, mainstream media. Undesired posts, opinions, and blogs can go viral and cause cracks in your brand if you do not manage this space proactively. Many online platforms offer features such as sentiment analysis, tracking trends, and social share of voice. When considering a platform, ensure it supports the various social media channels important for your organization.

Social media monitoring and strategy should be part of your day-to-day operations. When a crisis strikes, and you have hours or minutes to manage the message proactively, it may be too late to scramble to put a social media strategy together.

Brand Reputation Management

A brand is one of the most valuable assets to any organization. It refers to the distinctive qualities in your products and services that people recognize and perceive in a specific way. Brand reputation management is the process of influencing the perception of your brand. Building a brand takes years, significant resources, and expensive marketing campaigns, but only days and, in the worst-case scenario, hours to destroy.

When you experience a significant cyber event, your brand may also be under attack, and you need to defend it as vigorously as you defend your network. For this reason, as you leverage the SONAR framework to manage a crisis, brand reputation management should be your top priority.

We mentioned it before, but it is worth reiterating that perception trumps reality. Effective crisis communications strategies generate a positive perception of the company during a crisis, or at least help you reduce the negative perception stemming from the event. This is particularly important when responding to an oppositional crisis, and you need to reshape the perception in your favor.

This section provides strategies and considerations to assist you with managing your brand reputation during a crisis.

Key Takeaways

- Crisis communications are one of the elements of a successful crisis response. Corporate Communications often facilitates communicating with internal and external stakeholders, shaping the crisis perception, and protecting your organization's brand.

- Not all crisis events are equal. An oppositional crisis occurs when your stakeholders and the general public believe the crisis is your fault. On the other hand, a non-oppositional crisis occurs when your stakeholders and the general public are sympathetic toward you. You want to ensure the latter applies to you.

- Crisis communications typically have three distinct phases: identify, isolate, and manage. You must recognize early crisis indicators, isolate the event, and start proactively managing to ensure you control the message and perception.

- A brand is one of the most valuable assets to any organization. Effective crisis communications strategies generate a positive perception of the company during a crisis and help reduce the negative perception stemming from cyber events.

Chapter 21

Internal Communications

During a cyber crisis, your employees can be your strongest allies or worst enemies. When a cyberattack impacts employees, you must determine what information can and should be shared with them and clearly and concisely communicate that information.

How you manage employee communications directly impacts how they perceive the crisis, their morale, and what they share with their coworkers and the outside world. There are no secrets in the age of digital communication and social media, and effective internal communications can minimize the risk of a negative internal perception.

Moreover, employee communication can and should be bidirectional. As part of crisis communications planning, it is vital to document roles and responsibilities, including specific individuals assigned to those roles and their contact information. This does not have to be pages of lengthy and unnecessary details. A simple table with a few bullet points is sufficient.

When to Communicate with Employees

When a cyberattack negatively impacts employees' ability to perform work, leads to health and safety concerns, or requires them to adjust how they perform their tasks, the situation warrants employee engagement and communication. However, when the workforce is not impacted, or the impact is affecting only a subset of your operations, you may want to restrict what information is shared to minimize the risk of rumors, speculation, and negative perception.

For example, suppose a malware attack impacts manufacturing processes in a steel plant or an oil refining process in a refinery. In this situation, you will immediately communicate with employees for health and safety reasons and invoke business continuity plans where appropriate.

Also, when a crisis event becomes internal or public knowledge and when a message goes out, make sure your employees are among the first to know important announcements. Nothing can anger employees more than learning about the crisis from external sources, especially if their jobs and well-being may be at risk.

The reality is that your employees will talk about the situation whether you want them to or not. Why not leverage them as part of your crisis communications strategy and ensure they are your first line of defense in the public eye? At the end of the day, their experience and knowledge of the situation are more credible than that of a social media influencer or even a journalist scouring for information before the evening news. However, the employee communication strategy must be well thought out to ensure your employees are your allies and do not step on your external messaging.

You can assume that anything you say to employees will become public knowledge sooner rather than later. For this reason, equip your employees with messaging and provide a clear direction regarding what they can share and with whom. Furthermore, advise employees not discuss the matter with traditional media or initiate discussions on social media.

When Not to Make Internal Announcements

Not all crisis situations require notifying employees. Suppose an external threat actor gained unauthorized access to the network, established a foothold, and laterally moved within the compromised environment. Fortunately, your team detected and contained the intrusion before the threat actor gained access to highly confidential data or deployed destructive malware. In cases like this, it is doubtful you will have to engage the wider workforce and communicate information about the event.

In cases where a cyberattack does not impact business operations, lead to health and safety risks, or materially impact employees, it is critical to conduct a comprehensive investigation before notifying any employees. Then, based on the outcome, your legal counsel can advise if notifications to any impacted parties are required per applicable laws and regulations.

There are also cases where you have to communicate with employees about an outage, yet you do not have to share with them that a cyberattack has caused the outage. A prudent approach is to provide a generic message acknowledging a system issue and advise that the organization is working diligently to identify and remediate the root cause. In addition, you can outline high-level steps to stabilize and remediate the situation to induce a sense of confidence in the reader without revealing all the details and putting your organization at legal risk.

For the reasons mentioned above, it is essential that your Corporate Communications team identifies and isolates the crisis from a communications perspective, assesses it, and makes the right decisions about a communication strategy.

Understanding Employee Communication Needs

Now that you know when you should communicate with employees and other internal stakeholders, let's briefly cover the circumstances and the messaging you must consider as part of internal communications. Of course, every crisis is different. However, one key point to remember is ensuring the messages sent to various stakeholders are concise, consistent, and tailored and approved for the target audience. We explore this topic in more detail in the next chapter. The following paragraphs provide the most frequent internal communications scenarios that we've seen during our consulting engagements:

- **Health and safety concerns** – When a cyberattack creates health and safety concerns, you must communicate as soon as those concerns arise and ensure your messaging is concise and precise. For example, suppose a cyberattack impacts a manufacturing plant, and you suspect the threat actor can control manufacturing processes and cause employee safety risks. In that case, you must provide immediate instructions to personnel supporting the technologies in question and communicate any expectations from the plant employees, such as switching to manual processes or taking a paid leave of absence until your organization regains control of the systems.

- **Instructions to employees who cannot perform their work** – During an outage caused by a cyberattack, employees who cannot perform their job functions because of reliance on technology need direction. Your Corporate Communications team will collaborate with the impacted business unit's manager to draft messaging that provides instructions to those employees and sets expectations, such as taking a paid leave of absence, until systems are restored to an operational state.

- **Guidance on external communication** – It is a frequent occurrence that rumors spread during a cyber crisis, and employees speculate about the situation. For this reason, you must remind employees about internal protocols and provide clear instructions about not posting messages on social media regarding the crisis or providing comments to media outlets.

- **Managing expectations** – In business areas where manual process execution is still possible, your organization will likely invoke a business continuity plan. In such cases, your communication must be targeted and may come from a business unit manager. However, it is not unusual to experience operational issues due to technology glitches even after recovering the impacted business functions. Therefore, when the restoration is gradual and can result in intermittent service, you should consider including this information in your messaging and communicate when the organization will likely completely restore operations to a steady state.

Regardless of your communication strategy, we recommend you avoid discussing the crisis using terms such as cyberattack, breach, or data breach. In fact, it is better to avoid referencing security altogether to reduce rumors and speculations and minimize the risk of legal exposure. Instead, use generic terms to describe the situation, such as network outage or infrastructure issue. However, the part of the communications where you provide employees with essential information and instructions must remain clear, concise, and consistent with previous messaging.

Key Takeaways

- When a cyber crisis impacts your employees, determine what information can and should be shared with them and clearly and concisely communicate it.
- When your workforce is not impacted, or the impact is affecting only a subset of your operations, consider restricting what information is shared to minimize the risk of rumors, speculation, and negative perception.
- Ensure that the term "data breach" and other related terms, such as data leak or unauthorized data access, are not used in internal and external communications. Legal counsel and data privacy attorneys are responsible for determining if a data breach occurred per applicable laws and regulations and using this term appropriately, such as when communicating with regulators.

Chapter 22

Internal and External Communications

There are cases where you cannot prevent a cyber event from becoming public knowledge. In some situations, your organization must disclose a breach or information about a cyberattack to comply with laws and regulations. For example, when a breach leads to the unauthorized disclosure of Personally Identifiable Information (PII) related to employees or customers, jurisdiction-specific data privacy regulations may require your organization to notify the impacted individuals within a specific period. A prime example is a requirement to notify the SEC via a Form 8-K within four days of determining that an incident is material.

In other cases, information about a cyber crisis leaks into the public domain at the speed of light, putting your Public Relations (PR) team on the defensive from the outset. This phenomenon often occurs during destructive cyberattacks impacting business operations with a downstream impact on business partners, customers, or even the general public.

You must be ready to address your stakeholders when a crisis event becomes public knowledge. Otherwise, journalists, social media influencers, and bloggers will take you for a rough ride you are unlikely to enjoy. You want to control the message from the get-go and shape a positive crisis perception among external stakeholders.

Identifying External Stakeholders

The Crisis Communications team is at the forefront of managing a crisis, and their responsibilities may go beyond communicating with the general public. By definition, anyone other than your employees can be considered an external party or stakeholder, including:

- Current and potential customers
- The media
- Government agencies and regulators
- Business partners
- Social media influencers and bloggers
- Investors

In some cases, such as regulators and strategic business partners, senior leadership may own the relationship and communicate with those stakeholders directly. However, when it comes to mass communication or where direct contact is not possible, the Crisis Communications team typically crafts a PR strategy and provides messaging to those stakeholders.

Furthermore, it is common for Corporate Communications to maintain contact lists for stakeholder groups for internal and external messaging. For example, suppose a cyber crisis affects only a subsidiary company or systems hosted in a specific geographic location. The Crisis Communications team will leverage a contact list only for the impacted business areas or geographies in such a case.

The Role of PR in Brand Reputation Management

We live in a hyperconnected and dynamic world where information spreads at the speed of light. A positive brand reputation increases customer loyalty and builds confidence in products and services. However, inadequate handling of a cyber crisis can tarnish that reputation within days. For this reason, PR plays a critical role in crisis management.

When a crisis is not public knowledge, but your organization anticipates that the information will eventually leak or you will disclose it due to regulatory and legal reasons, PR can help you proactively prepare to handle the situation. This includes creating a messaging strategy that can encompass the following elements:

- Identifying stakeholder groups and their communication needs

- Drafting messages for those stakeholders
- Drafting press releases
- Preparing the company's spokesperson for potential media interviews
- Educating executives and senior managers about downstream communication within the organization, including the required messaging, its tone, and the desired messaging outcomes

An effective PR strategy can help you keep a crisis under wraps where possible. This is usually possible when your organization experiences a significant cyber event that does not require disclosure to the general public.

During a public crisis that requires a more reactive approach, at least in the initial phases, PR professionals can come to the rescue. They typically help turn reactive communication into a proactive strategy designed to create a favorable perception of how the organization responds to the crisis. In addition to the elements described earlier, PR can assist with the following:

- Acting as a single point of inquiry for media, reporters, and external stakeholders

- Handling press and media attention, including scheduling media interviews and social media posts, and managing holding statements on the company's website

- Drafting press releases and internal employee communications

- Moreover, once the dust has settled and the organization fully recovered its business operations, PR often continues with campaigns designed to draw public attention away from the crisis and toward more positive aspects of the brand.

Key Takeaways

- Identify external stakeholders for crisis communications and their messaging needs. When you can identify specific entities or individuals, ensure you have their contact information documented.

- Ensure your Corporate Communications team is ready to address external stakeholders and create a sound PR strategy to control the message from the get-go and shape a positive crisis perception among external stakeholders.

Chapter 23

Crisis Communications Strategies

In Chapter 20, we explained the difference between an oppositional and a non-oppositional crisis. The first step in your crisis communications should be to determine what type of crisis you are dealing with and craft your strategy accordingly. In our experience, a non-oppositional crisis is easier to manage. For example, if you are the victim of a sophisticated cybercrime group or a nation-state actor, use it to your advantage. For your stakeholders to become sympathetic, they need to hear it and perceive you as the victim, not the villain.

Do you remember when we also said in Chapter 20 that perception trumps reality? Perception is everything! You must carefully and strategically shape internal and external messages to create a favorable perception among your stakeholders.

Being proactive and consistent with your message is essential. Your first statement will set the tone for the rest of your communication. Therefore, you need to establish control over the message from the beginning. Also, ensure your message is consistent across all media channels and social media platforms. Discrepancies and mixed messages will likely give your stakeholders the impression of a lack of control and chaos.

Preparing for Crisis Communications

There is no question that when a cyber crisis hits your organization, preparation is essential to making internal and external communications a success. This section provides practical guidance on creating an effective communications strategy for your overall crisis response.

Over the years, we have encountered numerous organizations that aggravated a crisis by reactive and sometimes hostile messaging. In most cases, the issue stemmed from inadequate preparedness. The following paragraphs provide battle-tested advice on making your communications strategy work for your organization.

- **Understand the crisis** – It is challenging, if not impossible, to communicate with your target audiences without understanding the situation and its characteristics. As the first step, you must speak to the leaders and subject matter experts responsible for crisis response to ensure you know its nature and scope. Also, leverage their expertise in crafting messaging.

- **Identify and understand your target audience** – Your messaging content and distribution channels will vary depending on your target audience and their information requirements. For example, business partners have different information needs than employees or the general public.

- **Determine communication objectives** – As part of crafting a message for a specific target audience, determine the desired outcome you want to achieve. For example, you may want your messages to foster empathy and create a favorable perception of your response effort among the general public. In contrast, statements for investors and government agencies will be factual and written in precise language.

- **Decide on content** – Depending on the nature of the crisis, you may opt for open and transparent communication or take a more conservative approach to prevent potential legal exposure. When you craft your messaging, carefully evaluate the content and align it with the outcome you want to achieve.

- **Determine a distribution strategy** – Depending on your target audience and how widely you want to communicate, various distribution channels are available, including the company website, intranet, email, service desk, social media platforms, traditional media outlets, and call centers. You will likely need to leverage multiple channels to reach the intended audiences. So, determine how you will distribute the crisis communications to each target audience.

- **Determine update frequency** – When actively managing a crisis, you will likely need to provide specific status updates to your target audiences. For each audience, decide on an update frequency and consider setting expectations for how frequently they should expect new information. For example, as you recover applications and business services, you may want to inform your customers about their availability.

- **Evaluate** – Where you have the means, evaluate how effective your messaging is and whether it brings about the desired effect. For example, you can collect feedback from specific audiences, such as employees or business partners. In addition, if you have the tools to monitor social media sentiment, this is a great avenue to determine how the general public perceives the situation.

Before we dive into specific guidelines for handling crisis communications, we want to emphasize the importance of consistency between internal and external communications. For example, if you communicate to employees and other internal stakeholders that the sky is falling while your external messaging portrays the situation as under control and in good order, then it is just a matter of time before the media, bloggers, and lawyers identify the inconsistency and use it to undermine your credibility and trustworthiness. In some cases, this can also create legal exposure.

When to Activate Crisis Communications

As we mentioned in Chapter 20, communication failures often exacerbate a crisis. If you don't manage them properly, a minor event can spiral out of control into a fully-fledged crisis. For this reason, you must start managing communications from the inception of a crisis event.

Corporate Communications are the gateway to your stakeholders and should be activated when you observe crisis precursors. Ideally, when your organization identifies crisis parameters or precursors, you should engage Corporate Communications. It is a better strategy to err on the side of caution and avoid unpleasant surprises down the road, even when a potential crisis turns out to be a red herring.

In some cases, Corporate Communications detect early signs or precursors of a crisis. For example, suppose a researcher posts a message on social media that your organization has poorly configured security with plenty of vulnerabilities and legacy technologies. If you do not get ahead of the situation and actively manage it, social media influencers will surely put you on the defensive and take you for an unpleasant PR ride.

Of course, you can only plan for some situations, and sometimes activating a Crisis Communications team is an ad hoc decision that may fall outside the established plan.

Also, crisis communications are not always about mass communication and messaging. In many situations, especially when a cyberattack causes a crisis, the Corporate Communications team may prepare senior leaders for media appearances and prevent information leakage that can damage the brand and expose the organization to legal risks. We discuss this consideration later in this chapter.

Identifying Stakeholders

The scope of crisis communications depends on the nature and extent of a cyberattack. For example, suppose a ransomware attack cripples your business operations. Your communication strategy and messaging will be very different compared to a crisis caused by a social espionage attack that resulted in intellectual property theft.

An effective crisis communications strategy is often executed on a need-to-know basis and driven by the need to protect brand reputation. As part of your crisis communications strategy, you must consider the following entities and stakeholder groups:

- **Crisis responders** are members of the Crisis Response Team. You cannot have an effective crisis response without communication. Crisis response is a complex undertaking that requires horizontal and vertical communication and information flow between stakeholders participating in the response process. This group differs from the remaining groups because the response leaders facilitate communication within the response team instead of the Corporate Communications department. Also, crisis responders often have insights into the crisis that they do not share with external entities and employees.

- **Employees** require communication when a cyberattack impacts their ability to perform their work, leads to health and safety issues, or requires them to adjust how and where they work. For example, suppose destructive malware causes an operational outage. Certain employees may have to go on leave or default to manual processes, where possible.

- **The general public** requires information when a cyberattack impacts your ability to deliver products and services, especially when there are subscriptions or contractual obligations. For example, suppose a ransomware event impacts a health insurance provider, and their customer cannot file claims or get medical procedures due to a system outage. In that case, the company must consider its customers as part of its communication strategy.

- **Media** includes newspapers, TV, websites, social media, and other electronic sources that might publish a story about the crisis. Suppose it is inevitable that a crisis event will become public knowledge. In that case, you may want to proactively reach out to trusted media outlets to control the message and ensure favorable public perception instead of embarking on a downward spiral of negative publicity and public perception.

- **Government** agencies may require notifications if your organization operates in a heavily regulated environment and you are legally required to notify a specific agency or department about a crisis event. Furthermore, some laws and regulations require notification to a regulator within a specific time.

- **Partners** include strategic suppliers and business partners. Suppose a crisis event has a negative downstream effect on a strategic supplier. You should consider including those entities in your communication strategy.
- **Clients** include major buyers and strategic accounts who may experience product and service delivery disruptions and require a notification. If feasible, consider providing a tentative timeline for when deliveries might resume.
- **Investors** are financially vested in your business. A cyber crisis can impact their voting and investment decisions. If your organization is privately owned, investor communication requirements may differ from those for publicly traded companies. For example, in the United States, the Securities and Exchange Commission (SEC) requires public companies to report material events in their financial statements. This information could potentially influence how shareholders treat shares in the company.

Depending on the nature of your organization, you might identify other stakeholder groups that you may have to communicate with during a cyber crisis. Ensure that you consider their needs as part of your overall crisis communications strategy.

Handling Mass Inquires

Preparation is crucial when responding to a full-fledged crisis with a PR nightmare and many external inquiries. You do not want to be late to the game and let external forces shape the crisis perception. The following lists include some pointers for preparing for mass communication. However, before diving into the details, we want to emphasize that these measures require planning as part of crisis preparedness. Otherwise, you will have yet another task for an already stretched Crisis Response Team to manage when time is of the essence.

- **Call center** – If your organization serves a specific consumer market, you may experience a significant volume of calls exceeding your steady-state capacity. As it is rare for organizations to provide customized or customer-specific crisis updates, many organizations choose to play a pre-recorded message drafted by PR. The message can include general information about the crisis, direct customers to a holding statement on a website for further details or advise them to monitor social media for regular updates. Another way to handle the additional call volume is to use artificial intelligence (AI) with natural language processing (NLP) capabilities. You can employ this option during a crisis if your organization already leverages AI capabilities in a call center for day-to-day operations.
- **Publishing contact information for external entities** – During a crisis impacting business operations, your suppliers, business customers, and other entities with a stake in the situation might not be able to contact your organization through pre-established channels. Consequently, as part of your PR strategy, include information on how those entities can contact the organization for information. In many cases, relationship managers can facilitate communication. However, as appropriate, it is worth considering including contact information in a holding statement and other externally facing communications.
- **Communicating with business partners** – A cyber crisis can significantly impact business partners, whether the partner is a critical vendor or a large supplier. Smaller business partners can also be severely affected by the situation. They might need to obtain regular information beyond what you communicate to the general public to adjust production capacity or plan for a supply chain impact. Ensure you establish personal contacts with those entities and share the necessary information as legal counsel permits.

Social Media Sentiment Analysis

In the age of social media, you do not have days to prepare your PR strategy. If you are lucky, you may have a few hours to correct misinformation before it spirals out of control. For this reason, preparation is king! Even when you think you have a crisis event under control, the employee and public perception may differ. This is why social media monitoring and sentiment analysis are so crucial.

Social media sentiment analysis tools often leverage NLP to analyze and decipher how your organization, products, and services are perceived. When you experience a cyber crisis, and there is a spike in the number of your brand mentions, social media monitoring is an indispensable tool to provide early warning, correct misinformation and factually incorrect posts, and start shaping an external perception of the crisis. We recommend creating a protocol and training your social media team in handling messaging during a cyber crisis. Consider including legal reviews and approved roles to post social media messages and respond to posts on behalf of your company during a crisis. A benign message or meme that is appropriate during normal operations can cause harm and lead to legal exposure during a cyber crisis. In our experience, a senior and seasoned member of your PR team can fulfill this role.

Boilerplate Statements

A boilerplate statement is a short, standardized statement that you can easily customize for a specific situation. We have worked with organizations that take fundamentally different approaches to this matter. For example, one of us worked with a large media company whose Corporate Communications department did not utilize boilerplate statements. Instead, they believed they could not plan for every eventuality and drafting brief statements ad hoc was a more effective strategy. At the other end of the spectrum, we worked with a large services organization with an 80-page PR playbook with boilerplate statements for numerous situations.

No matter where your organization falls within the spectrum, ensure you can promptly draft and disseminate communication to control the message and manage internal and external perceptions. As part of this strategy, we recommend creating a document that outlines the facts and contains frequently asked questions (FAQ) and talking points for your leadership and your spokesperson. We will cover this topic in more detail in the next chapter.

Identifying the Right Communication Tools

Internal and external crisis communications can take several forms. For this reason, you must build an arsenal of communication tools to prepare for any crisis, including a cyber crisis. Moreover, when choosing the right communication tools, we recommend considering their communication speed, reach, and target audience. For example, a mass communication tool may be appropriate for sharing vital safety updates with the general public, while email is more appropriate for periodic internal announcements to employees.

The following list includes tools frequently used for internal communications:

- Email
- Organization-wide instant messaging channel
- Updates posted on the company's intranet
- Mass messaging software for critical events
- Call trees

In contrast, external communications options include:

- Social media, including X (formerly Twitter), YouTube, and Facebook, among others
- Statements posted on the company's website
- Press releases
- Regular media statements and interviews during severe crises

We recommend using multiple channels to reach your target audience effectively. When you choose this path, ensure message consistency to prevent confusion and a negative perception of how you handle the crisis.

What to Do When a Cyberattack Impacts Communications

As you have probably noticed by now, we broadly classify cyberattacks into two categories, destructive and impacting data privacy. In some cases, a cyberattack can impact the availability of communications tools, especially if your organization still hosts email, videoconferencing, and other communications platforms in on-premises data centers. This happens less and less as organizations migrate their communications systems to the public cloud and leverage Software-as-a-Service (SaaS) solutions.

Suppose a ransomware attack cripples your IT infrastructure, including email, teleconferencing, and instant messaging. In such a case, you must leverage out-of-band tools for employee communication and enable communication between the crisis responders.

Some of the recommendations in this section may appear to be violating a corporate policy or would not be allowed under normal circumstances. However, a crisis is not a normal circumstance, and firms often suspend corporate rules while the organization diligently works to restore business operations. It is all about getting things done in the shortest time possible. The following list provides communication tools you can use when your primary communication means are unavailable or compromised:

- **Personal email** – This solution might be required for the members of the Crisis Response Team to communicate. We have witnessed this approach countless times. Responders may have to use personal email when a destructive attack impacts on-premises email solutions, or a victim organization disconnects core enterprise services to prevent attack expansion. This is our least preferred approach, and we encourage you consider other solutions first. However, when a crisis evolves, you must evolve your solutions to respond to it. Remember to consider operational and legal risks in this choice.

- **Temporary enterprise email solution** – One option to facilitate asynchronous communication without using personal email is to set up a temporary email solution. With cloud-based solutions such as Gmail for business, all you need to do is to register a domain and sign up for a service with your credit card.

- **Cloud-based instant messaging platforms** – We often recommend provisioning a temporary business communication platform for responders to collaborate and communicate near real-time.

- **Direct manager communication with employees** – We typically recommend this approach for internal employee communications outside the response team or where only a small group of employees need to know about the crisis. Often, senior leadership mandates that communication cascade through the management chain to all levels of the organization.

- **Applications for critical event messaging** – If you need to send concise messages to a large group of employees or communication becomes urgent due to health and safety issues, critical event messaging platforms are an excellent choice.

We have also witnessed organizations using mobile messaging applications like WhatsApp or Signal. We typically do not recommend this approach because communication becomes chaotic and unsustainable when you scale out the response and add stakeholders to the various groups participating in the response process.

In rare and severe cases, organizations also choose to keep their employees and the general public informed about a critical situation through social media and website holding statements. For example, when Maersk, a global shipping company, experienced a NotPetya attack that impacted their operations globally, the company used

Twitter (now X) for communications.[13] However, it is essential to note that this approach blurs the line between internal and external communications and may not be appropriate in many cases.

Key Takeaways

- Preparation is essential to making internal and external communications a success. Before communicating with your stakeholders, understand the nature of the crisis and your target audience, determine communication objectives, and choose the right communication tools.
- Corporate Communications are the gateway to your stakeholders, and you must engage the team as soon as you observe crisis precursors. In some cases, your Corporate Communications team may even detect a potential crisis through social sentiment analysis before its symptoms become evident to other stakeholders.
- As part of crisis response preparedness, ensure you can facilitate mass communication and provide your customers and other external stakeholders with the necessary information.
- Monitor social media, prepare boilerplate statements, and identify the right communication tools to facilitate crisis communications with internal and external stakeholders.
- Be prepared for the worst-case scenario. When a cyberattack takes down your crisis communications tools, provision temporary tools to facilitate communication within the Crisis Response Team.

[13] Andy Greenberg, Wired, "The Untold Story of NotPetya, the Most Devastating Cyberattack in History," August 2018, available here: https://www.wired.com/story/notpetya-cyberattack-ukraine-russia-code-crashed-the-world/.

Chapter 24

Dos and Don'ts of Crisis Communications

As we mentioned earlier in this book, every crisis is different, and it is impractical or not even possible to script a 500-page playbook describing a response procedure for every conceivable cyber crisis event. In our experience, when it comes to handling a crisis, less is often more. Deliberate and well-orchestrated actions and messaging produce more positive outcomes than reactive and chaotic responses.

Pulling every possible lever to get a cyber breach under control is not always possible or desirable. This brief chapter provides some Dos and Don'ts of crisis communications that we have learned over the years.

How Much Communication Is Too Much?

Unfortunately, there is no universally accepted answer to this question. In our experience, an essential communication aspect is value. If frequent communication keeps employees informed and reassured about the situation, they get value. In such a case, daily bite-sized emails or text messages that are concise, relevant, and consistent may be a good approach. For example, suppose a ransomware attack impacts core business functions, causing a prolonged outage, and it will likely take several days or even weeks to restore business operations. If most employees cannot perform their work, it is essential to keep them informed. Your messages could include information about the restored functions, operational problems following recovery, and what to expect next.

On the other hand, if there are no updates or you cannot share information for specific reasons, such as legal considerations, consider reducing communication frequency. This approach will help you ensure that employees do not perceive the communications as corporate spam and pay very little attention to it, if any.

When considering the communication frequency, examine whether the communication is targeted to specific employee groups or involves the entire organization. For example, in some instances, you may opt for targeted communication or even instruct managers to have one-to-one meetings with their direct reports. In the latter case, managers must frequently check in with their direct reports to ensure they have the necessary information and remain assured about their employment and recovery. Organizations often combine mass employee communications with targeted messaging to address the particular needs of their employees.

Keep It Simple

Most crisis events are complex enough, and there is no need to make them more complicated with convoluted communication. Whether you communicate with employees, other members of the Crisis Response Team, or external stakeholders, keep it concise, factual, and straightforward. In our experience, vague or cryptic messages do not cut it for most audiences. Furthermore, when time is of the essence, stakeholders have no time to read overly long and cryptic messages that resemble academic dissertations more than human communication.

Also, during a crisis do not engage in political arguments, point the finger at others, or engage in passive-aggressive conversations. On the contrary, all of the Crisis Response Team members must put corporate politics aside, communicate candidly and openly with each other, and trust that everyone is working toward a common goal of solving the crisis. If this is not possible due to the corporate culture or other factors, then it may be time for a strong leader to take charge of the situation.

Be a human! During a crisis, your colleagues may work long hours and experience tremendous pressure and stress. Sometimes personal touch can bring a team together. For example, instead of sending formal emails or instant messages, pick up the phone and have a conversation. You will be surprised how many issues you can solve just by talking to the right people.

Breaking Bad News

Sometimes you just need to break bad news to your stakeholders. However, you can still deliver the information in a way that creates a positive perception and a desire to succeed. Whenever you are in a situation where you must communicate with employees or external stakeholders, consider making a sandwich statement. The technique is simple yet very effective. Here is the basic format:

1. Provide a positive statement about your team's progress and how they worked around the clock sacrificing time with their loved ones to address the crisis.
2. Deliver the bad news.
3. Provide a positive statement about the plan going forward. Discuss potential solutions and share a timetable to restore business operations if possible.

Explain your position positively and let the audience draw their own conclusions. For example, when post-ransomware recovery is not going according to plan, you can articulate the steps you have taken so far, then go over the challenges, and finish with a solution and a timetable to accelerate the effort.

Be Truthful

Whether you communicate internally with employees or externally with stakeholders, tell your story first, and be truthful and genuine. Do not make stuff up or tell half-truths or lies to get the situation under control. You will get entangled in a spiderweb of half-truths that will haunt you for months or years and seriously damage your brand. This point is crucial when information about an event leaks into the public domain or the breach negatively affects your customers and business partners.

Keeping quiet or being afraid of your shadow is also a terrible strategy. It can seriously hurt your business when well-connected and motivated journalists find out about a breach or information leaks through social media platforms. In other words, never go radio silent when a PR nightmare unfolds before your eyes.

A word of caution! We are not advocating for volunteering potentially harmful information to the press and other media or announcing on your corporate website to the entire world each time you experience a cyber event. In Chapter 21, we advised that not all crisis events require employee notifications or PR. In our experience, making general statements or drawing attention to specific portions of the truth are perfectly acceptable ways of creating a favorable perception. However, presenting false claims, covering key facts, or manipulating your messages is a perfect recipe for disaster. While your Crisis Response Team is diligently working to recover from a cyber crisis, reporters, bloggers, analysts, and plaintiff attorneys are also working to find cracks in your message, identify deficiencies in your response, and use their findings against you.

A perfect example of a PR nightmare caused by ingenuine communication is the 2017 Equifax data breach that affected the data of 143 million Americans. Equifax waited six weeks before announcing the breach despite millions of consumers being affected by the event. Furthermore, instead of notifying the victims, the company set up a website that was not fully operational during the announcement. To make matters even worse, Equifax initially asked the victims to waive the right to sue the company when offering them credit monitoring. The handling of the crisis was so bad that even six years after the event, PR and Crisis Management professionals use it as an example of how not to handle a cyber crisis.

The moral of this story is that reporting accurate information and being genuine and truthful is the most effective strategy to combat a negative perception and protect your brand. Controlling the message and playing offense rather than defense in a crisis is always better.

Managing Stress

A cyber crisis often causes tremendous stress, panic, and fear of the unknown. This observation is especially true for those who have never experienced a cyber crisis. A healthy amount of stress is sometimes necessary to motivate you and keep you going through the long hours of a crisis. However, overwhelming stress can often lead to analysis paralysis and the inability to make decisions.

The bad news is that you do not have time to take a stress management course or learn a new breathing technique during a crisis. The only way to learn how to handle crisis-induced stress is to go through immersive and realistic crisis response exercises and enroll in media training if you are a spokesperson. By conducting exercises that resemble realistic crisis events, you can develop immunity that will allow you to keep your stress at a reasonable level during a real crisis. It is like practicing martial arts sparring before going to a tournament. The only way to get good at handling a crisis and its associated stress is to practice, practice, and practice!

Key Takeaways

- An essential aspect of internal and external communication is value. Ensure that communication frequency, format, and means are appropriate for the target audience.
- Keep your messaging concise, factual, and straightforward. Also, avoid using vague or cryptic language in verbal and written communication.
- Use a sandwich technique to communicate bad news internally by padding a negative message with positive statements.
- Be truthful and genuine in your communication. Telling half-truths or deliberate lies makes crisis communications a potential nightmare when journalists, reporters, and plaintiff attorneys find cracks in your messages.

- Participate in crisis response exercises and attend media training to build immunity against crisis-induced stress.

Chapter 25

The Role of Leadership

As a leader, do not underestimate your role during a crisis. You must inspire your response team and raise morale when burnout becomes evident. At this point, the team may need extra motivation to get through the crisis. We have encountered leaders who have inspired an entire organization and led by example by participating in crisis meetings and actively reinforcing a positive message through the response. But sadly, we have also worked with leaders who could not handle their stress levels, used abusive language towards employees and contractors, and exerted unhealthy pressure on them to accelerate response and recovery. As you can imagine, this approach did not lead to positive outcomes.

As described throughout the Articulate section of this book, you must also be purposeful and intentional about communicating. Your communication and interaction can significantly affect the organization and how external entities perceive the response.

In this section, we provide battlefield-tested guidance that will help you handle crises effectively and get the response on the right foot from the outset of a crisis event.

A Bad Decision Is Better Than No Decision

As United States Army General H. Norman Schwarzkopf Jr. said, "When placed in command, take charge." During a cyber crisis, responders look to their leadership for direction, and you often do not have all the information you need or the time to strategize when a destructive cyberattack cripples your organization's operations. You must take charge of the situation and start making concrete decisions, even if those decisions are not perfect or do not lead to the expected outcome.

Analysis paralysis is the poison during crisis response when time is of the essence, and the next several hours or days may define the organization and its brand for years to come. For this reason, as a leader, start actively driving the response, set business priorities, and put a team in charge that can handle tasks under pressure and is not afraid to fail. Fail Fast is a philosophy typically associated with entrepreneurs and start-ups in Silicon Valley. However, we believe this philosophy applies equally to crises where making decisions is the only way forward, even if you must adjust the course of action or change the decision later.

For example, we worked with a client who decided to rebuild their network entirely from scratch following a destructive attack that disrupted their business operations. The client made that decision early on and committed resources to the process. However, after several days, the client realized that the complexity of this task would prolong recovery and put the very existence of their business at risk. As a result, the client worked with us to regain control of their environment from within the compromised network, focusing on securing access control first and then expanding outwards. A decisive leadership decision and clear direction for the recovery team allowed the client to adjust its course of action and stay in business.

We are not saying you should skip due diligence. As we've mentioned, arbitrary decision-making without considering the business context and listening to experts can be catastrophic. Instead, we advocate for strong leadership and decisiveness when you have limited information and time to make the perfect decision. As a crisis leader, you must become comfortable with uncertainty fast. Napoleon Bonaparte once said, "The winning general is the one who can best act on imperfect information and half-formed theories."

We also encourage organizations to engage external experts when they lack sufficient experience and expertise to even make an educated guess about the next step. Recognizing this deficiency and reaching out for external help is a well-founded decision.

Going to the Gemba

During a crisis, you genuinely want to understand the situation. As a leader, you are likely removed from details and need factual and actionable information to shape crisis communications and business decisions. In other words, you need to go to the Gemba and gain insights from those close to the work. Actively communicating with your employees will also help you understand different perspectives and make better decisions. *Gemba* is a Japanese term meaning "the actual place" where value-creating activities occur. The term was popularized in the West as part of the Toyota Production System (TPS).

Consider all people who may understand the cyber event and, if necessary, make them ad hoc members of your Crisis Response Team. Solicit input from those who have an intimate knowledge and understanding of the crisis, including:

- Senior managers who may understand specific communication requirements about their business areas
- Subject matter experts who can provide factual information about the investigation and restoration
- Corporate Communications professionals to assist with messaging and prepare a spokesperson for media interviews
- Legal counsel to review and approve the messaging before dissemination to ensure it does not expose the organization to legal risks

Getting to Gemba is crucial because it will allow you to understand the crisis better, eliminate incorrect assumptions, and make business decisions based on factual information.

Designating a Spokesperson

When a cyber crisis becomes public knowledge, and reporters impatiently demand a statement at the doorstep of your corporate office, saying nothing or making vague statements on X (formerly Twitter), Threads, or the corporate website is unlikely to cut it for them. You need a spokesperson, and you need them fast! The public subconsciously wants a knowledgeable and confident leader who controls the crisis.

We have emphasized perception several times throughout this book. Connecting with your audience is not about finding a perfect excuse for the crisis or creating a flawless logical argument. On the contrary, it is about clear, genuine, and truthful communication and connecting with your stakeholders to lead to empathy and create a favorable perception of the crisis.

Even astute and experienced leaders can make dumb and harmful statements under pressure and stress. For this reason, we recommend choosing a person who feels comfortable interacting with the media and can project confidence and psychological comfort when faced with difficult and uncomfortable questions.

As a rule, your spokesperson should also be knowledgeable and credible. Excellent soft skills and confidence are not enough. The person should speak in a straightforward and declarative manner and explain the complexities of the crisis in a language that the average Joe can understand.

During a non-oppositional crisis, your stakeholders can forgive you for small mistakes because they want you to succeed. However, you are on the defensive during an oppositional crisis, facing threat actors targeting you at every step. For this reason, you must ensure your audience can understand and relate to the spokesperson.

Getting Media Training

Have you witnessed a leader's media appearance or interview go wrong or when the leader said all the right things, but their body language did not match the words? Or, have you participated in a town hall or a corporate event where a leader gave a speech that lacked clarity, and you were not sure what the core message was? Now imagine the additional pressure and questioning the same leader can experience during a cyber crisis.

Situations like this occur because many organizations do not put leaders through media training and other programs to help them learn how to effectively communicate with the general public. Some leaders are natural communicators. However, many need training and preparation so they can project confidence and build a favorable perception of their organization during a crisis.

Even natural and confident leaders cannot project confidence unless they understand the crisis, how the organization is handling it, and what to expect over the next several days or weeks. For this reason, we strongly recommend providing media training to leaders. The following list also provides some practical guidance for media interviews:

- Understand the crisis sufficiently. The Corporate Communications team and the leaders managing the response should prepare the spokesperson for media interviews and ensure they have the necessary information to project confidence and create a favorable perception.

- Know your target audience and adjust the language to their needs. If you sound like a lawyer or use cryptic corporate jargon, your message is unlikely to achieve the intended outcome and lead to trust.

- Ensure your message is clear, concise, and consistent, and use action-oriented language. Ambiguous and inconsistent statements can lead to confusion and create a negative perception of how the organization responds to the crisis.

- Be honest and truthful. We are not saying you should reveal information that may expose the organization from a legal perspective. However, dishonest answers or stretched reality can have negative consequences, especially if your message becomes evidence in a potential legal proceeding. Moreover, people can subconsciously sense when leaders are dishonest and try to cover up ugly facts.

In addition, if you provide a written statement as a leader, we highly recommend engaging Corporate Communications professionals or even an external Public Relations (PR) firm to prepare it and send it on your behalf. PR professionals have the expertise and experience to craft a clear, concise, and appropriate message for the target audience.

Creating Alignment and Providing Direction

The role of a leader during a crisis is to ensure alignment between the technical and business response and provide an overall business direction to all functions involved in the response process. Effective communication is vital to achieving this goal. Leadership and communication are intertwined, and there are very few situations where an ability to communicate effectively is so critical as during a crisis response.

In our experience, communication gaps can severely impede decision-making. For example, suppose technical and business stakeholders do not effectively communicate or lack a strategic direction. In that case, neither side can effectively manage their activities because they depend on the other side's facts and guidance. Simply put, gaps in communication and inadequate leadership lead to bad decisions.

Vertical and Horizontal Alignment

Leaders must set clear objectives and priorities for crisis response and create horizontal and vertical alignment across the response groups. Using a military analogy, if troops do not know their marching orders, their response will likely be disjointed and ineffective. Top-down communication creates vertical alignment. Next, managers responsible for specific functional response areas can disseminate those marching orders horizontally to personnel responsible for executing particular activities and tasks.

As a leader, you must unite the entire organization around the same objective to protect brand reputation, recover from a crisis as soon as possible, and return to a steady state. We have observed that responders communicate more effectively and collaborate when there is clear direction from senior leadership, alignment, and a high-trust culture. Moreover, clarity and purpose allow those involved in response to see each other's work as mutually beneficial and remove roadblocks more effectively.

Direction and Response Priorities

As in a military mission, all the stakeholders involved in the response process need direction, clarity, and consistent messages from their leaders. Conversely, a lack of leadership, priority setting, and clarity often lead to unforeseen consequences such as prolonged recovery, inconsistent internal and external communication, and even headaches stemming from regulators taking an active interest in the crisis.

You can create alignment and provide direction to your Crisis Response Team by taking the following steps:

- Set and communicate business priorities for the response from the outset of an event, including prioritizing applications or business processes for recovery, the health and safety of employees and contractors, or preventing leakage of highly confidential information.
- Reinforce a positive message among employees, the general public, and other stakeholders that the organization dedicated the necessary resources to recover from the crisis and protect the impacted stakeholders.
- Articulate response protocols in health and safety, travel versus remote support, communication confidentiality and guidance regarding social media, speaking to friends and family about the crisis, and responding to media inquiries.
- Provide updates to regulators, investors, business partners, and other entities that may require engagement from the highest levels of the organization.
- Ensure that internal communication and messaging are clear, concise, and consistent. When you change priorities during the response, your role is to clearly communicate those changes and articulate new priorities and their reasoning.

We encourage organizations to set formal status updates at least once daily during a crisis to ensure communication continuity. However, during an event causing severe operational disruption, convening the response task forces twice a day is a more effective strategy. The purpose of each meeting is to go over a status update from each workstream, identify roadblocks and required resources, set up priorities for the next several hours, and clearly communicate priorities for the next 12 to 48 hours. The status updates are also an excellent time to identify opportunities for cross-functional collaboration and resolve items with cross-functional dependencies.

Finally, we emphasize that emotions often run high during a crisis. As responders reach burnout, your role as a leader is to motivate them, reinforce a positive message, and appreciate their work. Active leadership and communication are crucial to strengthening the message.

Key Takeaways

- Take charge of the situation and make concrete decisions. You may not know all the facts until a full investigation is complete, which can take days or even weeks. Act on the available information and adjust the course as new findings emerge.

- Go to the Gemba and gain insights from those close to the work. Speaking to Subject Matter Experts will eliminate incorrect assumptions about the crisis and enable you to make more informed decisions.

- Designate a knowledgeable and credible leader who can connect with people to act as a spokesperson. When faced with difficult or uncomfortable questions, the person must project confidence and psychological comfort.

- Provide media training to your spokesperson and senior leaders to ensure they do not easily fall prey to reporters trying to poke holes in their responses.

- Set clear business priorities and response objectives from the outset of a crisis and ensure they are communicated downstream to the response team.
- Set formal status updates and ensure that vertical and horizontal communication within the response team is ongoing.

Summary

Crisis response deals with the reality of a rapidly unfolding cyber event, and crisis communications are critical in the response process. Unfortunately, internal and external communication failures can worsen the crisis and damage your brand reputation.

This section covered several topics related to crisis communications and the role of leadership in this process. First, we discussed the fundamental issues associated with this domain and then articulated common crisis communications strategies. We also explained the difference between internal and external communications and advised you about specific techniques you can employ during a cyber event. Finally, we concluded the discussion by articulating the role of leadership in crisis communications. The following paragraphs provide key takeaways from this Articulate section and some next steps.

Key Takeaways

- Not all crisis events are equal. An oppositional crisis occurs when your stakeholders and the general public believe the crisis is your fault. On the other hand, a non-oppositional crisis occurs when your stakeholders and the general public are sympathetic toward you and want you to succeed.

- Brand is one of the most valuable assets to any organization. Effective crisis communications strategies generate a positive perception of the company during a crisis and help reduce the negative perception stemming from a cyber event.

- Corporate Communications are the gateway to your stakeholders, and you must engage the team as soon as you observe crisis precursors. In some cases, your Corporate Communications team may even detect a potential crisis through social sentiment analysis before its symptoms become evident to other stakeholders.

- An essential aspect of internal and external communication is value. Ensure that communication frequency, format, and means are appropriate for the target audience. Keep your messaging concise, factual, and straightforward. Also, avoid using vague or cryptic language in verbal and written communication.
- Be truthful and genuine in your communication. Telling half-truths or deliberate lies makes crisis communications a nightmare when journalists, reporters, and plaintiff attorneys find cracks in your messaging. However, do not carelessly put your organization at risk of litigation either. Instead, avoid the described communication traps that may hurt your organization long-term.
- As a leader, take charge of the situation and make concrete decisions. You may not know all the facts until a full investigation is complete, which can take days or even weeks. Act on the available information and adjust the course as new findings emerge.
- Go to the Gemba and gain insights from those close to the work. Speaking to SMEs will eliminate incorrect assumptions about the crisis and enable you to make more informed decisions.

Next Steps

- Create a Crisis Communications Plan. Preparation is essential to making internal and external communications a success. Before communicating with your stakeholders, understand the nature of the crisis, your target audience, and your communication objectives. Then choose the right communication tools.

- Include crisis communications in your Crisis Response Plan and ensure you are ready to address external stakeholders and create a sound PR strategy from the outset of a crisis event.
- Designate a spokesperson. The person should be a knowledgeable and credible leader who can connect with people to act as a spokesperson. When faced with difficult or uncomfortable questions, the person must project confidence and psychological comfort.
- Enroll executive leadership and your designated spokesperson in media training to ensure they do not easily fall prey to reporters trying to poke holes in their responses. Furthermore, conduct annual crisis response exercises to build immunity against crisis-induced stress.

Section 6

Remediate

"When solving problems, dig at the roots instead of just hacking at the leaves."

~ Inspirational author Anthony J. D'Angelo

Introduction

The lead author for this section is Andrew Gorecki, with significant input from and in collaboration with Christopher Scott.

Up to this point, you have diligently worked to stabilize and manage the crisis. Your teams have also tirelessly worked long hours and multiple shifts to plan remediation and recovery, performed a thorough intrusion analysis, managed internal and external communications, and assessed the crisis impact throughout the event.

The last phase in the SONAR framework is to remediate the compromised network and recover your systems to an operational and secure state. Arguably, this phase is one of the framework's most complex and challenging parts. You will likely work against the clock and experience tremendous pressure from the business to restore operations in the shortest time possible. Therefore, setting and managing expectations with business stakeholders and constant communication are critical to this process.

Throughout this last phase of the SONAR framework, we refer to remediation as an overarching term encompassing the remediation of security weaknesses and vulnerabilities, system restoration, and recovering the impacted environments to an operational state.

There is no one-size-fits-all approach to breach remediation and recovery. How you tackle these activities depends on your available resources, tools, skills, the event's impact, and other factors. Moreover, the work will require a lot of blood, sweat, and tears, and you will likely have to make tradeoffs between security and recovery.

This section of the book will guide you through considerations and approaches to eradicating the threat actor from the compromised network and recovering systems securely, so the threat actor cannot easily return to continue with their operations. It starts with identifying prerequisites and defining a breach remediation approach. Then, we discuss how to successfully execute the remediation and recover your systems to an operational and secure state. Finally, remediation does not end the crisis. In the final chapter, we provide considerations for post-breach remediation to ensure you can adequately secure your network and minimize the possibility of another cyber crisis.

Chapter 26

Identifying Remediation Prerequisites

Earlier in this book, we outlined the impacts organizations can experience following a cyberattack. This topic is important because understanding impact and severity will directly influence your remediation and recovery strategy. For example, remediating a network following a destructive cyberattack, such as ransomware, differs from a scenario where a threat actor engages in social espionage and exfiltrates highly confidential data.

Before delving into specific remediation topics, it is worth noting that cybercriminals often leverage double extortion tactics as part of their attack strategy. For example, ransomware operators historically focused on deploying ransomware to compromised networks. This activity aimed to encrypt data and systems and extort the victim to purchase decryption keys. However, now some cybercrime groups also exfiltrate confidential data from the compromised network to pressure the victim organization and increase the chances of payment.

In practical terms, this means that even if your organization has adequate and tested backup procedures and can restore business operations without paying the ransom to decrypt your data, the attack can still lead to a data confidentiality impact, data privacy implications, and a Public Relations (PR) nightmare.

Furthermore, in recent months we have observed triple extortion tactics. In addition to double extortion, some cybercrime groups have started to notify business partners, customers, and consumers whose data has been exfiltrated or launch a distributed denial-of-service (DDoS) attack if the victim organization refuses to pay the ransom.

In November 2023, the Black Cat/ALPHV ransomware group took the triple extortion tactic to the next level. Following the adoption of the SEC rule requiring victim organizations to disclose material incidents through Form 8-K, the group filed a complaint with the SEC alleging that their victim failed to disclose the cyberattack within the required four day period.[14]

The following sections outline considerations for remediating destructive cyberattacks versus those causing a significant data confidentiality impact.

Operational Impact

A cyberattack causes an operational impact when it negatively impacts the availability of systems and services supporting core business functions and processes. Depending on the nature and size of your organization, an operational impact can lead to a loss of revenue, impair the ability to receive, process, and fulfill orders, or halt manufacturing processes. An operational impact can cause health and safety concerns in the worst-case scenario. For example, over the last several years we have responded to ransomware attacks against hospitals that led to the cancellation of medical procedures and impacted the availability of medical data.

The following list provides essential considerations when remediating events disrupting business operations:

- Execute short-term containment to "stop the bleeding" and prevent further damage or event exacerbation during a destructive attack. This consideration especially applies to scenarios where you detect a threat actor's presence on your network before data theft and ransomware deployment. Our guidance is first to contain the event and then focus on investigation and longer-term remediation. We explored this topic in-depth in the Stabilize section of this book. You can

[14] BleepingComputer, "Ransomware gang files SEC complaint over victim's undisclosed breach," November 15, 2023, available at https://www.bleepingcomputer.com/news/security/ransomware-gang-files-sec-complaint-over-victims-undisclosed-breach/.

think of short-term containment as continuous stabilization during the entire crisis response process.

- Your organization will face conflicting priorities. On the one hand, analysts must investigate when and where the initial access to the network occurred and the scope of the attack. For this reason, you cannot simply destroy forensic data by restoring systems to a previous state. On the other hand, you will need to restore systems and data as soon as possible to resume business operations.

- Business resumption is often a priority, especially if an event causes health and safety concerns or threatens an organization's very existence. Clients often ask us for a pragmatic perspective. Industry standards and best practices prescribe a comprehensive investigation before executing restoration activities. However, you cannot afford weeks of downtime in the real world. For this reason, most organizations perform an investigation, recover business-critical applications, and harden the impact environments through parallel workstreams. We described the iterative nature of this process at the beginning of this book.

- Threat actors often execute destructive cyberattacks to extort the victim organization. Once they deploy ransomware or other destructive malware, the threat actor achieves their primary objective and awaits potential ransom payment from the victim. For this reason, you can take more risks when restoring systems and data. However, after resuming business operations, you will still have to harden and remediate the network. Otherwise, it is just a matter of time before you experience another significant event.

Data Confidentiality Impact

A cyberattack causes a confidentiality impact when a threat actor gains unauthorized access and potentially exfiltrates non-public data and information. The impacted data may include confidential business information, intellectual property, and data subject to local laws and regulations, such as customer and employee Personally Identifiable Information (PII). In the latter case, a data confidentiality event also leads to a data privacy impact that may require notifications to the affected employees and external parties, such as regulators. Note that confidentiality is a broad term. In various industry lexicons, you may also hear phrases such as data privacy, data leak, unauthorized data disclosure, data breach, and other similar terms.

The following list provides essential considerations when remediating events impacting data confidentiality:

- A comprehensive forensic analysis is a top priority to understand the scope of the event and enable a business analysis of the findings to inform third-party notifications. For example, analysts must establish which systems the threat actor accessed, which files they opened, or what data the threat actor exfiltrated outside the organization. Without this information, the business and its attorneys cannot determine the materiality and data privacy impact.

- A comprehensive forensic analysis is also required to inform containment and eradication. Planning remediation for several days or weeks and executing an immediate plan is counterproductive when the threat actor is interested in staying on your network. We have witnessed threat actors return to a network within days because management made assumptions and prematurely terminated an investigation before executing long-term containment and eradication.

Starting Remediation and Recovery on the Right Foot

Remediation and recovery planning begins at the outset of an investigation, typically in the Organize phase. However, the execution takes place when you fully understand the scope of the compromise and the prerequisites outlined in this chapter. Note that activities necessary to stabilize the crisis are an exception in this phase.

As we mentioned in the previous chapter, there are situations where business recovery takes precedence over other activities, including intrusion analysis and remediation. This approach is undesirable and carries a high risk of re-compromise. However, suppose you work for a medical facility and a cyberattack impacts the health and safety of patients. In this case, you will have to prioritize recovery and then harden the environments after returning to an operational state. For this reason, you must include business priorities in the planning process.

Regardless of the unique characteristics of a crisis, consider the following prerequisites before executing your remediation and recovery plans.

Conducting Comprehensive Analysis

We cannot emphasize enough the importance of conducting a comprehensive intrusion analysis before executing a long-term containment and eradication plan. This point is essential during network intrusions by sophisticated threat actors interested in fraud and social espionage. Those actors often remain on the compromised network as long as possible to exfiltrate confidential data or engage in fraudulent activities. Consequently, premature and inadequate remediation will likely only temporarily remove the threat actor from the network, and it is just a matter of time before they re-establish persistent access.

A thorough analysis of the compromised environments allows investigators to map the attack chain, identify the compromised systems, determine how those systems were compromised, and inform activities such as long-term containment, eradication, and hardening.

Besides informing containment and eradication, a comprehensive analysis allows the response team to establish a restoration point for systems and data based on when the threat actor compromised those systems.

Documenting Investigative Information

An intrusion analysis produces investigative findings that feed into the remediation plan. Remediating a breach without understanding how the threat actor operated in the compromised environment is incredibly challenging, if not impossible. For example, in order to eradicate the threat actor, you need to determine what vulnerabilities the threat actor exploited and what systems they infected with malware.

A detailed discussion on incident management and documentation is outside the scope of this book. However, we want to emphasize the importance of taking notes, tracking investigative findings, and producing comprehensive incident information. Without this information, you cannot create an adequate containment and eradication plan. Therefore, we highly recommend documenting your inventory of compromised assets and information related to tactics, techniques, and procedures (TTPs) employed by the threat actor.

We suggest you capture the following information:

- Compromised and attacker-created identities, including user and service accounts
- Compromised end-user workstations
- Compromised server systems
- A list of compromised domains if the threat actor moved laterally to multiple domains

Note that we list servers separately. You can easily re-image or replace a compromised workstation or laptop. However, you cannot take the same approach to server systems supporting core business functions. As a result, remediating servers requires a different approach that we discuss later in this section.

You must document all known Indicators of Compromise (IOC) and other information relevant to the threat actor's operations, including:

- Malware information, including hashes and other attributes required for blocking
- IP addresses and URLs associated with command-and-control (C2)
- Channels used for data exfiltration, including staging servers
- Vulnerabilities exploited as part of the intrusion
- Relevant threat intelligence necessary for building detections and blocking threat actor activity

Preserving Forensic Data

Data preservation is a critical but often overlooked prerequisite to remediation and recovery. You will restore or rebuild compromised systems as part of your eradication strategy. However, you may have to preserve forensic data from a legal standpoint, especially if your legal counsel anticipates civil litigation due to the crisis.

Unfortunately, organizations have rushed into restoring server systems and re-imagining compromised end-user workstations without data preservation considerations. This approach can expose your organization to legal risk and impede intrusion analysis.

During destructive attacks, we frequently encounter a scenario where the victim organization has insufficient storage capacity to retain compromised systems on the network while restoring systems from backup to resume business operations. For this reason, we highly recommend closely working with analysts and a Digital Forensics and Incident Response partner to acquire forensic images of compromised systems and secure them in a remote location or a secure cloud storage facility.

Assessing Readiness

Earlier in this book, we discussed short-term containment to "stop the bleeding" and stabilize the crisis. At this point, you have organized the response, negotiated a remediation approach, and articulated the plan to key stakeholders. However, before executing the plan, you need to take a step back and assess readiness. This step is necessary because crisis response is a complex process completed under tremendous pressure within a limited time frame. For this reason, missing essential elements or prerequisites can ruin your plan. Use the following lists to assess your readiness to execute the remediation plan.

- Ensure you completed a forensic analysis of the compromised environments and fully understand the compromise scope. Analysts usually conclude their investigation when they reach diminishing returns regarding new findings or are confident they identified all threat actor activity. This point is important because investigative findings feed into the remediation process.

- Validate that all the remediation prerequisites outlined earlier in this chapter are in place, including an inventory of assets for remediation, compromised accounts, and IOCs for blocking in security tools.

- Validate your remediation plan and rehearse it with all personnel involved, including technical staff, coordinators, and management. We recommend a dry run or walk-through exercise with all those stakeholders to ensure everyone is on the same page and you can identify weaknesses. We cannot emphasize enough how essential this step is. We have seen remediation go terribly wrong due to inadequate planning and siloed execution.

- Ensure you understand the operational impact associated with remediation activities and clearly articulate the impact to Senior Management and other vital stakeholders. The enterprise will have to manage any outages from a business perspective, including internal and external communications and invoking continuity plans.

- Verify that all logistics are in place, including communications, a physical location for a command center, and access to facilities and systems for employees and contractors. Also, ensure that you booked hotels for on-site personnel and ordered refreshments for the execution date.

- Finally, confirm that your Corporate Communications team drafted employee communications, external statements, and a script for a call center. Furthermore, validate that the team also prepared a holding statement for unforeseen situations, such as a prolonged outage caused by remediation. A holding statement is a short, prewritten statement that you issue shortly after an event to buy time to understand the situation, collect the necessary information, and provide more comprehensive messaging.

Consequences of Alerting the Threat Actor

As discussed earlier in this chapter, a threat actor's objective may be to dwell on the compromised network as long as possible. For example, this objective is typical of nation-state threat actors whose primary purpose is social espionage and data theft, often to advance economic activities in their home countries or gain political advantage. Another example is sophisticated cybercrime groups, such as Scattered Spider deploying exploits to bypass endpoint security.[15]

During an investigation and remediation planning, it is vital to take precautionary steps to minimize the risk of alerting the threat actor about efforts to eradicate their presence from the environment. For example, disconnecting specific network segments or systems from the network or deactivating compromised accounts can alert a threat actor. However, sometimes tipping off the threat actor might be unavoidable. The threat actor may react differently depending on their sophistication, resources, and persistence. This point is important because it will likely influence your remediation strategy.

Suppose your organization responds to a network intrusion by a nation-state actor whose primary purpose is social espionage. In that case, you must take extra precautions to ensure you do not alert the threat actor about your investigation and remediation planning.

[15] CrowdStrike Blog, "Not a SIMulation: CrowdStrike Investigations Reveal Intrusion Campaign Targeting Telco and BPO Companies," available here: https://www.crowdstrike.com/blog/analysis-of-intrusion-campaign-targeting-telecom-and-bpo-companies/.

Moreover, depending on the sophistication level of the threat actor, their response may be detrimental to the investigation. For example, threat actors may become dormant for a while, change how they operate, start destroying forensic data (aka anti-forensics), or even become destructive.

We advise this approach when there is no ongoing data exfiltration or risk of immediate system and data destruction through ransomware or other destructive malware. However, if the threat actor is getting ready to execute their objective, we strongly advise you to execute immediate containment to protect your assets and potentially avoid catastrophic consequences, such as data exfiltration or prolonged operational downtime.

We have observed the following threat actor reactions during breach investigations:

- **Becoming Dormant** – A threat actor may scale back their operations to avoid further detection and attempt to remain stealthy on the network. You may remediate compromised systems and secure your network. However, a persistent and patient threat actor will wait until you lower your defenses to plant additional backdoor malware, compromise additional user accounts, and solidify their presence on the network.

- **Changing Tactics** – Some threat actors may change how they operate in the compromised environment when they become aware of an investigation and remediation planning. For example, a threat actor may recompile malware to bypass anti-malware software, use different lateral movement techniques, or employ anti-forensics to evade detection. We have frequently encountered threat actors clearing log files to cover their tracks.

- **Becoming Destructive** – In some cases, threat actors engage in destructive activities, such as deploying destructive malware or encrypting systems and data for a ransom. This scenario occurs when a threat actor does not want your forensic analysts to determine how the threat actor operated in the environment or when the primary attack objective is destruction, such as ransomware.

Key Takeaways

- Conduct a comprehensive forensic analysis to inform long-term containment, hardening, and eradication to minimize the risk of network re-compromise.
- Document and share all investigative findings with the remediation team.
- Preserve forensic data. If storage capacity is an issue, work with your forensic analysts to identify an alternative means to accomplish this objective.
- Establish a quarantine network segment for securely restoring and hardening systems before releasing systems to the production network.
- Understand the applications, data, infrastructure, and enterprise services and their dependencies and establish a recovery order.

Chapter 27

Defining a Remediation Approach

In the Stabilize section of this book, we covered executing short-term containment activities to "stop the bleeding" and give you some breathing space to organize a crisis response adequately. However, that effort was short-term and focused on preventing further damage or attack exacerbation. Now, it is time to take a more comprehensive approach and define a strategy to eradicate the threat actor from the network and harden your environments to ensure the threat actor cannot easily return.

As part of remediation planning, you must consider the skills available within your team, resource capacity, the technologies and tools you have at your disposal, and support from technology vendors and security partners. These considerations are essential because the available resources will allow you to determine how much you can realistically achieve as part of breach remediation versus what security enhancements will fall within the post-breach remediation effort.

This chapter covers some of the most common approaches to remedying a cyber breach. However, the path to remediation depends on the nature of the event. For this reason, leverage the content as guiding principles. Moreover, with conflicting priorities and pressure from the business to restore operations as soon as possible, remediation no longer follows a sequential lifecycle model. Instead, you may have to iterate through some of the activities before you have confidence that you have eradicated the threat actor from the compromised network and can safely return to a steady state.

Regaining Control of Your Identity Platform

Identity compromises and privilege escalation are at the heart of many cyberattacks and are essential to enterprise breaches that involve lateral movement. Without elevated privileges, it is extremely difficult, if not impossible, for a threat actor to move laterally, exfiltrate data, or deploy ransomware.

Whether you host your systems on-premises, in the cloud, or in a hybrid environment, your identity platform holds the proverbial keys to the kingdom, allowing a threat actor often unrestricted access to your domain and resources. For example, a typical pattern for identity-based attacks may involve the following steps:

- Gain elevated privileges on the local compromised system to establish a foothold and move laterally.
- Enumerate and dump credentials on member servers to further escalate privileges and gain domain admin (DA) access to the Windows environment.
- Leverage the DA credentials to deploy ransomware across the Windows environment.

For this reason, securing access to your identity platform and hardening systems against credential harvesting techniques, such as credential dumping, should be the top priority for your remediation strategy.

There are many approaches to remediating an identity platform and securing privileged identities. Your overall plan will depend on the depth and breadth of the compromise, current security controls, and whether you are in recovery mode or trying to eradicate an active threat from your network. In extreme cases, you may even have to rebuild your identity platform from scratch and restore the schema and corresponding objects from a backup. The following list provides some common approaches we have leveraged during client engagements to remediate Active Directory Domain Services.

Access rights and privileges – Review access rights and privileges assigned to privileged identities and reduce them to only what is required. For example, during breach investigations, we frequently encounter over-privileged service accounts with interactive logon enabled or multiple and unnecessary members of the Domain Admin group in Active Directory. Auditing privileged identities and removing excessive access rights and privileges is often the first step in remediating your identity platform.

Vaulting privileged identities – Sometimes, we tactically use a Privileged Access Management (PAM) tool to discover and vault privileged identities. We use the term "tactical" because PAM rollout requires careful planning and a project ranging from a few to several months. However, you can tactically deploy a PAM tool for breach remediation, discover privileged accounts across your identity platforms, and vault them before a more strategic PAM rollout and Identity and Access Management (IAM) transformation.

Multi-factor authentication (MFA) – MFA is an authentication mechanism that requires two or more verification factors before allowing access to resources. MFA will help you to enhance protection against credential theft. At a minimum, we recommend implementing an MFA requirement for administrative access to servers and other enterprise resources, applications directly exposed to the Internet, and VPN access.

Password policy – We frequently encounter organizations with weak password policies that allow a threat actor to crack a password hash and use the credentials for lateral movement. Although complex passwords alone are not an effective strategy to secure digital identities, they can still be effective when combined with other controls such as MFA and digital vaults.

In some situations where clients had poorly segmented networks, we deployed tactical jump servers to prevent a threat actor from using compromised credentials to access Domain Controllers and identity platforms. A jump server, also referred to as a jump box, is a hardened system specifically used for privileged operational tasks. This control is especially effective when combined with micro-segmentation to restrict network access to your identity platform before re-engineering your access control as part of post-breach remediation.

This list is not comprehensive. Moreover, the enhancements described are tactical only. As part of post-breach remediation, we recommend performing a security assessment of your identity platforms and Identity and Access Management (IAM) practices and creating a more comprehensive strategy to improve the security and management of your digital identities.

Enhancing Security Posture

The core tenet behind enhancing the security posture of your network is to reduce the risk of potential exploitation and unauthorized access after remediation. For this reason, ensure that you establish a Remediation Team responsible for this task as part of the Technical Team outlined in the Organize section of this book.

Attack Surface Reduction

An attack surface is the area of your technology stack exposed to potential exploitation and unauthorized access. An attack surface is present in almost every component of your technology stack, including the operating system, web servers, application servers, and databases.

We recommend focusing on reducing unnecessary attack surfaces in your environments to enhance your network's security posture. Consequently, Attack Surface Reduction (ASR) focuses on reducing those exploitation areas to prevent unauthorized access.

During our consulting engagements, we have observed that organizations experiencing significant cyber events have often struggled with basic cybersecurity hygiene. As a result, during a cyber crisis, you may have to harden systems and implement security posture enhancements as part of your remediation efforts.

Of course, it is impossible to entirely secure a network and address technical debt during a heroic effort to address a cyber crisis. Instead, we recommend leveraging battlefield-tested measures you can realistically implement as part of breach remediation. Once the enterprise recovers from the crisis, the next phase is to plan post-breach remediation.

You can enhance your network's security posture by hardening systems and adding additional layers of controls. For example, system hardening includes changing security settings and configurations, disabling unnecessary software components, and strengthening password policy. Additional control layers may include blocking outbound traffic from server environments, tactical network segmentation, and securing access to your identity platform. We discuss system hardening in the next section.

Hardening Systems

Another vital consideration is creating hardening requirements for your workstations, server platforms, and critical infrastructure services before remediation and recovery. System hardening and eradication measures are necessary to ensure the adversary cannot exploit the same vulnerabilities and system weaknesses to regain access to the compromised environment.

Hardening goes beyond patching vulnerabilities and fixing security weaknesses exploited by the threat actor. Hardening aims to reduce security risk by limiting attack vectors and eliminating potential points of exploitation and entry into a system. By removing superfluous modules, accounts, open ports, and permissions and enabling native security features, you can make it much harder for threat actors to gain unauthorized access, drop malware, and leverage the system for further activities. Furthermore, hardening can often include adding additional layers of security through controls, such as:

- Installing EDR software
- Restricting software execution on critical systems
- Improving email security
- Enhancing authentication and authorization policies
- Enforcing security policies through a Network Access Control (NAC) tool

We recommend leveraging vendor best practices and industry benchmarks to create hardening guides for the platforms mentioned earlier, including:

- Windows server platforms
- Linux systems
- Active Directory (AD) Domain Services

- Golden images deployed to end-user workstations
- Network devices, including routers, switches, and firewalls
- Virtualization software
- Cloud computing resources

The Center for Internet Security (CIS) creates excellent hardening benchmarks and tools and makes them available free of charge.

In our experience, organizations greatly benefit from hiring external consultants with breach recovery expertise to assist with hardening and restoration. Firms with a proven track record often provide hardening guides and scripts to accelerate the effort. Furthermore, external consultants can augment internal staff and provide the expertise that may not be available within the IT department.

Establishing a Quarantine Network Segment

As part of remediation and recovery planning, we recommend configuring a quarantine network segment with restricted access. Isolate the segment from other networks and have no connectivity to the Internet. One option to implement a quarantine network is to configure a restricted Virtual Local Area Network (VLAN).

You will need a quarantine network segment to securely restore systems, harden them, apply patches, and install security tools before releasing those systems to the production network. This measure is necessary to ensure you do not unintentionally restore compromised or vulnerable systems to the production network.

In fact, we often advise organizations to establish a quarantine network segment as part of day-to-day operations to facilitate secure recovery following smaller incidents that may not necessarily lead to a cyber crisis.

It is worth mentioning that with the introduction of micro-segmentation technologies, also known as workload segmentation, you can leverage software to create logically isolated "bubbles" without moving systems between network segments. A micro-segmentation technology is an excellent and flexible alternative to a quarantine network segment if you can deploy it during a breach. We encourage you to explore this topic further on your own.

Enhancing Threat Monitoring

During intrusion analysis, you mapped the attack chain, created an inventory of assets for remediation, and compiled a detailed list of IOCs. The next step is to leverage the information, enhance your threat monitoring, and gain additional visibility into system and network events. This activity will allow you to detect potential threat actor activity if they remain on the network or attempt to return after remediation. Unfortunately, organizations often experience a cyber crisis because of insufficient threat detection capabilities and the inability to detect an attack in the early phases of the attack lifecycle before it leads to a material impact. Enhancing threat monitoring and detection includes:

- Deploying an EDR tool to end-user workstations and server platforms
- Deploying temporary network sensors
- Enhancing system logging
- Creating alerts for high-fidelity indicators of compromise
- Configuring systems to send event logs to SIEM
- Creating dashboards and automated reports in tools such as SIEM

Monitoring enhancements are especially important when eradicating a nation-state and other threat actors engaging in data theft and social espionage. Dwelling on the network for as long as possible is one of their objectives, and adequate threat detection is critical when they attempt to re-compromise the network after eradication.

Eradication

You likely have spent several days or even weeks enhancing the security posture of your network, regaining control of your identity platform, and enhancing threat monitoring. Now you are ready to eradicate the threat actor. Eradication is about removing a threat actor from the compromised network and ensuring they cannot easily return. Before we dive deeper into this topic, it is worth noting that you may come across the term *eviction* in some circles. For example, the U.S. Cybersecurity and Infrastructure Security Agency (CISA) has popularized the term *eviction* in government entities.

In our experience, many practitioners misinterpret eradication as merely removing malware from compromised systems. Although a necessary component, eradication is much more than that. An effective eradication strategy encompasses mapping the attack lifecycle, identifying the techniques the threat actor leveraged in each phase, and removing the threat actor's ability to access and operate on the network based on the investigative findings.

Eradication requires careful planning and resources. Poorly planned eradication may lead to attack escalation. A threat actor, such as a ransomware operator, may employ a "smash and grab" strategy by accelerating data exfiltration and ransomware deployment activities.

It is worth emphasizing that eradication is often executed in conjunction with other activities described in this section. This statement especially applies to ransomware and other destructive cyberattacks when you perform eradication and hardening as part of system recovery. Moreover, earlier chapters discussed the importance of conducting a comprehensive intrusion analysis before executing eradication. We cannot emphasize enough how essential this prerequisite is, especially if you are dealing with a threat actor who wants to maximize their dwell time on the network.

An effective eradication methodology starts with identifying the threat actor's entry point into the network. It revolves around mapping the attack chain through intrusion analysis and then working backward to identify the vulnerabilities and weaknesses that enabled the threat actor to progress through each phase of the attack chain. For example, suppose you determined that a threat actor compromised and leveraged a privileged service account for lateral movement. In that case, the sensible step in your eradication strategy is identifying the access control weaknesses that allowed the threat actor to abuse service accounts. For example, we frequently encounter overprivileged service accounts with interactive logons that rarely have their credentials rotated. Following this logic, you can map the entire attack lifecycle and determine appropriate eradication steps for each phase.

The MITRE ATT&CK framework has become the de facto standard for developing threat models and adversarial activity mapping. For this reason, we recommend leveraging it for planning your eradication strategy. Other popular frameworks you can leverage include Lockheed Martin's Cyber Kill Chain® or Mandiant's Targeted Attack Lifecycle. The following list provides examples of common eradication strategies employed during large-scale cyber events:

- Resetting credentials for privileged and other impacted identities
- Removing any accounts created by the threat actor
- Performing an enterprise password reset
- Patching vulnerabilities
- Rebuilding compromised end-user workstations
- Rebuilding or restoring compromised server platforms
- Removing malware and attacker tools from systems that cannot be restored or rebuilt
- Blocking network traffic to C2 infrastructure associated with the attack
- Blocking IOCs such as malware hashes
- Enhancing your identity platforms to prevent credential harvesting attack techniques
- Disabling protocols not required for operations
- Hardening systems

This list is not exhaustive. Moreover, a discussion of each technique is outside the scope of this book. However, we encourage you to familiarize yourself with each technique and conduct further research. Eradication can be complex, and you may have to make tradeoffs and set expectations with business leaders, especially if it can negatively impact business operations. For example, patching systems may require downtime, and resetting credentials for service accounts will likely disrupt business applications.

Key Takeaways

- Identity compromise and privilege escalation are at the heart of many cyberattacks. Your identity platform holds the proverbial keys to the kingdom. For this reason, hardening and securing it should be the top priority as part of your remediation strategy.
- Focus on reducing the unnecessary attack surface of your environments and hardening your workstations, server platforms, and critical infrastructure services. Attack surface reduction and system hardening are necessary to ensure the adversary cannot exploit the same vulnerabilities and system weaknesses to regain access to the compromised environment.
- Configure a quarantine network segment with restricted access or leverage micro-segmentation technology to securely restore systems, harden them, apply patches, and install security tools before releasing those systems to the production network.
- Enhance your threat monitoring and gain additional visibility into system and network events to detect potential threat actor activity if they remain on the network or attempt to return after remediation.
- Identify the threat actor entry point into the network, map the attack chain, and then work backward to identify the vulnerabilities and weaknesses that enabled the threat actor to operate on the network. Then, leverage this knowledge to plan and execute eradication measures.

Chapter 28

Executing Remediation

So far, we have focused our discussion on planning and organizing remediation and recovery. It is time to put all the effort into practice and cover execution. Remediation execution can take a phased approach, or you can carry out all the activities during a pre-agreed window. Each approach has pros and cons, and you must consider the risks of alerting the threat actor and their sophistication level when making the right decision.

During complex cyber events, remediation can consist of multiple work streams that require coordination and communication. Finally, there are considerations for returning to a steady state and dealing with operational issues that might arise following remediation and recovery.

This chapter covers all the necessary considerations to successfully execute remediation activities and return operations to a steady state.

Remediation Approaches

Two approaches to remediating a compromised network are executing activities during a predefined window and taking a phased approach. Each method has pros and cons, and the breach response community continues to debate the topic. For this reason, it is worth spending a few minutes discussing it.

Whether to execute remediation during a predefined time window or take a phased remediation approach depends on the attack impact and the level of sophistication of the threat actor you are dealing with. We have identified three scenarios that warrant different remediation strategies.

- Suppose a ransomware operator exfiltrated data from your network and deployed ransomware to most endpoints on your network. In this case, the threat actor achieved their objectives and is not motivated to remain on the network, and a phased approach is appropriate after the initial containment.
- In contrast, if you respond to a corporate espionage case by a highly motivated nation-state threat actor with unlimited resources, a phased remediation approach is not likely to eradicate the threat actor from the network. Instead, the most effective strategy is to create and execute a comprehensive remediation plan during a predefined time window, typically 12 hours but no longer than 48 hours. The rationale behind this approach is to isolate the compromised environment and then execute remediation activities to prevent the threat actor from re-accessing the environment and attempting to re-establish persistent access.
- A good compromise between the opposite approaches described above is a hybrid strategy with partial isolation. Instead of isolating the entire compromised environment or network segment, you isolate compromised systems and focus on gradually regaining control of your environment by executing containment measures and remediating the network. For example, you can progressively eradicate the threat actor by resetting credentials, locking down Active Directory, and enhancing monitoring and defenses. We sometimes compare this approach to establishing a beachhead on a compromised network and expanding outwards to regain complete network control.

Orchestrating Remediation

The purpose of orchestration is to align all the remediation activities into an end-to-end process and execute them in a coordinated fashion considering their dependencies. Let's briefly examine how you can orchestrate the entire process and ensure seamless remediation execution.

Command Center

A Command Center, also known as a war room or situation room, is a physical or virtual room you designate to gather key personnel leading the remediation process. In today's hybrid environment, you may establish a physical location with video conferencing facilities for remote personnel.

The following list outlines why establishing a Command Center is so essential:

- Provide a single location for command-and-control to orchestrate the remediation effort.
- Provide a centralized place for status updates and escalating issues.
- Facilitate rapid decision-making and improved communication.

You must dedicate the Command Center to orchestration and decision-making. Focused discussions related to specific workstreams should take place in dedicated breakout rooms. Furthermore, if you have personnel supporting remediation remotely, we recommend establishing separate conference calls for virtual breakout sessions to keep the communication focused and organized.

The following list provides field-tested advice for setting up a Command Center:

- Find a room with enough space to accommodate everyone and make them comfortable.
- Set the indoor room temperature to 68-70 degrees Fahrenheit (21 degrees Celsius).
- Set up video conferencing facilities for remote personnel.
- Provide a whiteboard and pens. If you do not have a whiteboard, we recommend a flipchart instead.
- Stock the room with supplies, including snacks, refreshments, and plenty of coffee.

We also recommend establishing instant messaging channels dedicated to each workstream to facilitate asynchronous communication and information sharing. Whether your organization uses Slack, Teams, or another messaging tool, create dedicated channels or group chats for each workstream, such as network, server hardening and recovery, and security.

If legal counsel directs the response, be sure to include appropriate legal markings in each channel and follow legal guidelines to minimize the impact of e-discovery if your organization anticipates a lawsuit.

Before Execution

Suppose you are responding to a nation-state threat actor and decide that the most appropriate strategy is to execute your plan during a predefined time window. Before starting the remediation process, gather all personnel and go through the following steps:

- Walk the remediation team through the plan and explain how the process is orchestrated.
- Ensure their understanding of the importance of commitment and focus for the execution to succeed.
- Emphasize the role of the Command Center and explain the escalation process.
- Explain logistics and communications.
- Allow time for questions and clear up any last-minute ambiguity.

Communication During Execution

During the execution window, communication must be on point and precise. This is because you have a limited time to execute a complex operation, and effective communication is critical to minimizing the risk of error and getting ahead of any issues.

We recommend establishing an hourly update cadence for each workstream to report their status update to the Command Center. The updates must be concise and to the point, and take no longer than a few minutes unless issues arise that warrant further discussion.

Furthermore, suppose a workstream experiences an issue with one of its tasks. We recommend an immediate escalation to the Command Center, even if the escalation is for information only. Escalating issues when they arise will enable the Command Center to assess the situation and respond rapidly should the need arise.

As mentioned earlier in this chapter, each workstream must take full advantage of instant messaging channels and dedicated bridges to facilitate both asynchronous and synchronous communication.

Managing Issues

As part of remediation preparation, you devised the perfect plan, socialized it with vital stakeholders, obtained executive buy-in, and ensured everyone was prepared and familiar with their roles and responsibilities. Unfortunately, we have some bad news for you. Remediation execution rarely goes perfectly, even if you micromanaged the entire process and thought about every possible situation that could go wrong.

In fact, your organization likely experienced a cyber crisis because of issues such as extensive technical debt, serious security weaknesses, poor governance, or a lack of alignment between information technology and security. Unfortunately, many of those issues surface during remediation. For this reason, you are likely to experience unforeseen problems during remediation planning and execution.

For example, we regularly encounter situations where the victim organization cannot upgrade unsupported legacy systems because upgrading those systems would break application dependencies. In one example, a recent client had Windows 2003 servers running legacy Java applications supporting manufacturing processes. Upgrading those systems could bring the entire manufacturing plant to a halt. This is common in healthcare, manufacturing, or entertainment, where specialized applications are tightly coupled with a specific operating system platform, and an upgrade or patching may not be feasible.

Another common issue is an inadequate understanding of system architecture and dependencies. Modern applications are distributed and have numerous internal and external dependencies. Insufficient documentation and mapping of data flows can make remediation extremely difficult, and during the execution phase you may unintentionally break those applications. Sadly, these situations are all too common. In our experience, organizations can experience one more of the following issues during remediation:

- Minor obstacles that do not impede the remediation effort and can be addressed post-remediation. For example, during execution, you discover that vaulting a service account breaks an application. In this case, you can appropriately plan and complete the activity within the first two weeks post-remediation while implementing specific monitoring measures for potential unauthorized use of that account.
- Issues that could impede some of the remediation efforts but are not severe enough to terminate the entire execution. For example, you discover that adjusting policies in security tools breaks applications developed in-house, and those policies are essential to eradicating the threat. In this case, you may continue remediation, but you must urgently address this issue within the first few days of the post-remediation phase.
- A significant event that forces you to terminate the remediation execution. This situation could occur when a remediation activity causes an unplanned significant operational impact that can lead to loss of revenue or impact manufacturing operations. For example, we encountered this situation when an organization upgraded its Active Directory servers and experienced an issue with its domain name system (DNS), leading to operational problems. A similar issue can occur if you do not identify system dependencies and upgrading a platform breaks applications that rely on older, unsupported Application Programming Interfaces (API).

Suppose you encounter the worst-case scenario. The best approach could be to terminate the remediation execution and move to a phased remediation approach, as described earlier in this chapter. In such a case, you must significantly enhance threat monitoring and gradually regain control of your environment by incrementally employing the techniques described in this book.

Returning to a Steady State

A crisis does not end with breach remediation. Organizations experiencing significant cyber breaches have dealt with the consequences for months or even years to come. This section briefly describes how to return to a steady state and minimize the risk of the threat actor re-compromising the network. In the next chapter, we describe post-crisis activities.

Employee Communications

We have emphasized the importance of internal and external communications throughout this book. As mentioned, communications are required when your organization experiences an event that disrupts business operations or remediates a cyberattack that causes outages.

Internal and applicable external communications are also required post-remediation, once you restore systems to an operational state and are ready to resume business operations. For this reason, communicate to employees when they can return to their day-to-day duties and what to expect. For example, suppose you forced a password reset for all users across your domains. The communication should include a message that users will be prompted to change their password when they log into the network. Furthermore, as previously discussed, ensure the message is consistent with your overall communication strategy. For example, if the breach is not public knowledge, avoid mentioning anything related to cybersecurity. We often recommend using generic terms instead. For example, you can say that "information technology resolved a network issue and restored systems to an operational state."

Monitoring for Threat Actor Activity

As part of the investigation and remediation, you created custom alerts, dashboards, and detection rules for the unauthorized use of privileged accounts. However, the monitoring does not end there. For example, suppose you responded to a sophisticated and motivated threat. The threat actor will likely attempt to return to the network. We have witnessed situations where a threat actor re-compromised the network within one week after eradication to continue their operations.

As part of the post-remediation effort, we strongly recommend putting your threat monitoring team on heightened vigilance for at least several weeks. Ensure they pay particular attention to all the alerts and dashboards mentioned in the previous chapters. This approach will enable early detection and containment before the threat actor escalates privileges and moves laterally again. Even if it feels at times like whack-a-mole, this effort will pay off by minimizing the risk of another cyber crisis.

Resolving Operational Issues

After experiencing a disruptive business event that requires you to recover multiple systems, you will likely experience operational issues. For example, during recovery, you may only have the time to perform basic functional and integration testing instead of unit, integration, and end-to-end tests, before moving systems back to production. As you try to recover as many systems as possible within a limited time, you will need a mechanism to deal with post-recovery problems. Recovery is not a binary activity. For example, organizations that experienced a highly disruptive event gradually restore business operations instead of waiting until all systems are fully operational before moving them back to production.

To effectively address the issues described above, we recommend establishing a temporary IT incident management process focused on prioritizing high-priority incidents. This approach is vital because most of your team is dedicated to recovering the remaining systems, and you will have limited resources.

We recognize that this approach will likely make many users or business leaders dissatisfied. However, it is important to emphasize that less pressing issues have to wait during a crisis. Furthermore, consider proactively communicating with users regarding problems, setting their expectations, and arming the Service Desk with the necessary information and instructions to manage their expectations.

Key Takeaways

- Determine whether you will execute remediation during a predefined window or if a phased approach is more appropriate for your situation.
- Set up a Command Center to execute the remediation effort. Also, establish separate conference calls for virtual breakout sessions and instant messaging channels for asynchronous communication.
- Organize similar functional tasks into workstreams and ensure coordination and communication between those workstreams.
- Ensure all personnel understand the remediation plan and know their roles and responsibilities.
- Be prepared to manage unforeseen issues during remediation that may arise from technical debt, obscure configurations, and system complexity.
- As you return to a steady state, send out internal and external communication (as required), monitor for threat actor activities, and determine how to manage operational issues arising from recovery and remediation.

Chapter 29

Recovering Operations

During a large-scale cyber event, recovery is often a complex and lengthy process that can take up to several weeks before your organization fully returns to a steady state. In the worst-case scenario, recovery activities can drag on for months. This experience especially applies to organizations with significant technical debt, poor asset management practices, and insufficient understanding and documentation of technologies and data supporting business processes.

In the Organize section of this book, we discussed the need to establish a Minimum Viable Company and its importance for a cyber recovery strategy. This chapter discusses the technical considerations when recovering systems following a cyberattack.

On-Premises vs. Public Cloud Recovery

Before diving into the technical details of recovery, it is worth discussing considerations for recovering systems and applications hosted in on-premises data centers versus those hosted in a public cloud. We assume you have a fundamental understanding of cloud computing concepts. If some of the terms we use below sound esoteric to you, we encourage you to explore them outside the scope of this book.

On-Premises Considerations

On-premises, you deal with wires, hardware platforms, virtualization, operating systems, middleware, applications, and data. For this reason, your recovery strategy must consider the entire technology stack, data, and dependencies between resources. Furthermore, many organizations still run legacy applications hosted on unsupported software platforms. This introduces additional complexity and considerations when rebuilding the entire system or system components from scratch. This chapter assumes you will likely need to restore or rebuild an entire technology stack.

Public Cloud Considerations

Recovery in the cloud depends on your cloud consumption model, the resiliency architecture of your applications, and the backup options your public cloud vendor provides. For example, suppose you leverage Infrastructure-as-a-Service (IaaS) to host your application. Apart from hardware and virtualization, your recovery strategy must include the entire technology stack and data, as in the case of on-premises systems. The only difference may be the cloud capabilities and tools necessary to aid recovery.

However, suppose your organization leverages a cloud-native approach for system development underpinned by a microservices architecture. In that case, your exposure to cyberattacks and recovery considerations will differ from those for on-premises environments.

Most destructive attacks that require recovery involve malware and system-level access. However, according to the shared responsibility model, when you leverage the Platform-as-a-Service (PaaS) and Software-as-a-Service (SaaS) consumption models, the infrastructure resources are abstracted away, and the cloud vendor is responsible for the security of the operating system. This approach removes a significant portion of your attack surface and the technology you must secure.

Furthermore, cloud vendors typically architect managed services for resiliency and durability, making a recovery more straightforward in the cloud. We encourage you to explore resiliency options and reference architectures for the major public cloud vendors to gain a more in-depth understanding of this topic. For example, Amazon Web Services (AWS) created the Well-Architected Framework that encompasses a set of best practices to help their clients design reliable and secure cloud-based systems using their platform.[16]

In our experience, many cyberattacks against cloud-native applications are identity-based or involve resource misconfigurations, often leading to data exposure or resource abuse. For this reason, traditional recovery may not be required. However, suppose you must recover resources due to data and system corruption. In that case, the recovery process typically involves rebuilding an application from a template or restoring it from a snapshot. For example, we encountered one case where a junior developer mistakenly deleted an e-commerce website hosted in a public cloud, and it took the organization less than 30 minutes to restore the website following the event. The support personnel spent most of that time diagnosing the issue and engaging a vendor. Restoring the application from a snapshot only took several minutes.

Ransomware and the Cloud

The discussion on cloud and recovery would not be complete without covering ransomware. Our clients frequently ask us how this threat applies to workloads hosted in a public cloud.

As we described earlier, ransomware is just another native software application that executes on a specific platform. A native application is a software program that runs on a particular operating system such as Microsoft Windows. This means a threat actor must have access to an operating system to deploy and execute ransomware.

In the shared responsibility model, ransomware is a concern if you deploy virtual machines leveraging the IaaS model and are responsible for their security. However, if you build cloud-native applications and leverage managed services for your workloads, the cloud vendor is responsible for the security of the underlying infrastructure. As a result, ransomware and other threats that require

[16] Amazon Web Services, AWS Well-Architected Framework, published October 3, 2023, available at https://docs.aws.amazon.com/wellarchitected/latest/framework/welcome.html.

system-level access to your resources are not part of your threat model because the underlying infrastructure is abstracted away and you have no system-level access.

This model is arguably more effective from a security standpoint because cloud vendors are motivated and incentivized to secure their cloud. Moreover, they often have top engineering and security talent that non-security organizations find challenging to hire and retain.

Restore versus Rebuild

One of the first considerations during cyber recovery is whether to restore compromised systems from backup or rebuild them from scratch. Consequently, you must carefully plan recovery to maximize time and minimize the risk of recovering your environment to an insecure state. In the following paragraphs, we discuss how you can decide what systems you can restore versus those you must rebuild.

Restoring Systems

System restoration is an ideal recovery strategy during a destructive cyberattack. This option can also minimize downtime during non-destructive attacks when you must remediate compromised systems as part of your eradication strategy.

Your ability to restore systems depends on several factors, including:

- How long the threat actor dwelled on the network. The farther back in time you must go, the lower the chances of having a last known good backup; that is, system backup taken before the compromise. For example, rebuilding systems from scratch is a more secure option if you retain virtual machine snapshots for two weeks, but the initial compromise occurred three weeks ago.

- The types of systems and backup technologies employed within your organization. For example, restoring physical servers is typically more challenging than restoring virtual machine snapshots.

- Whether backups are available and intact. For example, a threat actor can delete the backup data before deploying ransomware if your backup servers are on the same domain as the servers you back up. In other cases, backup data might be corrupted as part of the backup or replication process without the victim organization's knowledge. This happens when backups are not regularly validated, and restoration procedures aren't tested.

Note that we are talking about restoring systems supporting applications and enterprise services, not data handled by those systems. We address restoring data later in this chapter.

Let's briefly discuss the factors above to ensure you can make an informed decision regarding restoration.

As part of identifying remediation prerequisites, we emphasized the importance of a comprehensive investigation. One of the reasons why an investigation is so essential is to determine when the threat actor compromised the first system, also referred to as Patient 0. This initial access is crucial because it allows you to establish a recovery point for system restoration. We typically recommend going back five days before the access as a precautionary measure.

The breach timeline can extend from days to weeks, depending on the threat actor you are dealing with and their objective. For example, nation-state actors whose primary objective is corporate espionage often dwell on networks for months or even years in extreme cases before detection. When you respond to such a case, it is doubtful you can restore systems to a secure state. Therefore, your safest strategy is to entirely rebuild the compromised environment to ensure you eradicate the threat actor's access.

In contrast, ransomware and cybercriminals have a much shorter dwell time. For example, a typical ransomware operator conducts their attack within days up to three weeks, depending on how strong your defenses are. If you regularly backup systems and your backup retention policy is sufficient, you can restore systems based on the recovery point established during forensic analysis.

Rebuilding Systems

There are situations where you cannot restore systems from backup. In our experience, the following factors require rebuilding a system:

- Forensic analysts cannot identify the Patient 0 system and establish when and how the initial unauthorized access to the network occurred. This situation frequently happens when the victim organization does not collect sufficient log data to enable historical intrusion analysis.

- Your organization does not back up systems. For example, a compromised system is deployed in a development or test environment and does not require regular backup.

- Following the previous point, the impacted systems are not business-critical. Note that due to cost constraints, some organizations choose to backup only systems supporting business-critical processes. If there is no backup available, the only way to restore a system is to rebuild it.

- The threat actor has dwelled on the network for several months or even longer. In this case, your backup retention policy may not be sufficient to restore your environment to a secure state.

When any of the situations described above occurs, you may have no choice but to rebuild the systems in the scope of recovery. For this reason, it is essential that your organization documents system architecture down to a component level, including system dependencies and interfaces to other internal and external systems for all production systems.

In our experience, organizations with poor governance practices and inadequate disaster recovery practices learn the hard way during a cyber crisis why documenting system architecture is so critical. For example, we have witnessed situations where systems administrators rebuilt complex distributed systems through trial and error over several days or even weeks instead of a few hours. This painful and heroic effort was required because the engineers who built the system did not create system architecture documentation before leaving the organization.

As part of the system rebuild, we frequently recommend upgrading legacy technologies to supported and more secure versions. This point is relevant to situations where upgrading a specific technology may be required as part of the eradication strategy. However, there are situations where an application relies on a legacy protocol, and migrating to a modern protocol cannot be accomplished within several days. In such cases, we recommend taking a pragmatic approach and focusing on what you can achieve during breach remediation. You must address the remaining items through dedicated projects during post-breach remediation.

Another remediation consideration is end-user computing. Threat actors often compromise a user and plant malware on a workstation before pivoting to server environments. As a result, we recommend re-imaging the compromised user workstations as part of your remediation strategy to minimize the risk of a residual backdoor and other malware that would allow the threat actor to return to the compromised network. This strategy is appropriate if your end-user computing support group closely works with security analysts to acquire and preserve forensic data from the compromised hosts before re-imaging occurs.

Cleaning Up Compromised Systems

There are situations where neither restoring nor rebuilding a system is an option. For example, suppose a compromised system supports a core business function, and any downtime would lead to a loss of revenue or halt a manufacturing operation. In such situations, the only option may be to clean up and harden the system in an operational state.

While this approach has high risk, it may be necessary. For instance, attack residues, such as backdoor malware and undetected persistence mechanisms, can allow the threat actor to re-compromise the system later. However, we also recognize that some situations may not be black or white. In cases like the one we have just described, the business must make a risk-based decision regarding remediation.

As part of a rapid risk assessment, you will have to clearly articulate the pros and cons of remediating a system in an operational state and clearly outline the risk to enable business leaders to make an informed decision.

If you choose this approach, create a plan for how the systems will be hardened, including any eradication measures. Examples include:

- Installing an EDR tool
- Patching vulnerabilities
- Hardening system configurations
- Locking down access control
- Other necessary controls

Moreover, we also recommend heightened monitoring for such systems for several weeks to ensure you can detect any attempts to re-compromise the system. We described enhancing security and eradication in the previous chapter.

Restoring Data

Up to this point, we have discussed system recovery. However, recovering systems is not enough to resume business operations. You also must restore the data those systems handle. This point is essential because data often resides on a separate disk volume or an external data store, depending on how the system has been architected.

Data can reside on different storage media, including local disk volumes, physical file shares, Network Attached Storage (NAS), Storage Area Networks (SAN), and object stores hosted in a public cloud. Moreover, data can be represented in numerous formats, such as tables stored in relational databases and non-relational models leveraging key-value pairs. This point is important because, in some situations, you will have to consider application state and data consistency during recovery. For example, considerations like this arise when you are recovering an application that processes financial transactions or other data that must be highly accurate.

Once you have restored and hardened a system, the next step is to restore the corresponding data. As part of this process, we recommend validating data integrity. For example, suppose your organization employs near real-time data replication from the primary site to a secondary location and you experience a ransomware attack. In that case, your backup software likely replicated some corrupted data to the backup before you contained the attack. For this reason, you must ensure you only restore the last known good copy and validate that the data is intact before releasing the system into production.

Dealing with Distributed Applications

Most modern systems are distributed and employ various mechanisms to maintain a state. This is a vital consideration in cyber recovery. A distributed system consists of multiple components communicating over a network through Application Programming Interface (API) calls. Those components often comprise self-contained and loosely coupled applications that run independently and are usually written in different programming languages. We refer to this realm as microservices or Service Oriented Architecture (SOA). In contrast, a monolithic system is a system that handles multiple tasks through tightly coupled functions contained in a single software package, even if the software is deployed to multiple servers and the load is balanced between those servers. In other words, a single system contains the user interface, application business logic, data, and other system components.

State refers to the current status of your system. A stateful application maintains information or specific data related to your past transactions, such as items in the shopping cart, your user profile, or the balance on your bank account. On the other hand, a stateless application does not store any data about your past transaction. So, for example, if your session gets interrupted, it is not a big deal. You can start over.

The considerations above are critical to cyber recovery because system-centered recovery approaches do not work well for distributed systems, especially if you must consider transaction state. Consequently, when recovering a distributed application, consider the following requirements:

- Understand the workflow and dependencies between microservices, including their reliance on enterprise services such as your identity platform and DNS.
- Consider data workflows between the various microservices and the role of each service in the workflows. Some microservices are core to the system, whereas others may provide additional functionality, such as a geolocation lookup. Your users can likely live without it for several days!
- Implement observability for the system. Before processing transactions, you must ensure all the interfaces between microservices re-connect and re-authenticate. Without observability, you are not likely to determine if you successfully recovered a distributed system.
- Reconcile transactions to ensure data consistency. It is likely that some transactions fail or do not complete at the time of interruption. For example, a payment service may process your credit card transaction, but the service responsible for shipping a product may not be available. In this case, you will likely have to deal with many angry customers. You get the idea!

The considerations outlined above will enable you to get the recovery of distributed systems on the right foot and prevent unwanted surprises as your return to an operational state.

Putting It All Together – A High-Level System Recovery Approach

Your remediation and recovery strategy will likely include a combination of system restoration and rebuilding. In extreme cases, you may have to rebuild an entire network, such as in the case of the 2014 Sony Pictures Entertainment attack, where a group calling itself the Guardians of Peace destroyed systems and stole large quantities of personal and commercial data. At the other end of the spectrum, your recovery strategy may be restoring the impacted system from a snapshot. The following steps outline a generic procedure to recover systems to an operational state following a cyberattack:

- Assess the damage and determine the scope and extent of the compromise. As part of this step, determine what systems require restoration versus which you must rebuild.
- Determine a recovery point based on the earliest evidence of compromise.
- Review system architecture documentation and understand dependencies. This understanding is essential to recover system components in the dependency order and re-connect interfaces to internal and external applications.
- Establish a system component recovery order based on the system architecture and estimate the time it will take to recover each component.
- Determine the required hardening and eradication measures to implement in the recovery process.
- Restore or rebuild system components one at a time in the quarantine network, patch vulnerabilities, install security tools, and apply hardening configurations.
- Restore and validate data required by the system.
- Perform smoke testing and release the system to production. A smoke test validates critical functionality and stability of a system before more comprehensive testing is performed.
- Include the system in the scope of enhanced monitoring—this applies both to threat monitoring and observability to detect stability issues.

Key Takeaways

- When recovering your environments, focus on an end-to-end business process that considers dependencies between applications, infrastructure, and data supporting that process.

- Establish a Recovery Point (RP) based on the earliest evidence of compromise and determine whether a system should be restored or rebuilt.
- Restore and harden systems in a quarantine VLAN before releasing them back into production to avoid re-compromise.
- If restoration or rebuilding is not an option due to system uptime requirements, clearly outline the risk of remediating a system in an operational state to enable business leaders to make an informed decision.
- When recovering a distributed system, consider its state, interfaces between microservices, data persistence, transaction workflow, and component dependency.

Chapter 30

Defining Post-Breach Remediation

Responding to a cyber crisis does not end with breach remediation. You may be at a point when the dust has settled, and you have returned operations to a steady state. However, this is not the end of the crisis response process. Before you move on and the crisis becomes a thing of the past, you must conduct post-crisis activities, draft an improvement plan, and deliver post-breach remediation projects to minimize the risk of a similar event happening in the future. You may also consider disclosure obligations and potential litigation.

This chapter discusses post-crisis activities. We share practical advice on performing a root cause analysis, identifying response lessons learned, and ensuring you address weaknesses that contributed to the crisis in the first place.

Root Cause Analysis

Root cause analysis systematically discovers security weaknesses and systemic problems that directly and indirectly contributed to a crisis. In our experience, a single vulnerability or deficiency rarely leads to a crisis. Instead, it is often a combination of factors, such as insufficient detection mechanisms, poor governance and security practices, and inadequate threat detection and response capabilities, among other factors. A systematic and thorough root cause analysis will enable you to identify those factors. The outcome will then form the basis for drafting a post-breach plan.

We cannot emphasize enough the importance of conducting a root cause analysis. We regularly assist organizations believing that a cyber crisis is a one-off event that is unlikely to happen again. However, suppose your enterprise does not identify and address the security deficiencies and deeper organizational problems that contributed to the crisis. It is just a matter of time before you may experience a significant event again. We have witnessed this situation numerous times. For example, some clients chose not to implement our recommendations following a crisis only to call us within six months because another threat actor exploited the security weaknesses we recommended they remediate.

Furthermore, we have observed that organizations sometimes focus on technology and point to technical deficiencies and security control failures when identifying the factors that led to a breach. However, in our experience, technical deficiencies are often symptoms of deeper systemic issues, such as inadequate risk management practices, governance issues, corporate politics, and inability to attract and retain skilled professionals. As we mentioned before, typically it is a combination of factors compounded over time that leads to a crisis.

The following paragraphs discuss the Five Whys analysis method. We only cover the fundamentals here and encourage you to research this topic. However, we wanted to briefly mention the method because it can be extremely beneficial when executed correctly.

Five Whys Method

Five Whys is a simple and effective method to help you find the underlying causes that directly and indirectly contributed to the crisis. This method enables you to establish a cause-and-effect relationship between events and their underlying causes. The idea behind this method is simple. First, define a problem and then ask a series of consecutive why questions.

You can start with the question of why your organization experienced a crisis. However, we also recommend pivoting around specific areas. For example, you can leverage each of the following questions for separate questioning threads:

- Why did the threat actor gain access to our network?
- Why did our controls not prevent the initial compromise?

- Why did we not detect the threat actor activity after the initial compromise?
- Why did we not have appropriate telemetry and detective controls?
- Why was our response disorganized during the first two to three days?

Another approach is to focus on the attack lifecycle. For example, you can focus on attack phases executed by the threat actor if you are particularly interested in security weaknesses and vulnerabilities.

- Why did the threat actor gain access to our network?
- Why was the threat actor able to move laterally within our environment without detection?
- Why was the threat actor able to escalate privileges?
- Why was the threat actor able to deploy malware to systems?
- Why was the threat actor able to access and exfiltrate our data?

When you start asking the why question, you initially get technical answers. However, the further you progress through the process, the more likely it is that you will uncover deeper governance and organizational issues.

The recommended approach is to follow five times with the question "why?" However, this is not a hard and fast rule. For example, suppose that five iterations of the why question doesn't reveal the root cause. In such a situation, asking it seven or even eight times may be necessary and is acceptable. Asking the question is simple, but answering it well requires some thought and systematic thinking.

Lessons Learned

Crises vary in scope and complexity, and the threat landscape continuously evolves. For this reason, it is not feasible to develop a perfect crisis response plan in a single iteration and rest on your laurels. Instead, response planning is a continuous journey. Furthermore, a good process is just a part of the story. Effective crisis response requires collaboration and trust between the stakeholders involved in the process and a sound judgment of crisis characteristics. Developing those abilities can take months or even years in larger organizations.

While a root cause analysis enables you to establish the underlying causes that contributed to a cyber crisis, a lessons-learned process is essential to improving the crisis response plan and capabilities. Capturing lessons learned will allow your organization to learn from failures, reflect on positive aspects of the response, and reinforce effective behavior. For example, we have assisted the same clients with responding to numerous cyber events over several years. Unfortunately, some of those clients have experienced the same response challenges because they did not capture and implement lessons learned, or their organizational culture and misalignment between different functions made this task difficult to achieve.

You can identify lessons learned at any point in the crisis response process, and the personnel responsible for crisis coordination should document their observations. However, we encourage you to commence formal evaluation after returning to a steady state to ensure you remain focused on the response activities.

Before diving into practical guidance on identifying lessons learned, it is worth emphasizing that inviting stakeholders from different functional areas to the lessons learned meeting is beneficial. Moreover, our experience tells us that conducting two separate sessions, one for the Technical Team and one for the Business Team, is more effective in avoiding confusion among the participants and facilitating focused discussions. We recommend correlating findings across the meetings and distilling key observations highlighting both efforts' collective wisdom. The Crisis Manager is best positioned to participate in both meetings and perform this task.

The Lessons Learned Lifecycle

We created the following lessons learned lifecycle to allow our clients to effectively evaluate their response to a crisis, identify lessons learned, and implement specific improvements to the process.

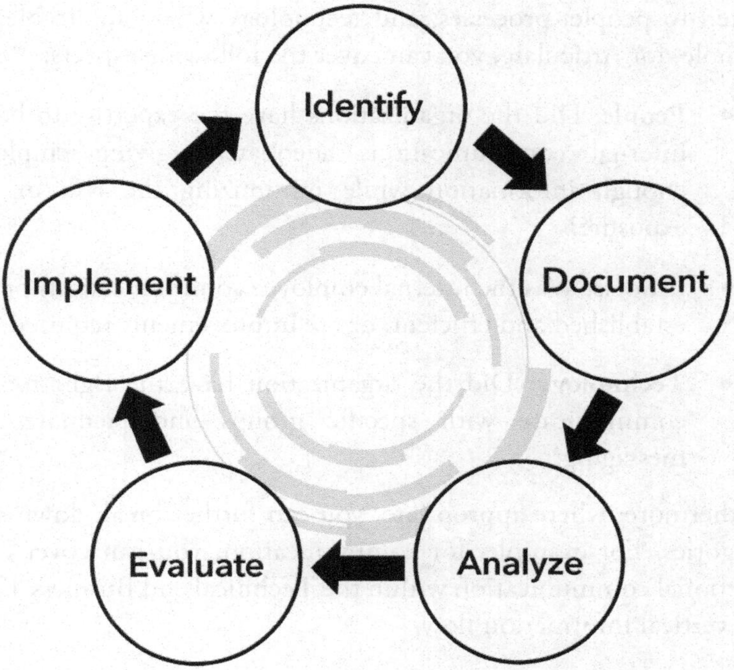

Figure 6 – Lessons Learned Lifecycle

The following list provides a brief description of each phase:

- **Identify** – Evaluate response activities to identify gaps and problematic areas.
- **Document** – Document gaps and problematic areas as part of the meeting.
- **Analyze** – Analyze each of the problematic areas and determine potential solutions.
- **Evaluate** – Evaluate the feasibility of each solution from technical and business perspectives.
- **Implement** – Implement the solutions.

For each phase of the SONAR framework, discuss information related to people, processes, and technology where applicable. For example, for Articulate, you can cover the following aspects:

- **People**: Did the organizations have the expertise to handle internal communications adequately, giving employees enough information while minimizing the risk of legal exposure?
- **Process**: Was the internal employee communications process established and efficient, or are improvements required?
- **Technology**: Did the organization have the right tools to communicate with specific groups and facilitate mass messaging?

Furthermore, where appropriate, you can further break down some categories. For example, for communication, you can cover cross-functional communication within the Technical and Business Teams and vertical information flow.

For each category, you need to ask the following questions:

- What worked well or positively contributed to the response?
- What went wrong or impeded the response?
- What must we improve to address shortcomings and make the process more efficient?

We recommend sharing this information before a formal lessons-learned process to make the meeting more efficient. In our experience, either of the following approaches can work:

- Send out a survey to the participants asking what worked during the response, what roadblocks they encountered, and what the organization could do to address the shortcomings. This approach will require some extra work. However, the extra effort will help you identify lessons learned and improvement opportunities before a formal meeting. Furthermore, you can prepare specific talking points for the meeting based on the outcome of the survey.

- Send out an agenda to the participants before the meeting outlining the response areas you want to discuss and ask the participants to come prepared for the meeting. This approach requires less effort from you. However, in our experience, many participants arrive unprepared for the meeting, and some might go off on a tangent and make it challenging to stay on track.

As with the root cause analysis, different approaches to identifying lessons learned exist. Regardless of the chosen method, preparation is vital to this process. The first step is to determine the response aspects you want to evaluate. We recommend starting with each phase of the SONAR framework: Stabilize, Organize, Negotiate, Articulate, and Remediate.

Conducting Effective Meetings

We have witnessed numerous root cause analyses and lessons-learned meetings that felt more like a checkmark in a process list and did not lead to tangible results and improvement. For example, we encountered an organization where the Security and IT organizations had an adversarial relationship, and the root cause analysis served a political purpose instead of leading to better security and operations.

Earlier sections provided practical guidance to identify the root causes of a crisis and lessons learned from the response. This brief section describes conducting an effective meeting to ensure fruitful outcomes.

Before the Meeting

Preparation is king. Arguably, the outcome will be proportionate to the quality of your preparation. Consider the following activities:

- **Identify attendees** – We recommend identifying stakeholders representing key business and technical areas. Where possible, keep the attendees to no more than fifteen. If this is impossible, consider scheduling separate meetings for technical and business teams or specific areas within those domains. This approach is necessary to keep the discussion focused and elicit responses from all the attendees.

- **Prepare a meeting plan** – Plan the meeting, including its structure and the content you want to cover. For example, for a root cause analysis meeting, establish the analysis method you will use and break down the content into meaningful sections such as attack phases. For a lessons-learned meeting, identify the process areas you want to evaluate.
- **Send out an agenda** – Send out an agenda for the meeting and articulate to the participants what you expect from them regarding meeting preparation and input. Moreover, as discussed in the previous section, you can send out a questionnaire or ask the participants to document their observations before the meeting.
- **Prepare a template** – Prepare templates for documenting a root cause analysis and lessons learned. A template will allow you to keep your notes organized and stay on track.
- **Plan logistics** – Be sure to book a conference room with enough space for everyone and send out a link to video conferencing for those who will join virtually. Where possible, we strongly recommend encouraging participants to participate in person. In our experience, face-to-face interaction often leads to more frank conversations and better outcomes.

During the Meeting

Now it is time to conduct the meeting. The following list provides considerations to ensure the session is fruitful and leads to positive outcomes:

- **Stick to the agenda** – Last-minute changes, unless necessary, can derail the meeting and lead to unproductive discussions. In our experience, if you have identified the essential participants and planned the meeting well in advance, you will likely not need last-minute changes to the agenda.

- **Keep the discussion focused** – Some people might change topics or focus on issues unrelated to the discussion. Acknowledging those issues and then bringing the conversation back on track is crucial. Also, ask participants not to use mobile phones, answer emails, or engage in other distractions that can be detrimental to the meeting.

- **Identify quiet participants** – Some participants may be introverted or feel uncomfortable speaking in front of others. However, their observations and contributions are likely as valuable as those who speak more openly. For this reason, directly ask quiet people for their comments and be sure to gather many different perspectives during the discussion.

- **Identify a lead and a note-taker** – Ensure only one person leads the discussion according to the agenda. Moreover, designate a note-taker. This approach will help you remain focused and organized.

- **Start on a positive note** – Start by thanking everyone for their effort to respond to the crisis and willingness to participate in the meeting. Additionally, if you are conducting a lessons-learned meeting, discuss what worked during the response. This approach will create a more positive and friendly atmosphere.

- **Banish blame** – Be sure to focus the discussion on identifying root causes and lessons learned instead of looking for a scapegoat for the crisis. Blame and finger-pointing will not help your organization to minimize the risk of similar events in the future. Instead, focus on what the organization must do to improve capabilities and respond to future events more effectively.

After the Meeting

In the Organize section of this book, we briefly mentioned post-breach remediation to address the security weaknesses you cannot fix quickly. This is where the post-breach remediation begins. Once you have determined the root causes of the crises and identified lessons learned following the response, it is time to create a plan to address the findings.

Below, we briefly describe the immediate actions following lessons learned and root cause analysis meetings. In the next section, we expand on the items you cannot address as part of day-to-day operations.

- **Document findings** – After the meeting, you need to clean up, organize, and save your notes to a file repository for future use and reference. A folder in a team file share or cloud-based storage facility is a good place to store your notes. You will likely need to include a summary of the root cause analysis and lessons learned in your final response report.

- **Assign owners to action items** – During the meeting, you identified action items and assigned owners to some of the action items. At this point, ensure every action item has a specific owner. Moreover, ensure the owners know the assignment and are comfortable with the action items. Without accountability, there is no improvement.

- **Disseminate the notes** – Disseminate the notes and communicate the next steps to all participants. We recommend assigning a specific person to follow up on the action items regularly. If you roll any identified improvements into a larger plan, as discussed later, a dedicated project manager will likely be responsible for tracking the implementation status.

Implementing Lessons Learned

After identifying lessons learned, the first step is to document them, determine specific improvements, and assign owners to action items. Create a plan, assign an owner, and track the status of immediate action items until you complete them. For example, suppose you must update a communications plan and the stakeholder list within your crisis response plan. This change is straightforward, and the plan owner or the custodian can make them as part of day-to-day operations.

In our experience, you can implement most lessons learned during day-to-day operations. However, there are circumstances where addressing specific findings may require resources beyond those allocated to day-to-day operations, including a budget, additional tools, or external expertise. For example, suppose your organization has immature crisis response capabilities, and a significant event surprises the organization. In such a case, a lesson learned may be to develop a crisis response capability, identify a cross-functional team, create a plan, procure the necessary technology, and train crucial personnel. To establish this capability, you must build a business case, gain leadership's support, and create a project with dedicated funding.

If you identify such significant lessons learned, they might be a root cause instead of a lesson learned. For example, maybe your organization identified a security event indicative of a threat actor on the network. However, because the organization did not respond adequately, the event progressed into a full-blown crisis within days or a few weeks. We discuss addressing more significant issues in the next section.

Post-Breach Remediation

After establishing the root causes of the crisis and identifying lessons learned, the next step is to focus on post-breach remediation and implement concrete measures to minimize the risk of similar events occurring in the future. This section describes a risk assessment and quantification and the creation of a remediation plan.

Risk Assessment

Winston Churchill is credited with saying, "Never let a good crisis go to waste." We have worked with numerous security leaders struggling to get funding to enhance their security programs until their organizations experienced an event that significantly impacted their operations or exposed them from a legal perspective.

In our experience, when an enterprise experiences a cyber crisis for the first time, the board of directors asks the following questions:

- Why did it happen?
- What must we do to prevent something similar in the future?
- How much money is it going to cost us?

The board often makes the necessary funding available to start post-breach remediation as long as the story and your business case are sound. However, even with all the budget you always wished for, you cannot boil the ocean and must prioritize remediation initiatives. Moreover, if your organization has mature risk management practices, you can align initiatives with wider risks the organization tries to mitigate.

This section is not about how to conduct a risk assessment. Many excellent resources are available to security professionals, including NIST Risk Management Framework[17] and ISO 31000:2018.[18] However, for this conversation, it is worth noting that a risk assessment typically includes the phases outlined below.

1. **Risk identification** – A breach root cause analysis should help you identify key risks that manifested during the crisis. However, you may also consider other known risks that did not directly contribute to the crisis.

---

[17] National Institute of Technology, Compter Security Resource Center, special publication NIST SP 800-37 Rev. 2, available here: https://csrc.nist.gov/pubs/sp/800/37/r2/final.

[18] International Organization for Standardization, ISO 31000 Risk Management, available here: https://www.iso.org/iso-31000-risk-management.html/.

2. **Risk analysis** – A root cause analysis is one of the techniques used to analyze risk following a crisis. The idea is simple. You must determine a corresponding risk, likelihood, and impact for each identified weakness and derive an overall risk score. This information will be critical to prioritizing post-breach remediation initiatives.
3. **Risk evaluation** – determining how to approach the risk. You can accept it, transfer it to another party through outsourcing, or try to mitigate it.

We strongly recommend leveraging threat intelligence as a basis for your risk assessment. As part of the assessment process, you must understand how threat actors organize their capabilities, conduct their operations, and execute their attacks from the initial compromise to data theft and malware deployment. This knowledge allows you to select and deploy the necessary controls at the system, business process, and organizational levels. Understanding risks and deploying controls that mitigate them is challenging without understanding threats. In addition, the findings uncovered during the intrusion analysis should be a critical input into the assessment.

Sadly, in our experience, many organizations still take a checklist approach to a risk assessment, even following a breach. Unfortunately, this approach misses a critical component in the risk management process: threats. Putting compliance and checklists before threat intelligence is the proverbial cart before the horse. For this reason, the investigative findings and threat intelligence should be crucial inputs into the risk assessment process.

A discussion of specific risk analysis techniques is beyond the scope of this book. However, we strongly recommend exploring this topic if you want to build a strong case for post-breach remediation leading to a positive risk reduction.

Risk Quantification

One topic we feel strongly about is risk analysis. The findings uncovered during the risk identification phase are often technical and sound cryptic to business stakeholders. Consequently, we needed the means to translate them into something business leaders can understand and leverage to make meaningful decisions regarding investments in post-breach remediation.

We advocate for risk quantification to translate technical and security jargon into quantifiable terms that executives can understand. One method to achieve this objective is to leverage Factor Analysis of Information Risk (FAIR), first mentioned in Chapter 2. The FAIR analysis framework breaks down risk into factors you can quantify (in counts, percentages, or dollar figures) to estimate the probable frequency and magnitude of loss associated with a specific event. In other words, FAIR can help you speak dollars and cents to the business instead of the traditional low, medium, and high-risk rating system.

Furthermore, the FAIR methodology considers risk as an uncertain event and focuses on what is probable instead of theoretical risks that may not even apply to your organization. When combined with threat intelligence and your intrusion findings, risk quantification is a powerful technique to predict the probable loss, frequency, and magnitude of events resulting from security weaknesses.

Once you have identified risks and quantified their potential loss, frequency, and magnitude, it is time to decide how to address them. In practical terms, this means deciding on solutions to mitigate the risks, creating projects, procuring services and technology, and implementing them.

Prioritizing Solutions

Not all security weaknesses are equal. Some can be relatively easy to address, while others require substantial funding and dedicated projects. Therefore, after identifying the root causes that led to the crisis and improvements to the response process, we recommend classifying improvement initiatives into the following categories:

- **Immediate** – items you can implement as part of day-to-day operations, usually within several weeks from the crisis closure. Also, immediate action items typically do not require additional funding or dedicated projects.

- **Tactical** – items that fulfill a specific security objective but do not significantly affect the strategic direction of your cybersecurity program. Suppose you discovered significant gaps around access control during the crisis response. Consequently, you create a project to implement a Privileged Access Management (PAM) solution and lock down Active Directory. Implementing tactical items requires funding and a dedicated project that may take several months.

- **Strategic** – items that change the overall direction of your cybersecurity program or require extensive implementation effort beyond tactical objectives. Examples of strategic items include outsourcing portions of your cybersecurity program to an external vendor, creating a project to segment a large corporate network, and building an entirely new function within the program. Implementing strategic action items requires substantial funding and projects that may last longer than six months.

As in the case of implementing lessons learned, we recommend creating a plan for immediate actions, assigning an owner, and implementing the plan as part of day-to-day operations. However, tactical and strategic remediation initiatives will require a business case and dedicated projects. This is why quantifying risk in financial terms is so crucial.

Creating a Remediation Plan

At this point in the book, you have probably identified and prioritized solutions to mitigate the issues identified during the root cause analysis and risk quantification. The next step is to create a plan describing how you will implement those solutions.

In our experience, some organizations attempt to boil the ocean and implement too many initiatives within a short time following a crisis. Unfortunately, this approach often leads to failure or half-baked solutions that give your organization a false sense of security. Instead, divide and conquer, prioritize initiatives, and create a roadmap.

As with the previous sections, the content presented here is not the ultimate project planning tool. There are many excellent project management methodologies available to enterprises. Instead, this section aims to highlight practical advice based on our consulting observations.

Developing a Roadmap

A roadmap is a strategic plan visually representing the desired post-breach remediation solutions with their implementation timelines and milestones necessary to reach their implementation. The projects and deliverables are presented on a timeline and provide a bird's eye view of your remediation plan.

In our experience, a roadmap is an excellent communication tool for senior management and stakeholders implementing the outlined projects. It also helps to understand the dependencies and relationships between those projects. The following list provides some tips that will help you develop an effective roadmap and start post-breach remediation on the right foot:

- Keep it clear and concise. Avoid unnecessary detail that may introduce clutter.
- Don't boil the ocean. Instead, start with projects that lead to the highest risk reduction.
- Focus on fundamentals first. For example, tackle areas such as asset management or securing your identity platform before spending your budget on the latest and shiniest tools.
- Consider areas that may expose the organization to legal or regulatory scrutiny, especially if your organization operates in a heavily regulated environment.
- Set realistic timelines. In our experience, many post-breach remediation projects underestimate time and effort. Understand their complexity and plan their timelines accordingly.

There are different approaches to producing a roadmap, such as a Kanban board, Gantt chart, or an agile roadmap. Choose one that suits your needs and your organizational culture.

Moreover, do not produce your roadmap in isolation. We recommend consulting subject matter experts (SME) and the members of the Technical and Business Teams about priorities and their needs. In our experience, collaboration and consultation are the first steps to getting stakeholder buy-in to implement post-breach remediation.

Validating Security Controls

Sometimes organizations invest millions of dollars in state-of-the-art security solutions and still experience significant breaches. Security and business leaders often ask us why their organizations experienced a cyber crisis despite allocating considerable resources to security. Unfortunately, there is no silver bullet answer to this question, and the potential solutions vary greatly from organization to organization.

However, enterprises frequently implement security controls without validating their effectiveness, building custom detections, and sufficiently tuning false positive events. Unfortunately, many organizations expect tools to provide immediate value with out-of-the-box configurations and solve pressing security problems. We believe that marketing hype and vendor promises often exaggerate this issue.

For example, suppose you implement a Security Information and Event Management (SIEM) solution to aggregate events logs for retention and security correlation as part of your post-breach remediation plan. Deploying a solution and configuring various platforms to forward logs into the SIEM is just the beginning. To make a SIEM successful, you must also consider logging standards for the platforms deployed within the enterprise, Identity and Access Management (IAM) hygiene, building contextual detection rules based on threat models, and ongoing tuning as your IT environments evolve. Of course, we assume that you already have mature asset management practices, can enforce configuration baselines across systems, and continuously identify non-compliant assets before you embark on a SIEM implementation project.

In most engineering disciplines, including software and hardware engineering, component and system testing are built into the system development and deployment lifecycle to ensure the end product works per functional and non-functional requirements. However, this approach to validating security control is infrequent. Given the critical requirement to protect your organization against cyber threats, we find the "deploy-and-forget" approach incomprehensible.

The validation process depends on the tools and solutions you deploy and can include:

- Penetration testing
- Adversary simulation to establish a detection baseline. Note that this domain is also commonly referred to as breach and attack simulation (BAS).
- Threat modeling use cases and creating test cases
- Attempting to bypass preventative measures based on the test cases

If there is one lesson we want you to take from this section, it is to validate the solutions you deploy as part of the post-breach remediation strategy. Do not take the deploy-and-forget approach, thinking you mitigated a key risk. Unfortunately, many organizations have learned the hard way that this approach does not work.

Key Takeaways

- Perform a root cause analysis to discover the security weaknesses and vulnerabilities that directly and indirectly contributed to the crisis. Often, a combination of factors compounding over time leads to a breach. A systematic and thorough root cause analysis will enable you to identify those factors.

- Conduct post-mortem sessions with the Technical and Business Teams and identify lessons learned from failures, improve the response process, reflect on positive response aspects of the response, and reinforce effective behavior.

- As part of crafting your post-breach remediation strategy, conduct a threat-driven risk assessment and quantify the findings in financial terms as part of the risk analysis process. This approach will allow you to translate technical terms into a language business leaders can understand to make meaningful decisions regarding investments in post-breach remediation.

- Prioritize solutions and create a roadmap. Don't boil the ocean as part of this process. Instead, start with fundamentals and focus on the solutions that will yield the highest risk reduction.

- Avoid a "deploy-and-forget" approach underpinned by out-of-the-box configurations. Instead, as part of project implementation, validate security controls to ensure they provide the intended outcome.

Summary

This final section of the SONAR framework guided you through remediation and recovery. After days of long hours, blood, sweat, and tears, your organization restored business operations, eradicated the threat actor from the network, and implemented tactical security measures to prevent the threat actor from re-compromising the network.

In the final part of this book, we guided you through eradicating the threat actor from the compromised network and recovering systems securely. First, we discussed executing the remediation and recovering your systems to an operational and secure state. Then, we concluded with considerations for post-breach remediation to ensure you can adequately secure your network and align long-term security initiatives with your organization's risk appetite.

The next step on your journey is to plan for post-breach remediation and institute long-term measures to improve your organization's security and minimize the risk of another cyber crisis. We wish you the best of luck and success in building and enhancing your crisis response program.

Key Takeaways

- Identify remediation prerequisites. Ensure you fully understand the impact, document investigative findings and assets in scope for remediation and recovery, and assess remediation readiness. Also, do not forget about the consequences of alerting the threat actor if you are responding to an espionage case or an attack where the threat actor will have the resources and patience to persist on the network.
- Carefully define your remediation approach. Critical aspects include regaining control of your identity platform, hardening

systems, and other attack surface reduction measures, and enhancing threat monitoring.

- You can execute remediation in a phased approach or during a pre-agreed time window. We encounter the former approach more frequently due to priorities and pressure to restore business priorities. However, the latter approach is still relevant when eradicating motivated and patient threat actors from your network.
- Understand when to restore compromised systems and data from backup versus when to rebuild systems from scratch. Furthermore, if you recover distributed systems composed of microservices, understand the workflow and dependencies between system components. Implement observability as part of recovery and reconcile transactions to ensure data consistency, if required.

Next Steps

As we mentioned in the last chapter of this section, responding to a cyber crisis does not end with breach remediation. You may be at a point when the dust has settled, and you have returned operations to a steady state. However, organizations experience cyber breaches leading to a crisis for a reason. Your next step after recovery and breach remediation is to conduct post-crisis activities, identify and quantify critical risks, draft an improvement plan, and deliver post-breach remediation projects. Only by identifying and addressing the direct and indirect causes of the crisis can you minimize the risk of a similar event in the future.

Conclusion

We live in a digital age where technology has created many opportunities but has also given rise to highly organized cybercrime, nation-state actors, and other threats. Often operating from jurisdictions outside the Western sphere of influence, those threat actors work tirelessly to infiltrate computer networks, gain access to highly confidential data, and negatively impact business operations for monetary gains and other malicious purposes.

When a cyber crisis rapidly unfolds before your eyes and causes severe damage to your organization, you must be ready to respond to minimize its impact and protect critical assets. The crisis response process is often messy and convoluted, and more than theory is needed to get the situation under control. You need a team of professionals working in concert to respond to and recover from the crisis in the shortest time possible. However, gathering the smartest people in your organization in a war room is not enough. You need a framework and process to guide the team through situations where emotions often run high, and chaos seems to rule the world.

In this book, we introduced The SONAR Method™, a battlefield-tested framework we have employed during numerous crisis events to assist our clients in responding to, stabilizing, and effectively managing those events. The purpose of this framework is to provide you with a structure and guidelines for handling even the most impactful cyber events. Moreover, its adaptability makes it ideal for building crisis response capabilities as part of crisis preparedness.

Throughout this book, we introduced concepts such as stabilizing an environment during a cyber-attack, organizing teams and resources, getting stakeholders on the same page, and communicating effectively to a broad range of stakeholders. We also emphasized the importance of detailing actions for remediation and recovery to return the organization to an operational state. You can use the SONAR framework to respond to and manage a range of cyber incidents, from singular events to the most complex cyber breaches and crises.

By writing this book and sharing our experience and advice, we hope to bring order to an inherently chaotic process. Even if a single paragraph or piece of advice in this book helps your organization respond to a crisis more effectively and reduce its impact, we will consider our mission accomplished.

Index

D

E

F

G

H

I

J

L

M

N

O

P

R

S

T

U

V

W

About the Authors

Andrew Gorecki is a cybersecurity professional and published author with over a decade of experience in technical, consulting, management, and executive advisory roles. He spent several years at IBM where he led investigations into large-scale breaches for Fortune 500 organizations and developed post-breach remediation strategies for clients impacted by significant cyber events. As an Executive Consultant, Andrew was also instrumental in building a cyber resiliency advisory program for IBM clients.

In his current role, Andrew is a Practice Lead at a leading cybersecurity vendor. He is responsible for the delivery of cloud technical advisory services in North America and developing new service capabilities. He combines cloud security expertise, threat intelligence, and unique methodology to advise clients about protecting their cloud environments against cyber threats.

Andrew is actively involved in the cybersecurity community. He has spoken at major cybersecurity conferences, including an ISC2 Security Congress and Black Hat, and received a certificate of appreciation from the United States Secret Service for contributions to law enforcement. He is the author of *Cyber Breach Response That Actually Works: Organizational Approach to Managing Residual Risk* published by Wiley & Sons and regularly writes about cybersecurity topics on his blog at www.agorecki.net.

https://www.linkedin.com/in/andrewgorecki/

Christopher Scott stands as a distinguished figure in the realm of global cyber security, renowned for his pivotal role in the investigation and remediation of some of the most critical and high-profile security incidents of the past decade. He is a key member of the Palo Alto Networks Unit 42 leadership team, delivering a cutting-edge offering designed specifically for Chief Information Security Officers (CISOs) and Boards of Directors.

Chris's expertise is technical and strategic, evidenced by his successful leadership in security engagements against threats including the Shamoon attacks in the Middle East and the NotPetya and APT attacks and insider threats in the U.S. and Europe. His leadership and strategic vision have made him a trusted advisor to board members, C-level executives, legal teams, and technical teams.

Before Palo Alto Networks, Chris was with the IBM Office of the CISO, where he led security innovation and remediation initiatives. His earlier roles include leading global remediation efforts for IBM Security X-Force and serving as a Director of Remediation at CrowdStrike Services, where he formulated and executed incident response, preparedness, and remediation strategies for a global clientele.

Chris's passion for security was ignited over 15 years ago at L-3 Communications, where he embarked on his journey to secure the digital frontier. This passion, combined with his extensive experience, positions Chris as a beacon of knowledge and leadership in the cyber security domain, making him an invaluable asset to CISOs and Boards of Directors navigating the complex challenges of today's cyber crisis management.

https://www.linkedin.com/in/chrisscott-u42/

Bill Bonney is a security evangelist, author, and consultant. As co-author of the Cybersecurity Canon Hall of Fame books the *CISO Desk Reference Guide: A Practical Guide for CISOs – Volumes 1 and 2*, Bill is dedicated to providing the practical advice needed to combat the ongoing scourge of cybercrime. Prior to co-founding CISO DRG Publishing, Bill was Vice President of Product Marketing and Chief Strategist at UBIQ, a maker of high-speed encryption software, Vice President of Product Marketing and Principal Consulting Analyst at TechVision Research, and Director of Information Security and Compliance at Intuit, maker of personal and small business financial products.

Bill holds multiple patents in data protection, access, and classification, and was a founding member of the board of directors for the San Diego CISO Round Table, a professional group focused on building relationships and fostering collaboration in information security management. Bill is a highly regarded speaker and panelist addressing technology and security concerns. In addition to co-authoring the two volumes of the *CISO Desk Reference Guide*, and the *CISO Desk Reference Guide: Executive Primer*, Bill has also written *Bring Your Own Cyber, A Small Business Owner's Guide to Basic Network Security* to help extremely small companies improve their security. He holds a Bachelor of Science degree in Computer Science and Applied Mathematics from Albany University.

LinkedIn Profile: https://www.linkedin.com/in/billbonney

Matt Stamper, CISA, CISM, CRISC, CDPSE, CIPP-US. As a senior security leader with both public and early-stage company experience, Matt brings a broad, multi-disciplinary knowledge of privacy and cybersecurity best practices to his clients. His diverse domain expertise spans IT service management (ITSM), cybersecurity, cloud services, control design and assessment (Sarbanes-Oxley, HIPAA-HITECH), privacy (GDPR, CCPA, CPRA), governance, enterprise risk, and IT risk management (ERM/ITRM). Matt co-authored the *CISO Desk Reference Guide, Volumes 1 and 2* with Gary Hayslip and Bill Bonney.

Matt's diverse experience also includes sales management and individual revenue contribution, new product and service development, and international experience in both Latin America and China. Matt excels at conveying complex privacy, cybersecurity, and IT concepts to boards of directors, executive management, and professional service providers. His executive-level experience with managed services, cybersecurity, data centers, networks services, and ITSM provides a unique perspective on the fast-changing world of enterprise IT, IoT, and cloud services. Matt has served as a Security Analyst and Research Director at Gartner and in multiple CISO roles. Matt is an IT Sector Chief for the FBI InfraGard program and a member of the Board of the San Diego ISACA chapter.

Matt received a Bachelor of Arts from the University of California at San Diego, graduating Cum Laude and with Honors and Distinction in Political Science. He earned a Master of Arts in Pacific International Affairs from the University of California at San Diego and a Master of Science degree in Telecommunications sponsored by AT&T. He is fluent in Spanish and has worked in executive roles in Latin America.

LinkedIn Profile: https://www.linkedin.com/in/stamper

Made in United States
Orlando, FL
04 November 2026

90200820R00184